The Ebb and Flow of Global Governance

The Ebb and Flow of Global Governance challenges the traditionally dichotomous distinction between international intergovernmental organizations and international nongovernmental organizations. Alexandru Grigorescu argues that international organizations are best understood as falling on an "intergovernmental–nongovernmental continuum." The placement of organizations on this continuum is determined by how much government involvement factors into their decision making, financing, and deliberations. Using this fine-grained conceptualization, Grigorescu uncovers numerous changes in the intergovernmental versus nongovernmental nature of global governance over the past century and a half. These changes are due primarily to ideological and institutional domestic shifts in powerful states. *The Ebb and Flow of Global Governance* assesses the plausibility of these arguments through archival research on a dozen organizations from the global health, labor, and technical standards realms. Grigorescu concludes that there has been a continuous ebb and flow in world politics, rather than an inexorable movement toward greater roles for nongovernmental actors, as existing literature contends.

Alexandru Grigorescu is a professor of political science at Loyola University Chicago. He is the author of *Democratic Intergovernmental Organizations?* (2015). Prior to his academic career, he worked as a diplomat in the Romanian Foreign Ministry and at the United Nations.

The Ebb and Flow
of Global Governance

Intergovernmentalism versus
Nongovernmentalism in World Politics

ALEXANDRU GRIGORESCU
Loyola University

CAMBRIDGE
UNIVERSITY PRESS

CAMBRIDGE
UNIVERSITY PRESS

University Printing House, Cambridge CB2 8BS, United Kingdom

One Liberty Plaza, 20th Floor, New York, NY 10006, USA

477 Williamstown Road, Port Melbourne, VIC 3207, Australia

314–321, 3rd Floor, Plot 3, Splendor Forum, Jasola District Centre, New Delhi – 110025, India

79 Anson Road, #06-04/06, Singapore 079906

Cambridge University Press is part of the University of Cambridge.

It furthers the University's mission by disseminating knowledge in the pursuit
of education, learning, and research at the highest international levels of excellence.

www.cambridge.org
Information on this title: www.cambridge.org/9781108495509
DOI: 10.1017/9781108850049

First published 2020

A catalogue record for this publication is available from the British Library.

Library of Congress Cataloging-in-Publication Data

ISBN 978-1-108-49550-9 Hardback

Contents

Figures

Tables

Acknowledgments

The idea behind this study was sparked by archival research I conducted for my previous book, *Democratic Intergovernmental Organizations? Normative Pressures and Decision-Making Rules* (Cambridge University Press, 2015). At that time, while reading about developments in international organizations (IOs) over almost two centuries, I began noticing global trends that seemed to repeat themselves across time. I was surprised that the study of IOs had not truly paid attention to such cyclical patterns and that, instead, almost all of the literature had been emphasizing recent linear trends. I was just as surprised to find that officials working for or with such organizations were not aware (and were genuinely interested to hear) that other practitioners had grappled with similar problems many decades earlier. The "ebb and flow of global governance" that I noticed would not have been as visible without considering the main idea of this book: that we have looked upon intergovernmental and nongovernmental organizations as dichotomous terms too long and that all IOs do, in fact, fall upon a continuum. Moreover, once I introduced the concept of a continuum, the all-important question of when global governance shifts across this continuum became an essential one.

As my main arguments crystalized, I began searching for the necessary evidence to assess the validity of my claims. Throughout the five years during which I conducted the research for this book, I was fortunate to have the support of dozens of women and men overseeing the archives and libraries of numerous IOs: Food and Agriculture Organization; International Association for Labour Legislation; International Bureau for Education; International Committee of the Red Cross; International Electrotechnical Commission; International Federation of Red Cross and Red Crescent Societies; International Labour Organization; International Organization for Standardization; International Telecommunication Union; League of

Nations; Office for International Public Hygiene; UN Educational, Scientific and Cultural Organization; United Nations; World Bank; World Health Organization; and World Tourism Organization. I am profoundly grateful to all of these individuals. Their dedication and expertise allowed me to uncover many essential original documents.

As I began writing the book, I benefitted from the advice and feedback of many colleagues and friends. I am especially grateful to Elizabeth Bloodgood, Angela Crack, Thomas Davies, James Gathii, Federica Genovese, Chris Hasselmann, Ian Hurd, Tana Johnson, Robert Keohane, Sarah Maxey, Molly Melin, Charles Roger, Peter Sanchez, Duncan Snidal, Theresa Squatrito, Jonas Tallberg, Felicity Vabulas, Lora Anne Viola, and Peter Willetts for their helpful comments and ideas.

A special thanks goes out to Claudio Katz and Vincent Mahler, two friends and colleagues who have not only read large segments of this book and helped me present my arguments in a much more complete fashion, but have also pushed me throughout the years to fine-tune my ideas and explain them more clearly in virtually all of my work. This brief acknowledgment cannot capture my tremendous gratitude to both of them for never saying "no" to my (too) many requests for their feedback and advice.

I would also like to thank the editorial team at Cambridge University Press for their very efficient and professional help throughout this complex process. I am particularly indebted to Robert Dreesen, who always replied quickly to all of my (often confusing) questions and who always found the best solution to my (often ridiculous) requests.

I benefitted greatly from the research assistance of the following graduate students: Caglayan Baser, Thomas Callan, the much too soon departed Kimberly Loontjer, and Paul Olander. I am grateful for all their hard work.

On a more personal note, I would like to thank Ron Linden, my longtime mentor and friend, who engaged in the unenviable task of transforming me from a physicist into a political scientist several decades ago. The unique mixture of his sharp mind, humor, and astute understanding of Romanians made this possible. As in all of my academic work, as I was writing this book, I often thought of the advice and scholarly approach that Ron passed along to me.

Most important, I am deeply grateful to my family, including its most recent generation. I believe that everyone who has written a book understands very well that without the love and support of those closest to you, such a long and complex endeavor can become a pain rather than something enjoyable. Thanks to my family, I enjoyed working on this book very much.

Acronyms

AESC	American Engineering Standards Committee
AFL	American Federation of Labor
AGTU	Austro-German Telegraph Union
AIIB	Asian Infrastructure Investment Bank
AIP	Apparel Industry Partnership
ANEC	European Association for Consumer Representation in Standardisation
AO	changes in relevance among existing organizations
ARC	American Red Cross
AT&T	American Telephone and Telegraph Company
BESA	British Engineering Standards Association
BIPM	International Bureau of Weights and Measures
CEN	European Committee for Standardization
CI	Consumer International
CIO	Congress of Industrial Organizations
COPOLCO	International Organization for Standardization Committee on Consumer Policy
ECITO	European Central Inland Transport Organization
ECOSOC	Economic and Social Council
ETSI	European Telecommunications Standards Institute
FAO	Food and Agriculture Organization
GA	United Nations General Assembly
GATT	The General Agreement on Tariffs and Trade
GAVI	Global Vaccine Alliance
GF	Gates Foundation
IAF	International Aeronautical Federation
IBE	International Bureau for Education
ICFTU	International Confederation of Free Trade Unions

ICI	International Commission on Illumination
ICRC	International Committee of the Red Cross
IEC	International Electrotechnical Commission
IEE	Institution of Electrical Engineers
IFTU	International Federation of Trade Unions
IGO	intergovernmental organization
IHC	International Health Conference
ILL	International Association for Labour Legislation
ILO	International Labour Organization
ILRF	International Labor Rights Fund
INGO	international nongovernmental organization
INTERPOL	International Criminal Police Organization
IO	international organization
IR	international relations
IRU	International Relief Union
ISA	International Federation of National Standardizing Associations
ISO	International Organization for Standardization
ITC	Inland Transport Committee
ITU	International Telecommunication Union
IUCN	International Union for Conservation of Nature
LNHO	League of Nations Health Organization
NDB	New Development Bank
NGO	nongovernmental organization
NO	new organization
OIHP	International Office of Public Health
OTIF	Intergovernmental Organisation for International Carriage by Rail
RF	Rockefeller Foundation
RTUI	Red Trade Union International
UN	United Nations
UNAIDS	Joint United Nations Programme on HIV and AIDS
UNCIO	United Nations Conference on International Organization
UNECE	United Nations Economic Commission for Europe
UNESCO	United Nations Educational, Scientific and Cultural Organization
UNICEF	United Nations Children's Fund
UNIDO	United Nations Industrial Development Organization
UNRRA	United Nations Relief and Rehabilitation Administration
UNSCC	United Nations Standards Coordinating Committee
WFTU	World Federation of Trade Unions
WHO	World Health Organization
WO	changes to rules within existing organization
WTO	World Trade Organization

The Intergovernmental–Nongovernmental Continuum in Global Governance

THE MAIN ARGUMENT DRIVING THIS BOOK

Despite the lack of a global government, many important global problems have been tackled by national governments, usually acting together through intergovernmental organizations (IGOs) such as the United Nations (UN), the Organization of American States (OAS), and the International Monetary Fund (IMF), and by nongovernmental actors such as Amnesty International, the World Federation of Trade Unions, and the Bill & Melinda Gates Foundation. The actions taken by such organizations to resolve global problems have been referred to as forms of "global governance."[1] In almost all of the global governance literature, it is assumed that the distinction between intergovernmental and nongovernmental actors is clear-cut, consequential, and self-evident.

This book takes the conversation beyond the rigid, dichotomous intergovernmental–nongovernmental conceptual divide. It starts from a two-step argument. First, it posits that individual international organizations (IOs)[2] can best be understood as falling across an intergovernmental–nongovernmental *continuum* defined by the degree to which governments actually control their work. The degree of such government control can be assessed across three

---

[1] For comprehensive discussions and definitions of this term, see, e.g., Rosenau (1992), Ruggie (2004), Dingwerth and Pattberg (2006), Murphy (2014), and Weiss and Wilkinson (2014); for an important recent discussion, see Zürn (2018).

[2] When referring to organizations that have previously been discussed as "intergovernmental organizations" (IGOs) and "international nongovernmental organizations" (INGOs) this book will utilize the broader umbrella term of "international organizations" (IOs), acknowledging that they all fall on an intergovernmental–nongovernmental continuum. In order to distinguish between the characteristics of various IOs I will refer to them as "intergovernmental IOs" or "nongovernmental IOs," often qualifying them as "very," "more," or "less" intergovernmental or nongovernmental to reflect their relative placement on the continuum.

different dimensions: decision-making, finances, and deliberations. Second, the book argues that the intergovernmental–nongovernmental nature of global governance in a specific realm at a certain point in time is determined by the aggregate intergovernmental or nongovernmental character of the most influential international actors (the main "global governors"[3]).

The idea that organizations are rarely, if ever, purely governmental or nongovernmental has long been discussed in the context of domestic politics (e.g., Bozeman 1987). The need for developing the concept of a governmental-nongovernmental continuum in domestic politics or the intergovernmental–nongovernmental one in the global realm has become apparent from the number of works that have used terms such as "quasi government" (Kosar 2008), "hybrid international organizations" (Archer 1983, 41; Willetts 1996, 2011), or "public-private partnerships"[4] (e.g., Andonova 2010; Hale 2015, 4) to describe important actors in the two realms. However, even such terms have been presented as additional categories rather than as specific points among many possible ones on a continuum.

In sum, therefore, the first step in my argument, regarding the need to develop an intergovernmental–nongovernmental continuum for individual IOs, is a novel one. By contrast, the second step of the argument, regarding the intergovernmental–nongovernmental nature of the aggregate character of global governance, builds on recent work (e.g., Abbott and Snidal 2009; Green 2014). What the present study adds to that literature is a broader view of the evolution of global governance, over a far longer period of time.[5] As this book traces the ebb and flow of global governance over more than a century and a half, it allows for observations of multiple shifts, *both* toward more nongovernmental approaches *and* toward more intergovernmental ones. It thus stands in contrast to most works discussing global governance that have focused only on recent developments and have generally only captured single instances of shifts. Moreover, the shifts that have been discussed in this literature all appear to have been unidirectional, toward more nongovernmental approaches.

The notion of an intergovernmental–nongovernmental continuum has important practical implications. First, by considering the degree to which governments control IOs, rather than adopting a formal intergovernmental versus nongovernmental dichotomy of such organizations, we gain a more complete understanding of the actual processes that unfold in the global realm and assess who is in fact behind them. Simply put, such an approach allows us to observe important phenomena taking place across a broad

---

[3] The term is discussed in greater depth in Avant et al. (2010).

[4] Most of the literature on public-private partnerships treats these entities as collaborative arrangements between purely intergovernmental and nongovernmental organizations, rather than as a separate type of actor.

[5] For an exception to the short time frame as well as for a discussion of the importance of studying developments over long periods of time, see Hale (2015, 5).

intergovernmental–nongovernmental "frontier,"[6] which are not visible when taking a dichotomous approach.

Second, the conceptualization of an intergovernmental–nongovernmental continuum, both for individual IOs and for the overall nature of global governance, allows us to observe the many subtle changes that take place across time. These changes are not as noticeable as when one simply takes a dichotomous approach to understanding such organizations. Indeed, one of the most significant findings of this study is that over the last century and a half, in virtually all issue-areas, global governance has experienced multiple shifts back and forth on the intergovernmental–nongovernmental continuum. This has important implications for future global developments.

Third, by examining a large number of shifts across this continuum, I can identify patterns of such variation and address the question deriving from my main argument: When is global governance likely to experience shifts toward a more intergovernmental or nongovernmental approach? This is an important question, as our potential solutions to global problems will be affected by our understanding of the *degree* to which governments or nongovernmental entities can best become involved in solving them.

More broadly, the introduction of an intergovernmental–nongovernmental continuum is as consequential for the field of international relations as many other similar moves from purely dichotomous to continuous understandings of political science concepts. For example, the shift from characterizing states either as democratic or autocratic to one considering multiple characteristics of political systems and placing them on a continuous autocracy-democracy scale has had a significant impact on the study of comparative politics (Marshall et al. 2010). Similarly, the move from a simpler understanding of globalization as a phenomenon that exists or does not exist, to one based on multiple facets that allows us to assess the *degree* and nature of globalization, has led to a better understanding of international developments (Dreher 2006).

The rest of this introductory chapter will discuss in greater depth the intergovernmental–nongovernmental continuum. I begin by briefly offering the issue-area of education as an illustration of this continuum and of the types of shifts across it. I then break down this continuum across three dimensions (decision-making, financial, and deliberative) and show that the three do not always go hand in hand and therefore need to be treated separately.

The following chapters will then turn to address the question regarding the conditions under which we expect to see shifts toward a more intergovernmental approach to global governance (discussed in this book as

---

[6] The term "frontier" was introduced by James Rosenau as a solution to a similar conceptual problem deriving from the oversimplified understanding of the domestic–international "boundary" as a clear line delineating the two realms. Rosenau argued that along this frontier was in fact a wide political space where "domestic and foreign issues converge, intermesh, and otherwise become indistinguishable" (1997, 5).

"intergovernmentalism") or a nongovernmental one (discussed henceforth as "nongovernmentalism"). I offer several possible answers to this question and assess their plausibility. Most important, I develop two hypotheses that emphasize how domestic ideological leanings and domestic institutions in the most powerful states can affect the intergovernmental–nongovernmental nature of specific IOs and of global governance. Specifically, I suggest that the need for ideological consistency of top-level national officials establishes connections between their domestic preferences and international ones. Additionally, new or empowered domestic institutions can promote the emergence and use of international organizations.

Of course, I acknowledge that other factors besides domestic ideologies and institutions in the most powerful states affect the intergovernmental or nongovernmental nature of global governance. I identify such additional factors by extending arguments from the existing literature to their natural conclusions. Many of these factors are derived from arguments based on the main international relations theoretical approaches, as well as from the recent literature discussing IGO-INGO interactions.

My findings have important theoretical implications in addition to the practical ones mentioned above. I discuss these implications briefly in this chapter and more broadly in the concluding chapter of this book.

A FIRST EXAMPLE: THE INTERGOVERNMENTAL– NONGOVERNMENTAL CONTINUUM IN THE EDUCATION REALM

In the second half of the nineteenth century and the early twentieth century, attempts to establish intergovernmental IOs to deal with education were unsuccessful. All international collaborative efforts in this realm remained very nongovernmental. This is represented in Figure 1.1 by the fact that only very nongovernmental IOs (i.e., ones in which governments had virtually no influence) are included among the main global governors, in parentheses, under the 1850–1924 time period. The aggregate nature of global governance in the education realm was therefore also very nongovernmental. I represent this by placing global governance on the left end of the intergovernmental– nongovernmental continuum in Figure 1.1.

After World War I, many nongovernmental IOs pressured states to have the new intergovernmental League of Nations take on questions of education. Yet the major powers that met in Paris to set up the postwar global institutional architecture ignored the issue (Rossello 1943, 48, 206–208).

By 1921, some states, most notably France, changed their positions and proposed that the League establish an office for international intellectual relations among schools and universities, seeking a shift toward the intergovernmental end of the continuum (Renoliet 1999, 16). This initiative is represented in Figure 1.1 with a dashed line below the continuum to show that the proposal was not successful. The vast majority of League members opposed this

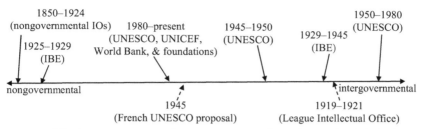

FIGURE I.I. The intergovernmental–nongovernmental continuum in global education governance.

plan and a League Council report concluded that "under present world conditions intellectual cooperation can best be advanced by means of voluntary efforts" (League of Nations Council 1921, 14).

By 1925, as it became clear that there would be no intergovernmental IO for international collaboration in the education realm, a handful of small and medium states, together with several nongovernmental IOs and foundations, established the International Bureau for Education (IBE). Although the IBE was very nongovernmental in nature, the role played by states in its founding and in its work imply that global governance of education in the mid-1920s shifted from its almost pure nongovernmental status quo before World War I toward greater intergovernmentalism, but only slightly. In 1929 the IBE was officially transformed into an intergovernmental IO (IBE 1929). This was an even more substantive shift toward intergovernmentalism, as illustrated in Figure 1.1. From its 1925 founding as a very nongovernmental IO, and even throughout its more intergovernmental years, the IBE's largest donor was the nongovernmental Rockefeller Foundation (RF), suggesting that the organization was controlled not only by governmental entities. While some major powers such as France, Germany, and Italy joined the organization, the United Kingdom and the United States did not. Due to this relative lack of support, the IBE remained a modest organization, with narrow goals and little power (Suchodolski 1979, 68–69). Many international cooperative initiatives in education were still driven by nongovernmental actors.

After World War II, when negotiations for the UN Educational, Scientific and Cultural Organization (UNESCO) began, two proposals emerged. The first, promoted by the United Kingdom and the United States, was for a very intergovernmental organization, where only governments would be represented and vote. The second, supported by France, called for an organization in which each state was to be represented by two delegates from governments and three from educational and cultural domestic NGOs. Each of these would count as a national delegate and would have its own vote, much like in the International Labour Organization (ILO) (Conference of Allied Ministers of Education 1945, 9–10; Laves and Thomson 1957, 36–40). The emphasis on nongovernmental actors in the French plan is illustrated in Figure 1.1 by representing with a dashed line the 1945 moment as an unsuccessful attempt to shift global governance of education toward the middle of the continuum. In the end, even though decision making in UNESCO remained almost entirely intergovernmental, the concessions made to the French proposal initially led the organization to give nongovernmental actors a greater role than elsewhere in the UN system. In its first years, UNESCO assigned projects to small and very nongovernmental IOs. When there were no such IOs to deal with the issues UNESCO sought to resolve, it funded their establishment (Sewell 1975, 110).

Throughout the first half of the Cold War, under pressure from the United States and, later, from the increasingly large number of Soviet Bloc and Third World states, UNESCO slowly shifted toward a more intergovernmental approach to education. In 1954, its Executive Board, which was intended originally to include 18 well-known intellectuals elected in their personal capacity, was transformed into a forum for government representatives. By the 1960s, UNESCO was relying less on nongovernmental IOs. In the late 1970s, many Western states began complaining about UNESCO's "statist" approach (Preston et al. 1989, 11–14). The United States and the United Kingdom cited this issue among the reasons for leaving the organization in the 1980s. At that time, the United States sought to shift the global governance of education toward other IOs, such as the World Bank and United Nations Children's Fund (UNICEF), that relied more on nongovernmental IOs to implement policies (Mundy 2010, 340). After the United States returned to UNESCO in 2003, it was able to coax the organization to broaden its collaboration with nongovernmental actors. Most important, in 2012 the organization adopted a "Policy Framework for Strategic Partnership" that formalized relations with the private sector. Powerful private organizations such as the Gates and Hewlett foundations have become active in international education programs through UNESCO and other IOs and, directly, on their own (Mundy 2010, 352). Private foundations now contribute more to UNESCO's educational programs through voluntary donations than governments do (UNESCO 2016).

As Figure 1.1 suggests, it is often difficult to pinpoint the exact *location* of global governance structures on a continuum. However, the above narrative illustrates that we can usually determine the existence and direction of *shifts* across an intergovernmental–nongovernmental continuum. This is important because the study will focus mainly on such shifts, seeking to explain why they take place, but not necessarily how far they move global governance across the continuum.

The shifts across the continuum can result from the emergence of new organizations (NO), from changes to formal or informal rules within existing

organization (WO), or from changes in relative importance of existing organization (i.e., changes among organizations: AO). This distinction can be
viewed as a version of the classification of institutional choices introduced by
Jupille et al. (2013).[7] The present study will consider these three types of strategies leading to changes in the intergovernmental or nongovernmental nature
of global governance.

The example of the international education realm illustrates that there is
indeed variation in the degree to which global governance in an issue-area has
been intergovernmental or nongovernmental in nature at a certain point in
time. Furthermore, it shows that such variation is the result of the emergence
of new IOs, of developments within IOs making them more intergovernmental
or nongovernmental (as in the case of the IBE and UNESCO), and of processes that led to the empowerment of some IOs and weakening of others, thus
affecting the aggregate intergovernmental–nongovernmental nature of global
governance in this realm.

This book seeks to show that the variation in intergovernmental and nongovernmental approaches to global governance is pervasive. It can be found
across virtually all historical periods and all issue-areas, beyond the one of
education. The present study will focus primarily on three global issues:
health, labor, and technical standards. It will show that they all changed their
character considerably across time.

Even when it comes to global security and trade, two of the most important and studied issues, we observe similar shifts. For instance, in the
security realm, governments recently appear to have given up, at least to
some degree, their monopoly over mediation of international conflicts to
nongovernmental IOs (Bercovitch and Jackson 2009). Also, private military and security corporations are seen as playing increasingly important
roles resolving civil conflicts, harkening back to times when states would
rely heavily on nonstate mercenary groups to fight their wars (Avant 2005;
Singer 2008; McFate 2014). In 1995, by contrast, governments finally agreed
to establish the very intergovernmental World Trade Organization (WTO)
as the principal forum for resolving global trade issues, fifty years after
turning down the proposal for the International Trade Organization. This
intergovernmental approach to global trade balanced the traditional role
that independent markets (together with intergovernmental agreements) had
played in this realm.

---

[7] According to Jupille et al. (2013), states can (1) use available international institutions, (2)
select from among existing institutions, (3) change existing institutional rules, or (4) create
new institutions. The last three strategies can all lead to shifts across the intergovernmental–
nongovernmental continuum.

CONCEPTUALIZING THE INTERGOVERNMENTAL–
NONGOVERNMENTAL CONTINUUM

IGOs are generally understood as organizations where government representatives come together to collectively seek and implement solutions to international issues. Conversely, international nongovernmental actors, whether INGOs, philanthropic foundations, international labor movements, transnational expert groups, or private businesses, are generally seen as entities that are *not* run by governments.[8] This traditional dichotomous approach to the main international actors leads to a similar dichotomous understanding of the possible approaches to global governance. Specifically, a purely intergovernmental approach to global governance is one where governments and IGOs are the only ones involved in resolving global collective problems. A purely nongovernmental approach is one where only nongovernmental actors seek and implement solutions to such problems and governments do not become involved at all. In fact, of course, virtually all instances of global governance fall somewhere in between these two extremes. This is true for at least two reasons.

First, as the literature has pointed out, it is rare that only one international actor is involved in an issue-area. Indeed, issue-areas usually involve many different actors, both intergovernmental and nongovernmental, that interact with each other in different ways (e.g., Biermann and Koops 2017). In fact, the growing number of IOs involved in various issue-areas has led some scholars to turn to regime complex theory when explaining the impact of interactions between multiple organizations on international relations (e.g., Raustiala and Victor 2004; Alter and Meunier 2009; Keohane and Victor 2011; Abbott 2012). While much of the literature has primarily

---

[8] Of course, these types of nongovernmental actors are very different in terms of how they function and the tasks they fulfill. However, the literature (and datasets) usually includes all such entities into the broader category of nongovernmental actors. An important exception to such classification is Abbott and Snidal's discussions of the "governance triangle" that consider the separate roles of governments, NGOs, and firms (2009). Like others before me (e.g., Andonova 2010, 26), I collapse the two types of nongovernmental actors discussed by Abbott and Snidal into one, considering that all nongovernmental entities are broadly treated similarly by governments. Specifically, when governments take a hands-off approach, they allow or encourage other actors (whether firms, NGOs, private-public partnerships, or philanthropic foundations) to take on a greater role. When activist governments play a greater role in global governance, they may "crowd out" one or more types of nongovernmental actors, pushing the system toward intergovernmentalism. This assumption that brings together all types of nongovernmental actors under one umbrella should not be viewed as one leading to a dichotomous approach and thus contradicting the main argument of this book. Indeed, I consider that all types of nongovernmental actors are influenced to lesser or greater degrees by governments and therefore all fall somewhere on the intergovernmental–nongovernmental continuum.

studied interactions between IGOs separately from those between INGOs (e.g., Grigorescu 2017; Schneiker 2017), there has also been an increased interest in how these two types of organizations work with each other, something that is, of course, relevant for a study seeking to explain the overall intergovernmental or nongovernmental nature of global governance. Such literature has shown that while at times the two types of actors may have different (even clashing) interests, most often, they have at least some common goals (e.g., Johnson 2016). Some of this literature has emphasized how IGOs have opened up to nongovernmental actors, including them in the deliberative process (Tallberg et al. 2013). Others have investigated processes through which IGOs "orchestrate" the work of multiple other international actors, many of which are nongovernmental (e.g., Hale and Roger 2014; Abbott et al. 2015). Yet others have sought to explain when these two types of actors are more likely to work together (e.g., Abbott and Snidal 2009; Green 2014; Hale 2015). However, as mentioned earlier, this literature has not considered how such interactions have led to shifts across an intergovernmental–nongovernmental continuum in global governance, as the present study does. Even the few studies that acknowledge that the end result in the global governance of an issue-area can be more intergovernmental or nongovernmental have only taken into account discreet positions on such a continuum, rather than continuous ones. In this sense, the present study can be considered to subsume existing ones by asking not only when intergovernmental and nongovernmental IOs come together to resolve global problems but also which types of actors are likely to take the lead and become the main global governors. As more intergovernmental or nongovernmental actors are empowered or weakened, the overall nature of global governance in a specific realm shifts toward greater intergovernmentalism or nongovernmentalism.

Second, I add to the existing argument regarding the possible shifts across the continuum due to interactions between individual global governors, another one positing that the character of each of these international actors involved in global governance is rarely purely intergovernmental (controlled entirely by governments) or nongovernmental (where governments have absolutely no influence). Indeed, like all concepts in the social sciences, the distinction between intergovernmental and nongovernmental actors is only a rough approximation of the real world. Intergovernmental IOs are often influenced considerably by nongovernmental actors, and nongovernmental actors are often influenced by governments. The interactions between them lead to complex relations, often making it difficult to ascertain whether and how they control each other.[9]

---

[9] For recent discussions of such interactions, see, e.g., Abbott et al. (2015) and Johnson (2016).

Therefore, I argue that all international organizations are better understood as falling along a continuum rather than within just one of these rigid
dichotomous categories.[10] The placement of the main global governors in a
certain issue-area at a given time on such continuums and their relative influence determines the placement of the overall character of global governance
on the intergovernmental–nongovernmental continuum.

In the social sciences, most dichotomies are the result of the analytic need to
distinguish clearly between concepts. Early on, when there were fewer international organizations, there was hardly any need and therefore very little effort
to distinguish between intergovernmental and nongovernmental international
actors. When the Union of International Associations (UIA; founded in 1907)
offered its first listings of international organizations in 1912, it included IOs
and private foundations without specifying their intergovernmental or nongovernmental character. The main characteristic used at that time to differentiate between organizations was the issue-area on which they focused (Union
of International Associations 1912).

When the League of Nations was established, Article 24 of the Covenant
stipulated that "international bureaux" should be placed under the "direction"
of the League. The concept of international bureau, once more, did not differentiate between the more intergovernmental IOs, such as the Universal
Postal Union, and the more nongovernmental ones, such as Save the Children.
Based on this article, the League Council initially requested the International
Bureaux Section to coordinate collaborations with both types of organizations, treating them equally (League of Nations 1922, i). The League eventually developed collaborative relations with more than 200 intergovernmental
and nongovernmental actors.[11]

Initially, the League attributed many nongovernmental actors a formal
status considered equal to those of the very intergovernmental IOs, described
as one of "participation without a vote" (Pickard 1956, 25–26, 54; Seary
1996, 23). Some nongovernmental IOs, given the position of "assessor,"
were even allowed to propose resolutions and amendments and to initiate
discussions (League of Nations 1922, i). Top League officials consulted
with such organizations on a regular basis and sometimes requested that
they submit reports to the League (League of Nations 1922, i; White 1951,
250). Nongovernmental IOs were represented in various League bodies such
as the Communications and Transit Committee, the Committee on Social

---

[10] The idea of a continuum moves beyond Willetts's argument that IOs belong in one of three
categories (intergovernmental, nongovernmental, or "hybrid") (2000). Earlier, Willetts considered more categories (1996, 8). Yet, even in that more nuanced approach, organizations
fell within distinct categories rather than on a continuum.

[11] See League of Nations Archives of Section of International Bureaus and Intellectual Cooperation
(various years).

Questions, or the Commission on Traffic of Women. These bodies often gave them "permanent seats" or positions of "corresponding members" (White 1951, 249). Representatives of nongovernmental groups were also invited to participate in League-sponsored conferences such as the International Finance Conferences or the Conference on the Abolition of Import and Export Restrictions.

Despite this formal equality between nongovernmental and intergovernmental organizations, in practice, the Bureaux Section began informally differentiating between them by the mid-1920s, primarily because its relatively small size did not allow it to tend to all these organizations' demands (International Union of League of Nations Associations 1921; MacDonald 1934). In 1925 the League reversed its initial decision to interpret the Covenant as allowing for equality among the more nongovernmental or intergovernmental IOs (Seary 1996, 22). Around the same time, the UIA also began emphasizing the distinction between private and public international organizations. In its 1924 edition, and since then in every *Yearbook of International Organizations*, the UIA has used the intergovernmental–nongovernmental dichotomous differentiation.

With the emergence of the UN and the increasing number of international organizations, the distinction became even more necessary in order to prioritize the new global organization's work. In fact, the term "non-governmental organization" was officially used for the first time in Article 71 of the UN Charter (Davies 2014, 132). As many government representatives considered that the influence of nongovernmental actors had gone too far during the League years, the new UN made it clear that while it would give INGOs so-called consultative status, this status would be limited only to the economic and social realm and, more important, they would not be granted the more influential observer status, reserved only for IGOs. Since then, the distinction between the two types of international organizations has become increasingly rigid, as their status has evolved to be the subject of differentiated formal agreements.

The advantages given to the more intergovernmental IOs in the UN and elsewhere led to an increased perception of prestige attached to IGO status. This contributed to some organizations, such as INTERPOL (Valleix 1998), altering their internal rules in order to gain UN observer status (which is conferred upon IGOs), rather than consultative status (conferred upon INGOs).

When it comes to international actors, the intergovernmental–nongovernmental dichotomy is based on the simple differentiation between entities in which governments have decision-making power and those in which they do not have such powers. However, this formal distinction does not offer much guidance with regard to the important question of whether governments actually control the organizations. For instance, the example above suggests that nongovernmental entities such as the RF (in the case of the IBE) or the Gates Foundation (in UNESCO) have had tremendous influence over the work of otherwise very intergovernmental IOs. Nongovernmental organizations have also been instrumental in the adoption of *intergovernmental* treaties, as was the case of the International Association for Labour Legislation, the nongovernmental predecessor of the ILO, or in the case of approximately 1300 INGOs that together launched the 1997 *intergovernmental* Mine Ban Treaty.

Conversely, many international nongovernmental actors have been accused of being too "governmental." Such an accusation usually implies that some governments have excessive influence over these actors. The extreme example of governmental influence is the one of so-called GONGOs (an acronym for "government organized nongovernmental organizations"), which are intended to appear nongovernmental in nature but, in fact, are organized and run by governments (Naim 2009). Of course, hardly any of the formally nongovernmental IOs are purely independent of governments, just as GONGOs are rarely entirely dependent on them.[12] Similarly, other types of nongovernmental actors such as foundations[13] or international labor federations[14] have been accused of being controlled, or at least influenced, by governments. Rather than be simply classified as fitting neatly within either the intergovernmental or nongovernmental category, virtually all global governors fall across an intergovernmental–nongovernmental continuum based on the degree to which governments actually control them.

I further argue that this continuum can be observed across three different dimensions: (1) decision-making, the degree to which governments or nongovernmental entities have voting rights in the organization's bodies; (2) finance, the degree to which governments or nongovernmental entities contribute to the organization financially and, implicitly, shape policies; and (3) deliberation, the degree to which governments or nongovernmental entities take part in the organization's debates and, implicitly, shape ideas. Simply put, the intergovernmental versus nongovernmental nature of international organizations can be assessed by answering three main questions: "Who votes?" "Who pays?" and "Who speaks?" Together, the answers to these three questions allow us to address the broader essential question of "who governs" that has long been asked by political scientists (Dahl 1961) and more recently by the global governance literature (Avant et al. 2010).

In the following sections, I discuss the continuous rather than dichotomous nature of IOs by focusing on these three dimensions. While my assessment

---

[12] One possible reflection of the *degree* to which nongovernmental organizations are influenced by governments is the proportion of funding that they receive from governments. See, e.g., Cooley (2010, 253).

[13] E.g., for the relationship between the Ford Foundation and US government, see McCarthy (1987, 105).

[14] E.g., see the blatant case of Soviet-Controlled World Congress of Red Trade Unions in Schevenels (1956, 140).

is based primarily on formal decision making, financing, and participation, I also consider important informal rules that guide the work of organizations. As a reminder, the placement of all major global governors on such continuums determines the aggregate intergovernmental or nongovernmental nature of global governance in an issue-area at a certain point in time. In sum, in this book, I will consider all changes to rules stipulating which types of actors can vote, finance, and participate in deliberations in IOs.

THE DECISION-MAKING DIMENSION OF THE
INTERGOVERNMENTAL–NONGOVERNMENTAL CONTINUUM

There are many different types of institutional decision-making arrangements in IOs. I focus here specifically on the ones that give voting power to governments or nongovernmental entities because the field of international relations has emphasized the distinction between IOs where solely states are members and have the formal right to vote (IGOs) and those where they are not members and do not have voting privileges (INGOs). This ubiquitous distinction is made in virtually all college introductory International Relations (IR) textbooks as well as textbooks focusing specifically on international organizations. It is also commonly used by policymakers and the press. The IGO-INGO dichotomous differentiation also appears in all research on global governance. Quantitative studies utilize datasets that have understandingly adopted this dichotomy for operationalization purposes (Shanks et al. 1996; Pevehouse et al. 2004; Rodgers and Volgy 2009; Murdie 2014). This dichotomous analytical approach further affects the literature on this topic, as the vast majority of research seldom takes into account the potential similarities of the two types of organizations and rarely compares the relative impact that they have in the international realm, implying that IGOs and INGOs are simply "different."[15] Of course, this dichotomous approach to empirical studies has meant that there have not been any analyses using the *degree* of intergovernmentalism/nongovernmentalism as explanatory or outcome variables.

Even if we were to base our understanding of the intergovernmental–nongovernmental character of global governance solely on this dichotomy, we would still observe considerable variation across time. Figure 1.2 offers a visualization of such trends across the past century. The lines in the figure reflect the changes in the total number of formal IGOs and INGOs established that year. The graph is based on the dichotomous conceptualization of IGOs and INGOs and on data from the *Yearbook of International Organizations*,

---

[15] For an interesting exception, see the reports of One World Trust, an organization that assesses and compares side by side the level of accountability of both IGOs and INGOs (Blagescu and Lloyd 2006).

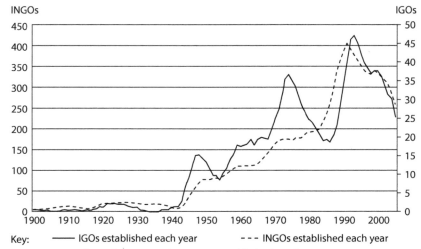

FIGURE 1.2. Number of IGOs and INGOs established each year.

generally considered one of the most authoritative sources (and the oldest) on international organizations (Union of International Associations 2015).[16] As expected, the number of INGOs established each year (see left vertical scale) is approximately ten times higher than the number of IGOs established each year (right vertical scale).

Figure 1.2 illustrates that although the increase and decline in the number of IGOs and INGOs have generally gone hand in hand (as emphasized by extant literature[17]), there have also been times when the number of new IGOs appears to increase faster than the number of INGOs and other times when the reverse is true. Figure 1.3, tracking the evolution of the *ratio* between the number of new IGOs and new INGOs established each year since 1900, offers a better illustration than Figure 1.2 of such differences.[18] It indicates that while in the interwar era and in the mid-1980s, for every

[16] It accounts for the establishment of all "Cluster I" international organizations, which include "type A" (federations of IOs), "type B" (universal membership IOs), "type C" (intercontinental membership IOs), "type D" (regionally defined membership IOs), and "type F" (organizations having a special form). Implicitly, it excludes all national organizations, "emanations," "subsidiaries," "treaties and agreements," etc.

[17] For discussions of how the emergence of INGOs triggers the emergence of IGOs, see, e.g., Boli and Thomas (1997, 1999); for discussion of IGOs generating opportunities for new INGOs to emerge, see, e.g., Reimann (2006) and Steffek (2014).

[18] The graph is based on data from Union of International Associations (2015). It represents the smoothed five-year moving average.

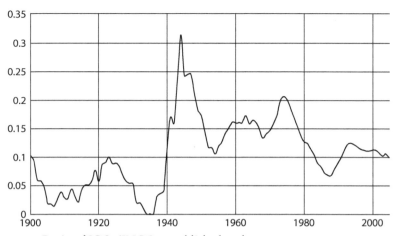

FIGURE 1.3. Ratio of IGOs/INGOs established each year.

new IGO established, there were more than ten new INGOs, in the immediate post–World War II era, for every new IGO there were only about three new INGOs. The ups and downs of the graph in Figure 1.3 can be interpreted as reflections of greater intergovernmentalism and nongovernmentalism, respectively.

In addition to this "first cut" discussion of the relative intergovernmental versus nongovernmental nature of global governance based on a dichotomous understanding of decision making, we can also identify *degrees* of governmental versus nongovernmental control. Moreover, there is significant variation across time with regard to such control. Indeed, many IOs such as the IBE and the UN World Tourism Organization started out by giving nongovernmental actors control over decisions and later formally granted control to governments (IUOTO 1969). Other organizations, such as Intelsat[19] and Inmarsat (Sagar 1999), were transformed from formal IGOs into private, nongovernmental entities. Additionally, IOs do not necessarily fall on one end or the other of the continuum. In some organizations, both governmental and nongovernmental actors are given votes. The first such mixed arrangements date back to the early international meetings of the mid-nineteenth century. For example, in the first International Sanitary Conference of 1851, states were each represented by two delegates, a diplomat and a physician (Charnovitz 1997, 5). After World War I, the ILO became the "poster child" of hybrid organizations. The International Union for the Conservation of Nature, founded in 1948, gives votes to almost

[19] See www.intelsat.com/announcement/2001-intelsat-privatization, accessed March 3, 2018.

a hundred governments and a thousand NGOs. Governments have three votes, international NGOs are given two votes, and national NGOs get one vote. Collectively, both governments and NGOs have veto power over the IUCN's decisions (IUCN 2017).

There are yet other cases of formal IGOs where although some organs are solely in the hands of governments, others offer nongovernmental actors decision-making power. For example, the World Commission on Dams, which was established by the World Bank and functioned from 1997 to 2001, included governmental and nongovernmental representatives with equal rights.[20]

Other IGOs have established bodies comprised of experts who vote in their individual capacity, not as representatives of states. This practice goes back to 1815, when it was adopted by the first formal IGO, the Central Commission for the Navigation of the Rhine. The Commission has altered its rules several times over the past two centuries with regard to the relative independence of its officials (Walther 1965).

Some of the best known examples of such independent experts are those of judges in the International Court of Justice and in the International Criminal Court. Even though studies have found some evidence of national bias in judges' decisions (Posner and De Figueiredo 2005), the overall nongovernmental nature of these bodies has remained fairly strong. Moreover, in practice, the independence of such experts varies across states and time.

In other well-known very intergovernmental IOs, the original nongovernmental nature of some bodies has eroded or been completely eliminated over time. For example, Article V of the World Bank's Charter provides for an advisory council to include nongovernmental representatives of banking, commercial, industrial, labor, and agricultural interest groups. Although a council was selected soon after the Bank's inception, it never truly functioned (Mason and Asher 1973, 32). As mentioned earlier, the rules guiding the work of UNESCO's Executive Board changed in 1954 so that members who were supposed to be elected in their personal capacity instead became official representatives of their governments, thus shifting the body toward greater intergovernmentalism (UNESCO 2009).

Of course, the intergovernmental nature of decision making in international organizations is not only reflected in the relative independence of top experts represented in councils, committees, and courts. It is also a product of the independence of the entire staff working for such organizations (e.g., Cronin 2002). Although officials from intergovernmental IOs are rarely directly part of the decision-making process, the information that they generate, the way they frame such information, as well as the information that they *leave out* of their official reports impacts decisions. Therefore, the degree to which

---

[20] See www.internationalrivers.org/sites/default/files/attached-files/world_commission_on_dams_final_report.pdf, accessed March 3, 2018.

intergovernmental IOs' formal and informal rules promote staff independence contributes to their nongovernmental character. At various moments, most obvious during the late interwar and early Cold War eras, such independence was eroded and, implicitly, international organizations slightly shifted away from nongovernmentalism.

Finally, we should note that even when nongovernmental actors are formally represented and vote in international forums, their nongovernmental character is a question of degree. Indeed, one of the greatest concerns in the ILO is that throughout the history of the organization, many labor and employer representatives have not been truly independent but rather controlled by their governments (Milman-Sivan 2009; Grigorescu 2015, 202–210). Conversely, in many formal INGOs, voting is organized through national delegations. This often allows for greater control by governments. In fact, one of the main reasons for the establishment of the very nongovernmental League of Red Cross Societies (LRCS) in 1919 was that the United States sought to gain greater control over the rival International Committee of the Red Cross (ICRC) founded fifty years earlier (Towers 1995).

Of course, throughout history, there were many far less subtle (but more successful) attempts by governments to control nongovernmental IOs. Recently, the literature discussed how some INGOs (dubbed "IONGOs" rather than GONGOs) are organized and controlled by IGOs (Steffek 2014).

THE FINANCIAL DIMENSION OF THE INTERGOVERNMENTAL–NONGOVERNMENTAL CONTINUUM

While even the apparently straightforward decision-making dimension of IOs allows for some differentiation across the intergovernmental–nongovernmental continuum, the other two dimensions of control (financial and deliberative) lead to especially subtle nuances. Indeed, the financing of IOs often blurs the traditional dichotomy. There are many organizations that are formally nongovernmental but that receive funding from governments. A 2006 study on humanitarian aid found that states tend to offer more funding through INGOs ($1.07 billion for that year) than through the major IGOs ($0.73 billion) (Cooley 2010, 253). In the United States, for example, government funds for nongovernmental IOs are channeled through several frameworks, including the US Agency for International Development, the National Endowment for Democracy, the Middle East Partnership Initiative, and the US Institute of Peace (NGO Monitor 2013a). There are, however, significant differences across IOs considered to be nongovernmental. While many organizations such as Doctors without Borders and the World Wildlife Fund receive government funding, others such as Amnesty International and Greenpeace refuse to do so (NGO Monitor 2013b). During the Cold War, the practice of funding nongovernmental IOs by governments became especially visible after numerous cases were reported of such organizations secretly being financed by the CIA or Soviet government sources (Willetts 2000, 41).

Organizations that on paper appear to be very intergovernmental are often funded by nongovernmental entities. The RF, for example, has long been one of the most generous donors to many different types of organizations, including intergovernmental ones. During the interwar era, not only did it fund the IBE both during its more nongovernmental years and later as a formal IGO, but it virtually singlehandedly kept the League of Nations Health Section alive with funds and personnel when governments had drastically reduced funding for the organization (Borowy 2009, 137). Recently, the Gates Foundation has contributed in similar ways to a number of intergovernmental IOs. For example, in 2012 it gave more than half a billion dollars to the World Health Organization (WHO), far more than any other voluntary contribution to the IO, including those from member-states (WHO 2013).

Some intergovernmental IOs, like UNICEF, rely substantially on nongovernmental funding. In 1998 nongovernment sources accounted for 38 percent of the IO's budget (UNICEF 1999, 5). By 2005, this proportion had grown to 50 percent (UNICEF 2009, 29). It is difficult to assess how intergovernmental these organizations really are, as one presumes they need to satisfy, at least to some degree, the interests of their nongovernmental donors as much as those of their member-states.

Funding also flows from the more intergovernmental to the more nongovernmental organizations. This practice can be found as far back as the first years of the League of Nations. Due to a stipulation in Article 24 of the Covenant that "the Council may include as part of the expenses of the Secretariat those of any bureau or commission which is placed under the direction of the League,"[21] the organization initially supported financially some otherwise very nongovernmental IOs, offering its facilities for their meetings and covering publishing costs of some of their documents (Inter-Parliamentary Union 1921, 1; White 1951, 251).

As I noted, in its first two decades, UNESCO also sponsored a number of very nongovernmental IOs, some of which would not have existed without such support (Sewell 1975, 110; Willetts 2000, 55). More recently, in 1996, when ECOSOC took on the reform of the UN's relationship with NGOs, it adopted Resolution 31 that called on the UN Secretariat to offer secretarial support for NGOs. This action, although not as substantive as the direct donations that were made by the League and UNESCO, nevertheless also brings into question the independence of such formally nongovernmental IOs.

---

[21] See League Covenant, available at http://avalon.law.yale.edu/20th_century/leagcov.asp, accessed March 3, 2018.

THE DELIBERATIVE DIMENSION OF THE
INTERGOVERNMENTAL–NONGOVERNMENTAL CONTINUUM

A third way of gauging the relative intergovernmental or nongovernmental nature of an IO is by assessing the degree to which representatives of intergovernmental and nongovernmental entities participate in deliberations taking place in each other's forums. Such deliberations shape ideas that, in turn, affect global governance. Very intergovernmental IOs indeed participate in conferences that are formally considered nongovernmental and play very important roles in setting agendas of the more nongovernmental IOs (e.g., Carpenter 2010).

Nongovernmental actor participation in intergovernmental IOs can take multiple forms short of voting or funding programs, discussed in the previous sections.[22] For example, many very nongovernmental IOs are involved in the implementation of programs of intergovernmental IOs. Nevertheless, such "IGO-INGO" interactions usually involve nongovernmental IOs performing tasks (and often competing to be given the opportunity to perform them) that have already been decided by the intergovernmental IOs, a relationship sometimes described as "orchestration" (Abbott et al. 2015), and that are not expected to give very much influence to nongovernmental actors. Therefore, of the various forms of nongovernmental IOs' participation in intergovernmental IOs discussed, this study considers that together with voting and financing work, access to deliberations is the most important because it gives nongovernmental entities the possibility to shape the ideational environment of formally intergovernmental IOs and, implicitly, their policies.

There is a great deal of variation with regard to nongovernmental actors' access to the deliberations in intergovernmental IOs, both across time and organizations. As mentioned, the initial status given to nongovernmental entities in the League of Nations, described as "participation without a vote" (Pickard 1956, 25–26, 54; Seary 1996, 23), was a very prestigious and influential one. The early inclusive nongovernmental approach of the League was replaced by the 1930s with a more intergovernmental one. Nongovernmental IOs were rarely allowed in League conferences after 1929, and the last assessors had their participation rights withdrawn in 1937 (Chiang 1981, 38; Charnovitz 1997, 21).

Nongovernmental actors were once again given an important role in global governance immediately after World War II. More than a thousand nongovernmental IOs took part in the deliberations leading to the drafting of the UN Charter (Seary 1996, 26). Due to this initial nongovernmental influence, Article 71 of the UN Charter stipulated that ECOSOC should make "suitable

---

[22] For a comprehensive discussion of the potential forms of IGO-INGO interactions, see Johnson (2016).

arrangements" for consultations with nongovernmental organizations. The number of such nongovernmental IOs with consultative status in ECOSOC increased rapidly in the UN's first two decades (Global Policy Forum 2011). However, in 1967 ECOSOC Resolution 1296 gave the NGO Committee greater control over which organizations could participate in UN activities (Chiang 1981, 161). In the following years, the proportion of nongovernmental IOs given consultative status declined slightly.

In the early 1990s, nongovernmental actors once more were given a greater role in the UN. The ICRC, the Sovereign Order of Malta, and the International Federation of Red Cross and Red Crescent Societies became the first such organizations to be granted observer status in the General Assembly (Willetts 2000, 197). Many very nongovernmental IOs were also increasingly present in UN conferences organized in the first few years of the post–Cold War era (Friedman et al. 2005; Martens 2011). This nongovernmental movement spurred then UN Secretary-General Kofi Annan to state that "The United Nations once dealt with governments. By now we know that peace and prosperity cannot be achieved without partnerships involving governments, international organizations, the business community, and civil society" (UN-NGO 1998). Yet, by the late 1990s, the movement toward increased nongovernmental actors' access to the UN slowed down again. Although the 1993–1996 review of ECOSOC's arrangements for consultation with NGOs allowed national and subregional organizations (and not just the internationally focused nongovernmental organizations) to gain UN consultative status, through this action, the UN is generally considered to have in fact diluted the role of larger and more critical organizations and opened the door to some government-sponsored IOs that were formally considered NGOs (Global Policy Forum 1996).

Figure 1.4 offers an illustration of nongovernmental organizations' access to the League and UN. It represents the ratio between the number of IOs considered by the *Yearbook of International Organizations* to be INGOs and that had an official working relationship with the League (as "assessors" or "corresponding members") and with the UN (in "consultative" status), and the total number of such INGOs in existence that year.[23] The graph illustrates that nongovernmental organizations' access to deliberations in these major intergovernmental IOs varied considerably across time.

One recent study has shown that the variation in nongovernmental actors' access is visible in many other formally intergovernmental IOs besides the League and UN. Moreover, it showed that there are important differences with regard to access among various intergovernmental IOs (Tallberg et al. 2013).

---

[23] The data are based on information from the League's *Bulletins of Information on Work of International Organizations* and the *Yearbook of International Organizations*, respectively. Also see Grigorescu (2015, 187, 190).

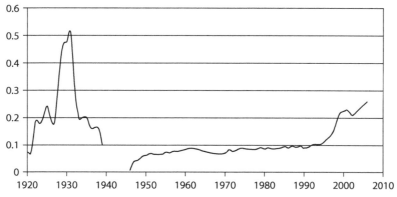

FIGURE 1.4. Proportion of INGOs working with the League of Nations and UN.

In some organizations, such as UNESCO, nongovernmental groups can participate in almost all forums, while in others, such as the Bank for International Settlements, virtually all nongovernmental entities are kept out of all forums. Of course, this variation affects the degree to which nongovernmental actors can influence the work of the very intergovernmental IOs and, implicitly, the overall nature of the organization.

POSSIBLE RELATIONSHIPS BETWEEN THE THREE DIMENSIONS OF THE CONTINUUM

Recent developments may suggest that the movement across the three dimensions of the intergovernmental–nongovernmental continuum go hand in hand, and thus imply that it may not be useful to distinguish between them. Indeed, the literature has shown how in the post–Cold War era, a number of organizations where decisions are adopted by nongovernmental entities, such as the International Accounting Standards Board or the Forest Stewardship Council, became the main global governors in their respective realms, taking on important issues that could easily have been handed over to more intergovernmental IOs (Slaughter 2004). This is a possible indication that global governance is becoming more nongovernmental in nature on the decision-making continuum. During this period, very significant donations from organizations such as the Bill & Melinda Gates Foundation (McCoy et al. 2009) and the UN Foundation, that began with $1 billion in funding from Ted Turner (Rohde 1997), have also raised awareness of the financial contributions of nongovernmental entities to very intergovernmental IOs. Similarly, research has shown that nongovernmental actors' access to intergovernmental deliberations increased dramatically after the end of the Cold War (Tallberg et al. 2013).

Nevertheless, this apparent simultaneous advancement across the three dimensions is deceiving. First, it is not clear whether the same IOs or issue-areas that experience increased degrees of nongovernmentalism across one dimension simultaneously experience it across the other two dimensions or whether, in fact, the shifts are across only one or two dimensions at a time. Second, even if there have been simultaneous movements across multiple dimensions in the past few decades, it is not clear whether the trends from other periods throughout history have also exhibited such connections between the three dimensions or whether this recent period is unique in the way it brings together these dimensions.

In fact, there are multiple examples of IOs and issue-areas experiencing opposing trends across the three dimensions. For example, while the ILO is one of the few IOs where representatives of fairly nongovernmental groups vote, it is also seen as one of the least open to participation of formal INGOs, in part because labor and employer representatives want to preserve their power in the organization and not share it with other nongovernmental actors (Thomann 2008). This may imply that IOs often occupy very different positions on the decision-making and deliberative dimensions of the continuum. Indeed, while one may believe that the decision-making dimension somehow "subsumes" the one of deliberation (because actors who can vote also can participate in deliberations), this example reminds us that, in fact, the two are independent of each other, as there are moments when some nongovernmental actors are being included in the decision-making processes while, simultaneously, others are being excluded from the deliberative ones. Conversely, there are moments when some nongovernmental actors are excluded from decision making while others are being included in deliberations. For example, as previously mentioned, in 1954 UNESCO turned its Executive Board from one where individuals were selected and voted in their own capacity into one where such individuals were government representatives. At that time, UNESCO nevertheless continued to maintain good relations with very nongovernmental IOs and include them in its deliberative processes.

Another relevant example is the League of Nations in the 1930s, which began limiting access for the more nongovernmental IOs to deliberations while the economic depression was making it rely more than before on nongovernmental entities such as the RF to fund its work. In a similar fashion, in UNESCO's first decade, although the IO had one of the highest numbers of NGOs with observer status (an indication that the organization was placed closer to the nongovernmental end of the deliberative continuum compared to other IOs), many of these organizations had been created and were funded by UNESCO, suggesting that on the financial continuum, global governance in this realm was very intergovernmental in nature (UNESCO 1951, 117).

Yet another example of how shifts across the three dimensions often do not go hand in hand is that the explosion in the number of formal INGOs with consultative status at the UN during the post–Cold War era has not translated into any changes with regard to their role in formal decision making. In fact, when the Joint United Nations Programme on HIV/AIDS (UNAIDS) was established, although it gave nongovernmental IOs a prominent role that was considered by many to be closer to that of "members" rather than of "observers" (Willetts 2011, 71), ECOSOC Resolution 1995/2, creating the new organization, stipulated clearly that "non-governmental organizations would not participate in any part of the formal decision-making process, including the right to vote, which is reserved for representatives of Governments" and, moreover, that "These arrangements for the participation of non-governmental organizations are not to be regarded as setting a precedent" (UNAIDS 2009, 14).

Finally, it is surprising to note that so-called hybrid IOs, where nongovernmental actors have formal voting power alongside governments, appear to receive a much greater proportion of their funding from governments than do many IOs where voting is solely in the hands of governments. For example, in the IUCN, one of the best known IOs that allow both governmental and nongovernmental representatives to vote, government and intergovernmental funding currently represents more than 90 percent of the organization's resources[24] while in IOs such as the WHO or UNICEF (where solely governments have decision-making power), this proportion is close to 50 percent.

This study therefore will not assume that global governance either experiences simultaneous changes across multiple dimensions of the intergovernmental–nongovernmental continuum or changes in different directions on these dimensions. Instead, I will begin by treating the above three dimensions as independent of each other and seek to determine if and when two or all three of them have experienced similar trends. What the above examples suggest is that there may be times, issue-areas, and organizations where similar factors lead to parallel trends across the dimensions. Alternatively, there may be instances where decision makers only promote changes across one dimension. They may even attempt to encourage a greater nongovernmental role on one dimension but compensate with a weaker role on another. Therefore, the present study seeks to assess the relationships between the three dimensions and the shifts across these dimensions rather than take them for granted.

For example, we may expect that changes to decision-making processes will not be as frequent as changes to funding and deliberations, especially if the latter two are more informal in nature. Similarly, we may expect that the main battles over the decision of which types of actors actually vote in an IO will unfold primarily at the founding of the organization. Those battles over

---

[24] See www.iucn.org/sites/dev/files/iucn_2015_-_audit_report_and_consolidated_financial_statements_with_2_signatures.pdf, accessed November 6, 2019.

the questions of who can and will finance the organization and who is allowed to take part in deliberations are expected to play out even later, throughout the existence of the IO. However, all such expectations need to be tested.

Despite their independence, the three dimensions nevertheless each represent an important aspect of the overall degree to which global governance is intergovernmental or nongovernmental. We can bring the three dimensions together to assess where global governance falls at a certain point in time on the aggregate intergovernmental–nongovernmental continuum.

In this sense, the three dimensions can be seen as analogous to other components of well-known aggregate measures such as democracy (Marshall et al. 2010) or national power (Singer et al. 1972). Various components of such measures (such as competitiveness of political participation, regulation of political participation, or constraints on the chief executive, in the case of the Polity democracy score) are brought together to give us a more refined and complete understanding of the concept that is being assessed. Similarly, the three dimensions of intergovernmentalism or nongovernmentalism, taken together, allow us to assess the overall placement of global governance at a given moment in time.

In fact, the images of global governance shifting across a single dimension as in Figure 1.1 should be interpreted as being ones of the aggregate measure of intergovernmentalism or nongovernmentalism. One could, of course, depict such shifts in global governance across a three-dimensional space defined by the three gauges of intergovernmentalism or nongovernmentalism. I will, nevertheless, represent them across only one dimension (as in Figure 1.1) because it is easier to visualize changes across one dimension rather than three in the two-dimensional pages of a book. Despite such simplifications in the illustrations depicting the intergovernmental–nongovernmental continuum, in the detailed case studies, I will discuss the three dimensions, as they give us a richer understanding of developments in global governance.

THE STRUCTURE OF THE BOOK

Having introduced in this chapter the notion of an intergovernmental–nongovernmental continuum to individual international organizations and to the aggregate nature of global governance in place of the traditional dichotomy, the following chapter turns to address the main question that derives from the existence of such a continuum: *When* is global governance likely to experience shifts toward a more intergovernmental or nongovernmental approach? This is a very basic question in the study of global governance, but for the most part it has not yet been asked, much less answered. It should be understood as both preceding and being preceded by another basic question in global governance scholarship, the more common and by now fairly ubiquitous one of when governments are likely to cooperate with each other and form IOs (e.g., Krasner 1983; Keohane 1984; Mearsheimer 1994; Shanks et al. 1996; Rathbun 2012). Indeed, even before seeking cooperation and the establishment of intergovernmental structures, states (at least the most powerful ones) first need to determine that they *want* to step in and deal with certain global problems rather than encourage or allow nongovernmental actors to become or remain the main global governors. For example, in the education realm, governments did not believe they should become involved in global governance up until the late 1920s. Some did not consider that they should deal with international education issues even as late as 1945.

Additionally, after governments decide that they do want to form organizations to deal with global problems, they may find that there is not sufficient agreement among them with regard to how such IOs should function (as in the case of the IBE discussed earlier in this chapter). When governments are not successful in establishing IOs, nongovernmental actors are more likely to take on important roles in global governance. In other words, the establishment of nongovernmental forms of global governance should be viewed as an alternative third possible outcome, in addition to the two usually discussed in the literature: (1) An intergovernmental IO is established or (2) no IO, whether intergovernmental or nongovernmental, is established.

More broadly, the emergence of intergovernmental IOs should not be viewed, as much of the literature has so far suggested, as simply the result of states' ability to cooperate with each other on a specific issue. It is also the result of governments deciding that such global issues need to be resolved by them (*and not others*) in the first place.

Chapter 2 offers a set of possible answers to the question of when global governance is more intergovernmental or nongovernmental. As this is the first study addressing this question, it cannot offer an exhaustive answer. I will therefore begin by emphasizing two hypotheses that offer the most explanatory power. They both involve mechanisms connecting domestic and global preferences of the most powerful states: one ideology-based and a second institutions-based. Both mechanisms explain how governments' domestic activist preferences are likely to lead to support for intergovernmentalism while domestic preferences for passivism generally lead to more nongovernmental approaches. Domestic preferences shaped initially by ideologies and institutions are then aggregated at the global level through the interactions of the most powerful states.

I add to those two main hypotheses several other arguments that derive implicitly from existing literature. Of course, by focusing primarily on only two mechanisms, even after mentioning briefly other possible explanations for the shifts in global governance, I am aware that I am not offering a complete answer to my question regarding the causes of shifts across the intergovernmental–nongovernmental continuum. Perhaps most important, an approach such as mine that emphasizes the role that governmental actors play inevitably leaves out explanations focusing on actions and reactions of nongovernmental actors. Indeed, although the present study offers examples of nongovernmental entities acting fairly independently and affecting the nature of global governance, future research on intergovernmental–nongovernmental shifts should look more closely at these actors. However, in this first cut attempt to answer my main question, I purposefully chose to focus primarily on governments because I join others who consider them to be the most important drivers of such processes (e.g., Green 2014, 6–8). This choice is based on the observation that when powerful states truly want to shape the nature of global governance (and agree on how to do so), they can almost always bring about the changes they desire. A study that covers developments over the past century and a half, such as mine, offers many examples (especially in the interwar and Cold War eras) of instances when statist and autocratic governments have reined in nongovernmental actors.[25] In other words, I argue that the apparently powerful and independent role of nongovernmental actors has been overemphasized due to the literature's primary interest in explaining recent developments. Indeed, when focusing solely on the past few decades we are, in fact, witnessing the result of a strong neoliberal approach promoted by powerful Western states that has given nongovernmental actors a greater role. However, such strong roles for nongovernmental actors should not necessarily be viewed as generalizable to past, or especially, future developments.

After presenting the arguments regarding the likelihood that global governance will be more intergovernmental or nongovernmental in nature, Chapter 2 concludes by laying out the research design that allows me to assess the plausibility of these arguments through in-depth case studies. Chapters 3–5 then follow the evolution over the past century and a half of three important global issue-areas: health, labor, and technical standards. The research for these chapters is based on both primary and secondary sources. The primary sources include documents from archives, libraries, and websites of multiple IOs: Food and Agriculture Organization, International Association for Labour Legislation, International Committee of the Red Cross, International Electrotechnical Commission, International Federation of Red Cross and Red Crescent Societies, International Labour Organization, International Organization for Standardization, International Relief Union, International Telecommunication Union, League of Nations, Office for International Public Hygiene, United Nations, World Bank, and World Health Organization.

---

[25] The anticorruption issue-area offers an interesting recent example of governments purposefully allowing nongovernmental actors (primarily Transparency International) to take the lead, only to become more active (especially through the intergovernmental World Bank, Organization for Economic Cooperation and Development and UN Office of Drugs and Crime) when they felt it was in their interests to do so (see Gest and Grigorescu 2010).

These empirical chapters serve two purposes. First, they offer additional support for the argument that global governance needs to be understood across an intergovernmental–nongovernmental continuum with distinct dimensions. The cases are chosen to represent issue-areas that traditionally have been considered to reflect very different approaches on the intergovernmental–nongovernmental continuum to show that even though they are generally viewed as being intergovernmental (in the case of health), hybrid (in the case of labor), or nongovernmental (in the case of technical standards), in fact, they have each varied across time back and forth on the three dimensions of the continuum.

Taken together, the three chapters suggest that when looking across time, regardless of the issue-area, global actors have sought both intergovernmental and nongovernmental solutions to collective problems. Therefore, we should not take for granted that the present forms of global governance, even if they have been in place for some time, are the only ones possible, or even the "best" for a specific issue-area.

Second, the three case studies assess the plausibility of the main hypotheses regarding the causes of shifts across the intergovernmental–nongovernmental continuum. I purposefully choose issue-areas where there have been at least some attempts to develop global collaborative arrangements for more than a century. Such long time frames allow for a more complete study of the variation across the intergovernmental–nongovernmental continuum and thus avoid the inherent problems faced by studies of issue-areas that are fairly new (such as the environment or anticorruption) and focus solely on recent decades when the few relevant shifts may all appear to take place in the same direction. The evolution of the three issue-areas includes instances of the emergence of new global governors; changes of rules in the way IOs work, thus making them more intergovernmental or nongovernmental nature; nongovernmental actors being preferred over intergovernmental ones; intergovernmental organizations replacing nongovernmental actors; and governments and nongovernmental actors vying for power within IOs and, more broadly, within an issue-area. Such variation gives us dozens of opportunities (that can be seen as numerous successive cases, rather than three single cases) to assess the strength of the arguments. Also, the diverse set of global problems discussed in the three chapters allows me to determine whether the main arguments "travel" not only across time but also across issue-areas.

By answering an identical set of five questions in each chapter, I am able to compare the evolution of events in the three issue-areas. I summarize the answers to these questions in similar tables at the conclusion of each empirical chapter. This allows me to bring together my findings in the concluding Chapter 6 into one overarching analysis of almost a hundred shifts across the intergovernmental–nongovernmental continuums in the three realms. The conclusions sum up both similarities and differences between the issue-areas and identify the broader patterns across time. The concluding chapter also considers some additional explanations of the shifts across the intergovernmental–nongovernmental continuum that derive from the three cases. While these explanations may appear to be "ad hoc" in each case discussed in the book, together they allow for broader generalizations that have important implications.

Chapter 6 further discusses the relevance of the findings in theoretical and practical terms. I mention here only the two most important such conclusions. First, in analytical terms, by moving beyond the dichotomous intergovernmental–nongovernmental approach to global governance, we can develop a much more accurate understanding of how to best seek solutions to the world's problems. After all, such problems, from security, trade, environmental, health, labor, human rights, standardization, and many other realms, affect billions of lives and it is therefore important that we allow for more nuanced understandings of how to best approach them. Implicitly, the answers to my questions regarding the degree to which intergovernmental or nongovernmental actors take the lead in global governance are just as consequential as the analogous ones from the domestic realm, of whether and to what degree governments or nongovernmental actors become involved in various issues such as health care, minimum wages, or consumer safety standards.

Second, the observation that global governance has moved both back and forth across the intergovernmental–nongovernmental continuum over the past century and a half implies that we should not draw hasty conclusions regarding future developments based solely on the past few decades, when several powerful Western states appear to have shifted global governance toward greater nongovernmentalism and a weakening of the state (Vernon 1971; Ōmae 1995). The more hands-on or hands-off government approaches to global governance across time have also been affected by the powerful states' preferences that are, in turn, strongly shaped by their domestic ideologies and institutions. In fact, one of the most important findings of this book, that the ideologies of powerful states indeed shape global governance, coupled with recent apparent domestic ideological shifts, as well as in the power shifts among the world's most influential states, may indicate that we will soon witness, yet again, important changes to how the world is governed.

2

Causes of Intergovernmentalism
and Nongovernmentalism

As discussed in Chapter 1, the observation that global governance varies across an intergovernmental–nongovernmental continuum begs the question of how we can explain such variation. In other words, *when* is global governance likely to experience shifts toward a more intergovernmental or nongovernmental approach?

In this chapter, I address this question by considering the factors expected to affect the likelihood that global governance be more intergovernmental or nongovernmental. As the present study is the first to seek direct answers to this question, it does not purport to offer an exhaustive analysis, going into the same amount of detail for all potential explanations. Instead, it emphasizes one powerful type of explanation for the variation across the intergovernmental–nongovernmental continuum that previous literature has only tentatively or indirectly touched upon: the link between the domestic and global preferences of the most powerful states.

I begin this chapter by showing that there are indeed strong connections between domestic shifts toward governmental activism or passivism and those between intergovernmentalism and nongovernmentalism, respectively. I offer some prima facie evidence of such linkages by focusing on important US foreign policy decisions that have led to shifts in global governance over more than a century.

I then proceed to explain these linkages by emphasizing the processes through which domestic ideologies and institutions come to affect international decisions. A first such process is based on political elites' need to have a high degree of coherence between the policies that derive from an ideological approach. A second process involves the establishment or empowerment of domestic institutions (often as a result of changes in ideology) that, in turn, alter a state's international preferences. I then explain how, once domestic preferences are projected to the international realm, the interactions between state representatives lead to aggregate overall intergovernmental or nongovernmental approaches to global governance.

I also mention other factors, mostly at the system level, that can influence the intergovernmental or nongovernmental nature of global governance, although I do not go into the same depth when discussing them as I do for my two main hypotheses. I identify such additional factors by developing a series of arguments that follow logically from existing literature.

These other factors are not viewed as alternative explanations, but rather additional ones. The complex processes that lead to shifts across the intergovernmental–nongovernmental continuum allow for multiple factors acting separately as well as simultaneously. There is no a priori reason to believe that the systemic and state-level factors affecting the intergovernmental or nongovernmental nature of global governance always go hand in hand. Systemic pressures for changes to global governance do not necessarily trigger domestic ideological or institutional reactions nor necessarily impede them. Alternatively, powerful states are not always successful in projecting their domestic preferences to the global level. I begin from the assumption that such system- and state-level factors are independent of each other. In the concluding chapter, I will seek to identify patterns across the almost 100 shifts discussed in Chapters 3–5 that will allow me to assess, among other things, whether and when system-level and state-level factors act together or separately.

The chapter concludes with a discussion of the research design I use to assess the plausibility of the hypotheses generated by the theoretical arguments. I explain the choices for the issue-areas considered in the following chapters and identify a common set of questions that I seek to address in each case.

INITIAL EVIDENCE OF THE DOMESTIC–INTERNATIONAL GOVERNMENT ACTIVISM LINKAGES

In virtually all states, governments have struggled with questions regarding the degree to which they should involve themselves in resolving collective problems. When the "government sector" does not act to resolve such problems, one of the other two domestic sectors (the business and voluntary nonprofit sectors) often steps in (Salamon and Anheier 1999). Alternatively, when governments take on more active roles, nongovernmental entities such as markets, nongovernmental organizations (NGOs), private foundations, or private-public entities are often crowded out of the governance process.

The distinction between the two other sectors, besides the government one, suggests that nongovernmentalism at the domestic level can be the result of either a laissez-faire ideology, which purposefully gives a greater role to markets, or a democratic pluralist one, which purposefully increases the role of the voluntary nonprofit sector. Conversely, governmental activism can be the result of statist or authoritarian ideologies. What these two ideologies have in common is that they both call for governments to play a greater role and for nongovernmental actors to play a smaller one. Of course, the multiple ideologies supporting activism or passivism do not necessarily go hand in hand.[1] There are instances of authoritarian states embracing laissez-faire economic policies and of democratic states adopting activist economic and social policies. I show below that in the case of the United States, and of many other states, the rise and decline of such ideologies at the domestic level has also impacted preferences for intergovernmentalism or nongovernmentalism at the global level.

At the end of the nineteenth century and the beginning of the twentieth century, progressives and socialists in powerful European states such France, Germany, and the United Kingdom sought to empower governments and give them a greater role in important social issues such as education, health, housing, and labor (Kloppenberg 1988). In the United States, when Theodore Roosevelt became president, his strong support for progressivism (as well as that of Taft, his hand-picked successor) materialized primarily in "trust-busting" policies and legislation through which the government intervened to rein in corporate actions. Woodrow Wilson's brand of progressivism, despite maintaining a strong emphasis on governmental activism, also promoted partnerships between governmental and nongovernmental actors more than Roosevelt had. These activist domestic policies coincided with increasing American support for intergovernmental initiatives, such as the failed efforts to establish the International Bureau of Education in 1914 that the United States strongly supported (Rossello 1943), and, of course, the establishment of the League and ILO after the war. Figure 1.2 indeed reflects this spurt in the number of newly established intergovernmental IOs soon after World War I, many of which were supported by the United States at that time.

The ILO, in particular, offers an example of a fairly intergovernmental IGO that began focusing on an international issue that had previously been dealt with solely by transnational labor movements and the nongovernmental International Association for Labour Legislation. While Wilson promoted an intergovernmental approach to the issue, he also sought to develop strong governmental-nongovernmental partnerships in the ILO that were similar to the ones he was promoting domestically. As will be shown, he supported, but with less success, a similar "hybrid" partnership in the global health realm.

Soon after World War I, support for intergovernmentalism was substantially eroded in powerful countries. This was true especially in the United States, as clearly illustrated by the Senate's rejection of the country's

---

[1] Ideologies do not map out perfectly on the political party spectrum of individual countries. For example, in the United States, there have been Democratic administrations with laissez-faire orientations and Republican administrations that took a hands-on approach to governance. Some policies of President Clinton (who famously declared that "the era of big government is over") offer examples of the former and some of the Nixon administration (including the establishment of the Environmental Protection Agency) illustrate the latter.

membership in the League. This trend accompanied President Harding's "return to normalcy" toward reduced domestic governmental activism of the 1920s. US-based nongovernmental actors such as the American Red Cross and the Rockefeller Foundation began filling gaps left open by the government and in some cases were supported by government officials who promoted nongovernmental approaches at both the domestic and global levels (Borowy 2009). At that time, the United States also opposed the establishment of very intergovernmental IOs, such as the IBE (as discussed in Chapter 1) and the International Relief Union (promoted by the Italian government starting in 1921) (Hutchinson 2001, 253).

The Roosevelt administration that adopted New Deal policies domestically was also responsible for the promotion of intergovernmental solutions to a number of economic and social issues. This was seen as early as the 1930s when it contributed to the establishment of intergovernmental IOs such as the Bank for International Settlements and became active in existing ones such as the ILO (which it joined in 1934) and the League itself, where it supported the Bruce Committee's work. The Committee considered the important question of expanding the League's tasks to the economic and social realms (Lavelle 2005). US domestic governmental activism during and immediately after World War II went hand in hand with the strong degree of American support for intergovernmentalism soon after the war. US leadership led to the establishment of many very intergovernmental IOs at that time, as reflected in Figure 1.2. The strong link between US activism in the domestic and international realms immediately after World War II has been mentioned before in the literature (Strange 1982; Burley 1993; Borgwardt 2005).[2]

Domestic governmental activism in powerful Western states declined soon after World War II, especially in the United States, where in the early 1950s, a Republican Congress began rolling back policies that had been in place for two decades of Democratic administrations. US support for intergovernmentalism also declined. In the late 1940s, Congress even hesitated to ratify membership in intergovernmental IOs that the United States had initiated (Farley 2008, 66–67).

Both domestic activism and global intergovernmentalism generally increased throughout the 1960s and early 1970s. However, in the 1980s, the United States, together with the United Kingdom and several other Western allies, began promoting deregulation and once more rolled back the role of government. The Reagan administration also emerged as an opponent of intergovernmentalism, refusing to back the creation of several new organizations (Brinkley 1987; Abbott and Snidal 1998, 5; Bennett and Oliver 2002, 342; Schechter 2005, 85). During the 1980s, the United States threatened to leave some intergovernmental IOs and, in the end, followed up on its promise in the case of UNESCO (Preston et al. 1989, 10).

---

[2] In fact, Susan Strange has argued that the global institutions that emerged after World War II were an attempt to "remake the whole world in the image of the U.S.A." (1982, 482).

Soon after the end of the Cold War, the United States experienced an increase and later a decline in its domestic activism. During the first of these two periods, it also went through a period of greater support for intergovernmentalism. For example, it is relevant that the post–Cold War era saw the emergence of organizations such as the World Trade Organization (WTO), about five decades after proposals for a similar intergovernmental IO was not accepted by the United States. Yet, by the 2000s, the United States and other powerful states began supporting the emergence of more nongovernmental entities that would deal with global issues that the more intergovernmental IOs had not yet tackled, as in the case of the International Accounting Standards Board.

Overall, the preceding brief narrative offers some initial support for the argument that, at least in the case of the United States, the broad changes in domestic levels of governmental activism mirror the shifts that powerful countries experience in terms of their support for intergovernmentalism. How can we explain such domestic–international linkages? The following sections will offer a survey of the literature discussing these linkages and then will lay out two arguments that allow me to explain the projection of domestic activism to the global realm.

LINKING DOMESTIC PREFERENCES TO INTERNATIONAL
OUTCOMES: EXISTING LITERATURE

The first major attempts to explain the domestic factors affecting foreign policies can be traced to the early decision-making literature of the 1960s and the work of scholars such as James Rosenau (1969) and Graham Allison (1969). Rosenau's research on foreign policy decision making was path-breaking in its focus on domestic factors that influenced international decisions. Yet his taxonomy of "linkage politics" did not lead to more extensive research on the specific domestic preferences that were being connected to the international ones. Allison's seminal work on the Cuban Missile Crisis offered three models of understanding foreign policy outcomes. The bureaucratic politics model is particularly useful for answering the main question of this book. This model emphasizes that foreign policy decisions are often the result of an interplay between individuals representing various interests within governments (Allison 1969, 707). The interests of top officials can be explained, at least in part, by the differing views of the organizations that they represent when coming together to make foreign policy decisions. Such high-ranking individuals often come to believe that the "health of their organization is vital to the national interest" (Allison 1971, 167). Therefore, when seeking to shape foreign policy decisions together with government officials from other national institutions, they will take into account the well-being of their own organization.

As the structural theoretical approaches of neorealism and neoliberal institutionalism dominated international relations literature in the 1970s and 1980s, the ensuing research of that period shifted to emphasize the similarities between state interests at a given time rather than the differences. After all, faced with the same structural constraints, states as different as the United States and Union of Soviet Socialist Republics (USSR) appeared to be seeking the same types of goals (Waltz 1979). Neorealism, in particular, has always prided itself in moving away from "atomistic" approaches because it sees state preference formation primarily as the product of interstate interactions, rather than being "home grown" (Grieco 1988).

By the mid-1980s, a number of scholars began questioning, once more, whether structures alone could explain international decisions. In one of the most relevant critiques for the purposes of the present study, John Ruggie argued that to understand the emergence of international regimes, we need to consider how structural power considerations are "fused" with legitimate social purpose (1982, 382). According to Ruggie, such social purpose varies, depending on the preferences of the most powerful states (1982, 384).

Similarly, although neoliberal institutionalism, one of the main theoretical approaches to challenge neorealism, has also focused on explanations at the system level (in part, to show that even when starting out from the same assumptions as neorealism, one can reach different conclusions regarding conflict and cooperation), Robert Keohane, the main proponent of this approach, has long recognized that material structures alone cannot tell us everything. For example, in an argument also particularly relevant for this study, he mentioned that to understand the difference between American and British hegemony at different times, one needs to also consider each state's *willingness* to lead in the international realm (Keohane 1984).

Starting with the end of the Cold War, international relations theories began focusing more on the processes that led domestic preferences to affect international outcomes. This turn was in part due to the recognition that the most convincing explanations of the groundbreaking events leading to the disappearance of the USSR and, with it, the bipolar system, relied at least partially on developments within states, rather than solely on the ones between them (e.g., Lebow and Risse-Kappen 1997).

In the late 1980s and early 1990s, constructivism quickly emerged as an important approach both challenging and complementing neorealism and neoliberal institutionalism. For example, Alexander Wendt, who contributed substantially to shaping this approach, argued that one of the main reasons neorealism and neoliberal institutionalism could not agree on whether relative gains or absolute gains guided states' decisions was that neither one had a theory of where such preferences came from in the first place. According to Wendt, the two approaches had a "behavioral conception of both process and institutions: they change behavior but not identities and interests" (1992, 392). Constructivism, on the other hand, does not take interests as given, but rather sees them as being socially constructed. While some authors initially focused more on how the construction of such interests was based on a history of *interstate* interactions (in great part to show that realist arguments also focusing on such "top down" approaches were incomplete) (e.g., Wendt 1992, 1995; Finnemore 1996), others moved to add explanations of preference formation based on *domestic* norm-driven processes (e.g., Katzenstein 1996). As part of this growing literature, a number of works have emphasized how domestic norms such as those of civil society participation (Tallberg et al. 2013), anticorruption (McCoy 2001), and transparency (Florini 2003; Grigorescu 2007) first became powerful at the domestic level and then traveled to the international realm, shaping global governance.

The emergence and increased influence of constructivism can be seen as part of a broader trend that has emphasized ideational approaches to international relations in the post–Cold War era. Goldstein and Keohane explained the "revival" of the study of ideas on foreign policy by emphasizing the need to complement the growing prominence of rationalist explanations that "called into question old assumptions about whether the substantive content of people's ideas really matters for policy" (1993, 4). Within this broader emerging strand of literature, some have discussed the importance of ideologies in shaping foreign policy decisions. However, such works have so far only emphasized how the ideological similarities and differences between states (Haas 2007; Moravcsik 2010, 241–242) or between key domestic actors (Milner and Tingley 2015) affect international interactions. Surprisingly, the literature has not, however, touched upon the most important element of ideologies: their coherent character that allows them to bring together ideas across issue-areas and, essential for this study, across the domestic–international divide. I argue in more detail below that the changes in great power ideologies are to a large degree responsible for the global governance shifts across the intergovernmental–nongovernmental continuum.

Just a few years after the emergence of constructivism, yet another important theoretical approach addressed in a comprehensive manner the question of how domestic preferences shape international outcomes. This approach, coined new liberalism by Andrew Moravcsik, took a number of previous arguments of domestic preference formation, especially from the decision-making and constructivist bodies of literature, added others, and included them in a broader theoretical framework connecting the domestic and international realms. This new form of liberalism emphasized how domestic ideas, material interests, and institutions shape foreign policy. The three different elements lead us, according to Moravcsik, to three variants of liberal theory: ideational, commercial, and republican (1997).

Ideational liberalism considers the impact of a state's social identity and values on its foreign policy. Such identities and values are defined as shared preferences regarding the proper *scope* and nature of public goods provision (Moravcsik 1997, 525). Some of the "democratic peace" literature is considered to fall within this strand of liberalism, as it emphasizes how democratic identities and values have an essential impact on states' international behavior (e.g., Russett 1993, 5–11; Weart 1998). Yet another important type of social identity emphasized by liberalism as shaping foreign policy is "the nature of legitimate socioeconomic regulation and redistribution" (Moravcsik 1997, 525), something of particular relevance in explaining powerful states' decisions related to *whether* to become involved in dealing with global issues.

Commercial liberalism offers explanations of state preferences based on market incentives that domestic (and transnational) economic actors face. More specifically, it suggests that domestic and global economic structures impact costs and benefits of trade and, implicitly, shape states' trade policies (Moravcsik 1997, 528). This second form of liberalism may be relevant for explaining the emergence and use of IOs such as the WTO (or failure of the International Trade Organization [ITO]), but it is not as useful for explaining the broader question of this study, regarding the emergence and empowerment of more intergovernmental organizations, rather than encourage a reliance on nongovernmental actors.

The third variant of liberalism, called republican by Moravcsik, focuses on the processes through which domestic institutions aggregate interests and shape foreign policies (Moravcsik 1997, 530). The various forms of domestic structures can lead even states with apparently similar preferences to take different actions in the international realm if institutions aggregate the original preferences in different ways (Risse-Kappen 1991). One should note that some of the most prominent authors whose scholarship is considered to exemplify this strand of liberalism have acknowledged that there is a direct link between the older foreign policy decision-making literature, especially Allison's work on bureaucratic politics, and their own work (Putnam 1988, 431).

The main arguments of the present study draw from liberalism, specifically from its ideational and republican forms. While I accept that some of the shifts across the intergovernmental–nongovernmental continuum are affected by changes in system-level factors (that I discuss below), I consider that the immediate causes of such shifts involve changes in domestic preferences. Indeed, even in some cases when global structural factors such as conflict or increased levels of peaceful state interactions (represented by economic and information flows) alter the incentives to embrace a more intergovernmental or nongovernmental approach to global governance, it is the most influential individual actors in the system, the great powers, that need to step in and establish or change existing international institutions. The actual choices that they make in responding to the system-level changes are based on domestic preferences (Moravcsik 1997, 519).

I further posit that there are two principal mechanism connecting governmental activism in the domestic realm to activism in global governance. The first mechanism can be considered a form of the ideational liberal approach, as it focuses on the impact of ideologies. The second, related mechanism emphasizes the impact of domestic institutions on the formation of international preferences, thus falling closer to republican liberalism. The two approaches, ideational and institutional, have a great deal in common and are often considered to complement rather than supplant each other (Checkel 1997). Therefore, as I show below, the mechanisms discussed here lead to similar predictions and often can be difficult to disentangle from each other. Nevertheless, I will suggest some important differences between the two mechanisms as well as some ways to understand the connection between them.

TWO MECHANISMS CONNECTING DOMESTIC AND INTERNATIONAL GOVERNMENT ACTIVISM

How exactly do domestic preferences translate into states' global preferences for intergovernmentalism and nongovernmentalism? A first mechanism connecting the domestic and international levels is generated by ideologies. The second is based on the impact domestic institutions have on international preferences for intergovernmental or nongovernmental solutions.

As expected, the literature on ideologies was especially prominent in the early part of the Cold War. Political scientists focusing on this topic started out by distinguishing them from other ideational forms, emphasizing that ideologies were coherent sets of ideas (Naess et al. 1956; Lane 1969; Sartori 1969; Mullins 1972). They "cluster" beliefs, thus giving them a rigid character (Sartori 1969). In fact, although many of the relatively disparate definitions of "ideology" may not always overlap with each other, they all share an understanding that ideologies offer a high degree of coherence between different ideas (Gerring 1997). Ideological approaches are therefore considered the opposite of pragmatic ones that imply individuals choose belief systems that work best in a given situation, regardless of whether they come together (Sartori 1969).

The constraining effect of ideologies impacts beliefs and actions not only across issue-areas but also across the domestic–international divide. For most individuals, the connections between domestic and international beliefs may simply be the result of their seeking consistency to avoid cognitive dissonance.[3] For instance, it would be difficult for an individual to support the reduction of national bureaucracies domestically while simultaneously embracing the creation and expansion of intergovernmental IOs with large bureaucracies. For political elites, the connections may be even stronger than for ordinary individuals. Even if they do not personally feel the need for consistency, they may be pressured to promote similar policies at the domestic and international levels because

---

[3] Cognitive dissonance theory has been incorporated in the literature on foreign policy decision making for some time. See, e.g., Jervis (1976, 406).

otherwise, domestic and even international audiences may question their sincerity. The discrepancies between domestic and international actions may weaken the ideology and, implicitly, the arguments backing important existing policies.

The relevance of ideologies for domestic–international linkages has been discussed by a number of scholars, including some who have specifically used such connections to explain the emergence (e.g., Mazower 2009)[4] and work (e.g., Steffek and Holthaus 2018) of intergovernmental IOs. I posit that ideological connections between domestic and international policies may lead public officials to promote activism simultaneously at both the domestic and global levels. For example, Roosevelt expressed such connections in his "Four Freedoms" speech, considered one of the first steps toward American global engagement in World War II, when he argued for the promotion of the freedoms to the international realm, not only at the domestic level: "Just as our national policy in internal affairs has been based upon a decent respect for the rights and the dignity of all of our fellow men within our gates, so our national policy in foreign affairs has been based on a decent respect for the rights and the dignity of all nations, large and small."[5]

Conversely, when governments embrace ideologies of limited government domestically, they are unlikely to support activist intergovernmental solutions in global governance. For example, at the 1981 UN Conference on New and Renewable Sources of Energy, the United States was among the main opponents of establishing an intergovernmental forum for this issue. At that time, the Reagan administration did not want to create an international agency funded solely by governments and argued instead for a nongovernmental approach based on public-private funding (Brinkley 1987; Schechter 2005, 85). This position implicitly suggested that there was indeed a need for such an international body, but not an intergovernmental one. The administration's arguments at the international level were consistent with its opposition to large bureaucracies and governmental activism at the domestic level. The intergovernmental International Renewable Energy Agency was established only in 2009, when the United States supported greater governmental activism.

A more explicit example of how anti-activist ideologies simultaneously affect domestic and international policies was expressed by Margaret Thatcher. In 1988, she argued against giving greater power to European institutions, stating that "We have not successfully rolled back the frontiers of the state in Britain, only to see them re-imposed at a European level."[6]

---

[4] It should be noted that the domestic–international linkage provided by ideologies that I discuss here is different than another important one emphasized by Rathbun (2012) in his study of IGO emergence. His argument is not based on ideological preferences for greater or less governmental activism but, rather, on behavioral differences between representatives on the left or right due to their inclinations to trust others.

[5] See http://voicesofdemocracy.umd.edu/fdr-the-four-freedoms-speech-text/, accessed March 3, 2018.

[6] See www.margaretthatcher.org/document/107332, accessed March 3, 2018.

The need for coherence among multiple ideas, operating at either the domestic or international level, provides the "glue" that allows us to connect developments at the two levels. In fact, for a theoretical approach that seeks to explain linkages between domestic preferences and international outcomes, it is somewhat surprising that liberalism has not emphasized the importance of such ideologies more. It is especially surprising because most ideologies focus on essential ideas about how domestic (and global) governance should work and, therefore, the actions that are based on ideologies should be easily observable.

The literature points to another characteristic of ideologies that has important implications for this study: They generally characterize beliefs of narrow groups within society, usually political elites (Sartori 1969; Mullins 1972; Bawn 1999). This makes these beliefs different from norms that are the focus of much of the constructivist literature. Norms are seen as being shared by individuals across large societal segments, regardless of their political inclinations.[7]

This understanding of ideologies implies that top-level elites are responsible for domestic–international ideational connections. In fact, the ideological approaches are most likely to provide connections between the domestic realm when they are promoted by the highest government officials (presidents, prime ministers, and representatives speaking directly on their behalf in international meetings) because they decide on policies in multiple issue-areas and levels where such consistency is important. By contrast, lower-level bureaucrats, who are not supposed to reveal their ideological leanings and who remain in position even when governments change, are not likely to be responsible for the domestic–international ideological linkages.

This argument suggests that ideological preferences for domestic approaches to governance and, implicitly, international preferences of states for more intergovernmental or nongovernmental approaches, are most likely to shift after new elites come to power. Such changes can take place either through peaceful means (usually through elections) or through violent ones (such as revolutions or internal putsches). While not all changes in national leadership will lead to ideological shifts, the sheer frequency and number of such changes in governments (especially in democratic systems) suggests that domestic factors allow for more opportunities for variation across the intergovernmental–nongovernmental continuum than the often slow-changing system-level factors. Of course, another possible cause for the shifts across the intergovernmental–nongovernmental continuum implicit in this ideology-based argument is the rise and decline of powerful states. Such systemic changes lead to different states, often with elites embracing different ideologies, playing greater or smaller roles in the promotion of intergovernmentalism or nongovernmentalism in global governance.

---

[7] For a widely accepted definition of norms, see Finnemore (1996, 22).

A second explanation for the domestic–international linkages focuses on the role of domestic institutions. Specifically, I expect that states are more likely to promote intergovernmentalism after government institutions are established or empowered to deal with similar domestic problems. Conversely, I expect states to embrace nongovernmentalism in global governance when domestic nongovernmental institutions are established or empowered. That is because domestic institutions come with bureaucracies that develop expertise and vested interests to establish and join IOs.

In the example from the international education realm discussed in Chapter 1, this mechanism was noticeable both when France became the strongest supporter of an intergovernmental education IO in the interwar era and when the United Kingdom and the United States pushed for establishing UNESCO after World War II. France was one of the few powerful countries with an education ministry in place in the 1920s. After the United States established the Bureau of Education in 1939 and the United Kingdom created an Education Ministry in 1943, officials from these two new domestic institutions took the lead in promoting an intergovernmental approach to international education immediately after World War II (Sewell 1975, 37).

We should indeed expect that officials from domestic specialized offices who represent their countries in international forums often will become the principal actors responsible for the domestic–international institutional linkages. As mentioned, the international relations literature has long noted that such officials may promote both their country's interests and their narrower organizational ones (Allison 1969). Organizations, in turn, are seen as rational goal-oriented actors seeking their own survival and growth (Downs 1966; Pfeffer 1997, 20). Growth is especially important in the organization's first years of existence. At that time, before having developed routinized relationships with major partners, it is seen as being in potential danger of surviving (Downs 1966, 9–22). Of course, even in later stages, the organization has incentives to expand its work in order to gain material resources and prestige.

An obvious way in which a domestic institution may grow is by taking on international work. By doing so, it can seek collaborations with counterparts from similar institutions in other countries, acquire valuable experience from other bureaucracies that have already sought to resolve analogous domestic problems, increase its budget and personnel, and garner prestige that often comes from participating in international forums.

There are many examples of government officials from domestic specialized institutions spearheading international initiatives leading to the creation and empowerment of IOs. Immediately after World War I, it was Leon Berard, the new French Minister of Public Instruction, who initiated the efforts to establish a League of Nations office for international relations among universities and schools (Renoliet 1999, 16). Similarly, just two years after the US Bureau of Education was established, some of its top officials sought (unsuccessfully) to form an intellectual and educational intergovernmental organization for

the Western Hemisphere (Sewell 1975, 56). Perhaps most important, the original plans for UNESCO originated in London during the war, when Richard
Butler, who was overseeing at that time the creation of the first British education ministry, launched discussions with education ministers from eight governments in exile in the United Kingdom to plan for postwar educational
reconstruction (Mylonas 1976, 93).

The interests of domestic bureaucracies are visible not only in the interactions leading to the establishment of new organizations but also in those surrounding the empowerment or maintenance of existing ones. For example, it
is noteworthy that the US Department of Education was one of the principal
advocates for continued US participation in UNESCO in the 1980s when
the Reagan administration sought withdrawal from the IO (Preston et al.
1989, 160).

Of course, there are also many instances of officials from domestic nongovernmental institutions promoting nongovernmentalism. For example, when
UNESCO was established, leaders of many national NGOs were among the
strongest supporters of the French hybrid proposal for the organization, giving votes not only to governments but also to nongovernmental representatives, like them (Sewell 1975, 65–66).

The two mechanisms hypothesized to connect domestic and international
activism do not exclude each other. One or both can take place at a given
time, linking developments across the domestic-global divide. In fact, one can
argue that the emergence or empowerment of domestic institutions is often
the result of domestic ideological shifts. Viewed this way, this second, institution-based mechanism can be considered as an indirect way through which
domestic ideologies can affect the global shifts across the intergovernmental–
nongovernmental continuum. The indirect mechanism can act simultaneously
with the more direct one discussed earlier. One should point out, however, that
the emergence of new domestic institutions or the empowerment of domestic
institutions is not always the result of ideological shifts. Changes in material
incentives (whether originating at the domestic or global level) can also lead
to institutional changes, even when the ideological environment remains the
same.

The possible linkages between domestic governmental activism and intergovernmentalism are represented in Figure 2.1. One can envision an analogous
figure depicting the connection between domestic and international support
for nongovernmentalism.

Because of their potential to take place simultaneously, the two mechanisms sometimes overlap. Ideologies can simultaneously lead to the establishment of new domestic institutions and the promotion of international ones
(see bifurcated arrow 1 in Figure 2.1). When domestic institutions are established or expanded, they increase the likelihood that international institutions
will be created or empowered because their bureaucracies have interests to
expand their work to international projects (arrow 2 in Figure 2.1).

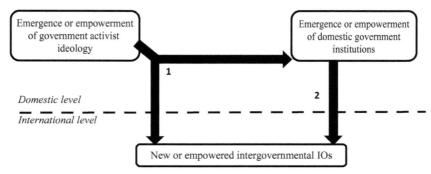

FIGURE 2.1. Connections between increases in governmental activism and increases in intergovernmentalism.

It is difficult to distinguish between the effects of these two mechanisms. However, the above discussion offers several indications of ways in which we can gain a better understanding of the specific mechanism that has unfolded. First, ideological linkages apply to multiple levels of both governance and issues. Decisions for greater governmental activism (or for rolling back government) cross issue-areas because they are influenced by similar belief systems. Institution-based mechanisms, however, function only narrowly, within one issue-area. For example, officials from domestic education institutions are expected to promote intergovernmentalism only in the education realm. Neither their vested interests nor their expertise should lead to changes in other areas.

Second, as suggested earlier, ideological arguments are likely to be made by top elites rather than lower-level officials coming from domestic institutions. By contrast, an institution-based linkage will be made by representatives of specialized domestic institutions. For these reasons, I consider the direct involvement of the latter group in the processes that lead to the establishment or empowerment of international institutions as necessary evidence of the institution-based mechanism unfolding.

Last, but not least, one can distinguish the institutional mechanism from the ideological one based on the types of arguments used by those promoting changes to global governance. As mentioned, ideologies differ from other sets of beliefs because they reflect a coherent (clustered) set of ideas. Therefore, arguments that are based on ideologies need to be seen as generalizable. In other words, they need to be applicable to other similar circumstances, whether these unfolded at other times or in other issue-areas. Ideological arguments thus often include references to analogies, to the ways that governmental activism or passivism in the domestic realm or in one issue-area worked well and therefore should also be applied to the issue at hand. Institution-based mechanisms, in contrast, will be reflected in more technical and pragmatic arguments regarding the greater effectiveness of either an intergovernmental or a nongovernmental approach. The latter arguments focus on the usefulness of a certain solution for the situation at hand without making any references to analogies across the domestic–international divide or across issue-areas.

THE AGGREGATION OF STATES' PREFERENCES AT THE INTERNATIONAL LEVEL AND HYPOTHESES

While the previous sections argued that individual states tend to export their domestic preferences to global governance, it is important to also consider the aggregation of preferences across states, leading to greater overall intergovernmentalism or nongovernmentalism in the global system. Indeed, liberalism looks to such two-stage processes where states first define their preferences and then "debate, bargain or fight to particular agreements" (Moravcsik 1997, 544).

The study of such aggregation is especially important when preferences vary across states. As the following chapters will show, over the past century and a half, there have been differences even between the United States and the United Kingdom, two great powers that often share similar views. Of course, there have been even greater differences between the United States and USSR throughout the Cold War and between the United States and China in the post–Cold War era.

To explain such aggregation, I first posit that the most powerful states play by far the greatest role in shaping the nature of global governance. As the examples in Chapter 1 from the realm of education suggest, we should expect the most powerful countries' ideologies and institutions to overwhelmingly affect decisions for adopting a more intergovernmental or nongovernmental global approach. The decision to not establish a more intergovernmental IO for education immediately after World War I as part of the League of Nations structure was primarily made by the United Kingdom and France. The United States did not weigh in on the decision because, at that time, it was becoming clear that it would not join the League. Later, although France, Germany, and Italy (and some smaller states) joined the IBE, the lack of support for this IO by the United States and the United Kingdom eventually led it to have only a minor role in global governance.

Additionally, I posit that the intergovernmental or nongovernmental nature of global governance results from a compromise between multiple powerful states, not solely from the preferences imposed by the dominant power. This complements previous literature that has emphasized only the role of hegemons in shaping global governance structures to match their own preferences (e.g., Ruggie 1982; Keohane 1984; Burley 1993). For example, the establishment of the League of Nations originated simultaneously, albeit based on different models, in several powerful states, most important in the United States, the United Kingdom, and France (Miller 1928). Similarly, ideas underlying the establishment of the UN originated in the US State Department. In December

1941, they were discussed with British officials. In 1943, the Soviet Union was also brought into the negotiations.[8]

When officials from the two to three most powerful states[9] come together to decide on the establishment of new international institutions or changes within existing ones and when their preferences are similar, the result will reflect their consensus and will sometimes lead to global governance shifting close to one or another end of the continuum. This was the case, for example, when virtually all powerful states refused to form a more intergovernmental IO for education immediately after World War I.

Yet, in most cases, powerful states' intergovernmental or nongovernmental preferences differ and clash. In many such instances, global governance is less likely to experience changes, as was the case in the first unsuccessful attempts to establish a major IO dealing with education before World War I. However, other times, the different positions of states can nevertheless lead to changes, but ones where the end result is not a purely intergovernmental or nongovernmental approach; rather, it is one of compromise that falls closer to the middle of the intergovernmental–nongovernmental continuum. This was true in the negotiations leading to the establishment of UNESCO, where the United States and the United Kingdom promoted greater intergovernmentalism while France sought an organization with greater nongovernmental elements. In later Cold War clashes over UNESCO's character, the USSR pushed for a more intergovernmental character for the organization while the United States and the United Kingdom promoted a more nongovernmental one. After the two Western states withdrew from the organization in the 1980s, the two sides of the Cold War appeared to reach a compromise that placed UNESCO, once more, closer to the middle of the continuum. Overall, I expect global governance to be more intergovernmental in nature when most of the great powers have embraced governmental activism domestically.

All of the above arguments and examples lead to the two following hypotheses linking domestic and international preferences.

H$_1$: Global governance is likely to shift toward intergovernmentalism when ideologies of domestic governmental activism become stronger in the most powerful states.

H$_2$: Global governance is likely to shift toward intergovernmentalism when domestic governmental institutions are established or enhanced in powerful states in a specific realm.[10]

---

[8] The Dumbarton Oaks Conference also brought the Chinese and French into the process of shaping the UN. Nevertheless, their impact on the organization was much smaller than that of the "big three."

[9] For tests in support of arguments that domestic preferences of the most powerful one, two, or three states affect the degree of intergovernmentalism in global governance, see Grigorescu and Baser (2019).

[10] The wording of the hypotheses shows that the ideology-based mechanism functions across multiple issue-areas while the institution-based one functions narrowly within only one issue-area.

Of course, I expect reverse shifts (toward nongovernmentalism) to take place in global governance when domestic ideologies and institutions favor passivism over activism.

ADDITIONAL EXPLANATIONS

Although this book emphasizes two primary mechanisms that lead to the export of domestic preferences to the international realm, it acknowledges that other factors can also affect the variation I seek to explain. First, there are, of course, other domestic actors besides top government officials and bureaucrats from domestic institutions who can play a role in projecting domestic preferences to the international realm. In most states, multiple other veto players (Tsebelis 1995) can deny (or at least delay) the executive branch the opportunity to promote either intergovernmentalism or nongovernmentalism. Most important, the legislative branch can slow down or even stop international plans initiated by the executive. This is especially true when the two branches are controlled by different parties that embrace different ideologies (e.g., Milner and Tingley 2015). This argument suggests, more broadly, that the structure of government and of the party system in a state may affect the ability of top elites to promote their ideologies internationally and of bureaucracies from domestic institutions to push for the establishment or empowerment of international institutions. This implies that the aforementioned distinction between shifts due to the establishment of new intergovernmental IOs (that usually require ratification by legislatures) and those due to changes to rules within existing IOs or to the increased use of some IOs rather than others (decisions that do not require ratification) is important not only to describe the evolution of global governance but also to explain it.

Additionally, a number of other nongovernmental actors, besides those pushing directly for a more nongovernmental approach to global governance (as was the case of the nongovernmental organizations promoting a hybrid approach to the functioning of UNESCO at its founding), may sometimes shape the government's overall approach to global governance. The empirical chapters will note when domestic groups representing business interests or professions, or ad-hoc coalitions of various groups, have influenced the degree to which the executive branch has ended up supporting intergovernmentalism or nongovernmentalism.

While acknowledging the role all such domestic actors can have, and the differences across states due to governmental structures, I posit that, all other things being equal, the ideological leanings of the elites in power and the emergence and empowerment of domestic institutions are likely to have a strong effect on a country's support for or its opposition to changes in the intergovernmental or nongovernmental nature of individual IOs and, more broadly, on global governance. Moreover, I suggest that even if other domestic actors play roles in determining countries' preferences for a more intergovernmental or nongovernmental international approach, these roles are only secondary, compared to the one of the executive. After all, it is individuals from the executive branch or from domestic specialized institutions who usually represent the country in the international arena and who adopt international agreements. Other domestic groups have only an indirect role in shaping this position (e.g., Krasner 1978, 11; Ikenberry et al. 1988; Brooks and Wohlforth 2008). In sum, as a first study seeking to explain the intergovernmental–nongovernmental shifts, the present book will focus primarily on the most relevant actors involved in such domestic processes but will also point out when other domestic factors appear to affect outcomes.

A discussion of the possible causes of global shifts across the intergovernmental–nongovernmental continuum needs, of course, to consider not only the domestic determinants of such changes but also system-level ones. First and foremost, it should be pointed out that as the main argument of this book is that domestic preferences of the most powerful states shape global governance, the systemic changes in the distribution of power are, of course, expected to influence the intergovernmental or nongovernmental nature of world politics.

There are other system-level factors beyond global power shifts that derive from existing literature and that I will also consider. The first strands of international relations literature directly relevant for identifying possible systemic factors leading to intergovernmental or nongovernmental trends emerged in the 1970s and 1980s. Despite emphasizing slightly different aspects of the establishment and work of IOs, complex interdependence theory (Keohane and Nye 1977), regime theory (Krasner 1983), and neoliberal institutionalism (Keohane 1984) all moved beyond the simplifying realist assumption that such organizations are nothing more than reflections of international power distributions (e.g., Mearsheimer 1994). They each discussed at great length the relationship between interstate cooperation and intergovernmental IOs, concluding that the two are both a cause and a consequence of each other. Indeed, the vast majority of the international relations literature has associated the emergence of intergovernmental IOs with the ability of states to cooperate (e.g., Krasner 1983; Axelrod and Keohane 1985; Snidal 1985; Oye 1986).

As mentioned earlier, this study goes beyond these basic arguments and considers that intergovernmentalism first requires governments, at least the ones of the most powerful states, to believe that they *should* become involved in resolving specific global problems and not leave global governance to others. Only afterward do they consider cooperating through IOs (or acting through informal institutions or even acting alone) to find solutions to such problems. Of course, this implies that the conditions allowing for interstate cooperation or impeding it, *as well as* the willingness of individual powerful states to take on global problems, are both necessary for intergovernmentalism to develop. Therefore, I will list below some of the factors the literature has discussed as leading to cooperation as I acknowledge that they need to be taken into account in a study focusing on the decision of whether to establish and empower intergovernmental or nongovernmental global governors.

Existing literature discussing the system-level factors affecting the emergence and empowerment of intergovernmental IOs suggests that one of the most important such factors is military conflict between states. International conflicts reduce interstate cooperation and, implicitly, the likelihood of governments adopting common (intergovernmental) solutions to their problems. The literature has found that intergovernmental IOs are more likely to be established immediately after major conflicts, when states seek ways to alleviate the problems leading to wars in the first place (Wallace and Singer 1970, 257; Shanks et al. 1996). Figure 1.2, which follows the variation in the number of new intergovernmental IOs each year, indeed shows that such numbers increased considerably after World War I and especially after World War II. However, the research suggests that this effect may simply be due to the fact that the continuous trends of IO establishment are interrupted during wartime and, therefore, what we see after wars is nothing more than states catching up with the "accumulated pressures" to create such organizations (Singer and Wallace 1970, 536).

While conflictual interstate relations are seen as reducing the likelihood of shifts toward intergovernmentalism, peaceful international and transnational interactions are expected to increase it. Indeed, functionalists have long made the argument that as interstate informational flows increased, and as production and markets became more international in nature, governments were under greater pressure to seek collaborative solutions to their growing number of common problems (Mitrany 1966). In other words, governments are more likely to become involved in global problems when they are sufficiently salient to warrant their collaborative efforts. Some of these initial arguments have been further developed by Keohane and Nye, who emphasized how increased interdependence led to a greater need for international regimes (1977, 290–292), as well as by others seeking to explain the emergence of intergovernmental IOs (Shanks et al. 1996, 618). These works have argued that interactions, whether between state actors or transnational actors, are conducive to cooperation and the emergence and use of intergovernmental solutions to global problems. Interactions can take multiple forms, such as transborder flows of information (including beliefs and ideas), goods, finances, and persons (Nye and Keohane 1972).

Sociologists, proponents of world polity theory (e.g., Meyer et al. 1997; Boli and Thomas 1999), have been particularly interested in how increased peaceful international interactions have led to the emergence of a global polity characterized by a common world culture. According to them, this culture, in turn, has been responsible for the increasing number of intergovernmental IOs (and of nongovernmental IOs). Their research has indeed shown that the degrees of interstate communication, trade, wealth, and development correlate very strongly with the number of IOs in the world (Boli and Thomas 1999, 26–27).

In addition to these system-level factors affecting the likelihood that states will embrace an *intergovernmental* approach, there are also a series of arguments regarding the overall strength of *nongovernmental* actors at a given time and, implicitly, the likelihood that global governance will be more nongovernmental in nature. Some of these arguments coincide with the ones regarding intergovernmentalism. Indeed, lack of conflict, or economic and informational interactions, may have positive effects on the emergence and empowerment of both intergovernmental IOs and international nongovernmental actors (Keohane and Nye 1977; Boli and Thomas 1999).

Nevertheless, I do not expect such effects to be equally strong. The *rates* with which intergovernmentalism versus nongovernmentalism increase at times of peace and intense economic and informational interactions are likely to differ (as Figure 1.3 suggests). For instance, it has been argued that while the internet has allowed both governmental and nongovernmental interactions to become more intense, the latter generally have benefited more than the former from this innovation, as governments have a more difficult time maintaining their monopoly over information flows across borders than they did in the past (Florini 2003). Similarly, in most cases, trade is a relationship that directly affects private (nongovernmental) producers, exporters, and importers, and only indirectly governments. As I will show, this explanation has been among those given for the fact that private actors rather than governments are usually the first to react to changes in technology and the first to seek common standards for goods that cross borders. Based on such arguments, one generally expects increased trade and informational flows to favor "transnational relations" (between nongovernmental actors) over "intergovernmental relations."[11]

Similarly, international conflicts reduce the likelihood of cooperation through both intergovernmental channels and nongovernmental ones. However, while conflicts lead governments to focus both their international and domestic efforts almost entirely on the war efforts, many nongovernmental actors may remain committed to cooperation with their counterparts from other states, even during such difficult times. This is because their main goals are not necessarily related to the conflict, as in the case of governments. Implicitly, I expect intergovernmentalism to be more affected by international conflicts than nongovernmentalism is.

An additional argument involving the degree to which global governance is nongovernmental builds on an observation from the domestic realm: Just as in domestic politics where nongovernmental entities are more likely to emerge and become powerful at times of greater democracy, global nongovernmentalism will develop when the number and strength of democracies worldwide is higher. This argument has been explained both on the basis of the spread of domestic democratic participatory norms to the more intergovernmental IOs

[11] For this distinction, see Keohane and Nye (1977, xii).

(Tallberg et al. 2013) and on the decentralizing domestic mechanisms that allow civil society groups to organize and become powerful internationally (Andonova et al. 2017). Overall, we expect nongovernmentalism to increase during "waves of democracy" and to decline during "reverse waves of democracy" (Huntington 1991).[12]

The literature has also pointed out that the empowerment of nongovernmental actors at the state level is strongly related to that country's level of development, especially to its relative wealth (Skjelsbaek 1971, 83–84; Boli and Thomas 1999, 26–27; Reimann 2006, 45). Indeed, as many nongovernmental actors rely on funding that is made available from societal disposable resources, we expect them to fare well during strong economic times rather than economic slowdowns. When projecting this argument from the domestic level to the international one, we conclude that overall global income should lead to a relative increase in nongovernmentalism.

However, the reverse trend, of governments taking on fewer activities during difficult economic times, has not been given the same attention. This latter development implies that when global wealth declines, intergovernmentalism also will be eroded. Just as in the case of competing trends resulting from high levels of economic and informational interactions and from conflict, discussed earlier, I expect one of the two trends resulting from changes in global wealth will be more powerful than the other. For example, one can argue that due to the relative ability of large nongovernmental foundations to weather economic crises better than governments, their influence will increase during such times, and global governance is likely to become more nongovernmental in nature.

In addition to this broad scholarship discussing the factors related to the emergence and empowerment of intergovernmental *and* nongovernmental actors, there is a burgeoning body of literature that asks a question directly related to the one of this book: When is it more likely for intergovernmental IOs *rather* than nongovernmental actors to emerge or become more powerful (Abbott et al. 2016; Andonova et al. 2017)? Some of these works draw from the rational choice institutionalist literature and have shown that there are important global changes when there is a high level of "organizational density," that is, when the number of IOs increases and they find themselves competing for the limited resources available. At such times, the literature has argued that entry costs of formal IGOs compared to lower costs of flexible nongovernmental actors will lead decision makers to prefer the latter over the former (Abbott et al. 2016).

It should be noted that virtually all of the system-level factors mentioned above can be considered as deriving either from the rational choice

---

[12] This argument differs from the main one that domestic ideologies in the most powerful states (including democratic ideologies) impact the degree of nongovernmentalism in IOs and in global governance as it refers to global trends across *all* states, rather than just within one or two great powers.

institutionalist literature or the sociological institutionalist literature. The former emphasizes how exogenous factors alter material cost-benefit calculations of states and, implicitly, lead to changes in IOs (e.g., Koremenos et al. 2004). The latter emphasizes the importance of norms in establishing and changing IOs (e.g., Finnemore and Sikkink 1998).[13] Yet, there is a third type of institutionalism, historical institutionalism, that may also be considered relevant for understanding the changes in global governance discussed in this study. Although much of this third strand of institutionalism has emphasized in the past the "stickiness" of organizations and the difficulties of altering them in any way (e.g., Mahoney 2000; Pierson 2000; Jervis et al. 2002, 175), more recent work has offered a number of explanations of changes in IOs (e.g., Fioretos 2011; Rixen et al. 2016). A particularly relevant type of change for the present study that is discussed by historical institutionalism is "layering," which is generally understood as a gradual transformation involving new elements that are attached to existing institutions and that eventually alter their structure and functions (Thelen 1999). This suggests, once more, that the previously mentioned distinction between changes *within* organizations (often discussed in historical institutionalist literature) and those involving the establishment of new organizations is important for explaining the shifts taking place on the intergovernmental–nongovernmental continuum.

The present study will seek evidence of all such additional arguments, especially of those that operate at the system level. It will assess whether global conflict, economic and information flows, waves of democracy, global wealth, and organizational density have led to changes in the intergovernmental or nongovernmental nature of global governance. It will also seek to identify the strategies used for such changes, whether they involved the creation of new IOs, changes in rules of existing IOs, or fluctuations in the relative use of some IOs rather than others.

THE RESEARCH DESIGN

As a reminder, the present book has two main goals. First, and perhaps most important, it seeks to show that the intergovernmental–nongovernmental continuum indeed exists, and that, over time, global governance in various realms has experienced back-and-forth shifts across this continuum. Second, it seeks to explain these shifts. These two goals led me to conduct a series of in-depth case studies, rather than utilize statistical analyses or formal models. In fact,

---

[13] As mentioned earlier, norms are different from ideologies. They are generally seen as becoming relevant (and bringing about change) once they reach a "tipping point" as large proportions of agents internalize them (Finnemore and Sikkink 1998). Because of that, it takes longer for norms to lead to global shifts, as they are not simply dependent on subsequent elections that can bring to power different groups of elites with a different ideological leanings.

all of the strengths of case studies noted by George and Bennett in their comprehensive discussion of this methodological approach (2005) are important for the purposes of the present book.

First, case studies are seen as especially useful for analyses where new concepts are introduced because they allow for high levels of conceptual validity and help avoid conceptual stretching (Sartori 1970; Collier and Mahon 1993). Specifically, it is important for the present book to assess whether the various shifts across the intergovernmental–nongovernmental continuum, at different times and in different issue-areas are, in fact, comparable phenomena or whether they are "apples and oranges" with very little in common (Locke and Thelen 1998).

Additionally, case studies, especially those that apply new concepts, allow for a greater degree of refinement. They help researchers identify the meaningful characteristics of a concept and eliminate the superfluous ones (George and Bennett 2005, 19). Indeed, in a previous study, together with my co-author, we were able to show that there is a strong relationship between a government's degree of domestic activism and its proclivity to take an intergovernmental approach to international problems (Grigorescu and Baser 2019). However, our findings were based on statistical analyses that used existing measures both for the main outcome and explanatory variables. Due to lack of available data, we were not able to discern and compare the effects of domestic preferences on shifts across each of the three dimensions of the intergovernmental–nongovernmental continuum, as I do here. Perhaps more important, the lack of comprehensive data made it difficult for us to distinguish between the two main mechanisms hypothesized to connect domestic and international developments: ideological and institutional.

Third, the literature points out that it is particularly useful to rely on in-depth case studies when one needs to explore the specific causal mechanisms at play, especially in the initial stages of theory development, as I seek to do in this book (George and Bennett 2005, 21–22). For the present research, it is important to disentangle the multiple causal factors considered to contribute to shifts across the intergovernmental–nongovernmental continuum because many of them go hand-in-hand. High levels of interstate interactions are expected during times of peace. Such interactions are often associated with high levels of global wealth. In fact, one of the important studies of the evolution of global governance has shown that not only have multiple systemic factors gone hand in hand with nongovernmentalism but also the number of intergovernmental and nongovernmental IOs established (measures that offer good reflections of the degree of intergovernmentalism and nongovernmentalism at a certain point in time) advanced in step (Boli and Thomas 1997, 1999). Of course, as discussed, ideologies of governmental activism often lead to the emergence of new domestic institutions (the two main explanatory variables of this study) as well as to new global ones. By considering developments in various issue-areas across time, I can focus on the causal paths connecting domestic and international developments rather than on simple correlations between phenomena unfolding in the domestic and international realms.

Last, but not least, case studies are useful because they help us identify when existing arguments are *not* supported. By uncovering "deviant cases," we can generate additional hypotheses (George and Bennett 2005, 21). As the present study is the first to analyze the causes of shifts across the intergovernmental–nongovernmental continuum, it is important to understand whether there are additional factors, beyond those discussed earlier, that can also lead to shifts across this continuum.

The following three empirical chapters will offer in-depth discussions of the evolution, across more than 150 years, of three global issue-areas: health, labor, and technical standards. The developments surrounding the changes in each of these issue-areas, in fact, constitute more than just three "cases." Each successful or unsuccessful attempt to shift global governance in one direction or the other of the intergovernmental–nongovernmental continuum is, in fact, a separate case. Together, the almost 100 shifts across the decision-making, financial, or deliberative dimensions of the intergovernmental–nongovernmental continuum allow for fairly thorough tests of the two hypotheses. They also allow me to assess whether any factors other than those discussed in this chapter have contributed to the changes in individual IOs and in global governance.

There are multiple reasons for choosing these three particular issue-areas. First, they are considered in the literature to be very different with regard to their intergovernmental versus nongovernmental character. The health realm has generally been viewed as intergovernmental in nature, the labor realm as a hybrid, and the technical standards realm as nongovernmental. These views appear to be accepted by many scholars because, *currently*, the main global governors in these realms (the World Health Organization, the International Labour Organization, and the International Organization for Standardization, respectively) are indeed each identified as falling into one of these three categories. By showing that all three realms experienced considerable variation across the intergovernmental–nongovernmental continuum, I can offer support for the main argument of this book that such a continuum is relevant for understanding global governance and that shifts across the continuum are common, regardless of the issue-area. Additionally, by choosing three issues that are seen as being different, I gain greater confidence that my hypotheses regarding the causes of shifts in global governance truly are generalizable.

Another important reason for choosing these three issue-areas is that they have a long history of global governance, of more than 150 years, and therefore allow for the study of multiple shifts across the intergovernmental–nongovernmental continuum. They differ from issue-areas where there is only a short history of global governance (of only several decades) and where the few shifts that have taken place usually do not allow for generalizable conclusions (Hale 2015, 9). The broad time frames for the three issue-areas discussed in this book allow me to assess whether the very noticeable recent trends to which the literature often pays a great deal of attention can also be found in the past and thus can indeed be explained using the same comprehensive analytical framework.

Last, but not least, the issue-areas were chosen because they are truly important and affect the lives of many people around the world. All three have led to some institutionalized form of global governance (whether intergovernmental or nongovernmental) for some time. The continued existence of institutional global governance structures suggests that the issues have been significant enough to warrant international efforts in order to deal with them, whether through more intergovernmental or nongovernmental channels. The study of the intergovernmental–nongovernmental balance in each of these three realms is just as important as the numerous studies explaining when governments or nongovernmental actors are likely to be involved in resolving *domestic* collective problems of health, labor, and technical standards.

Each chapter will identify the changes in the intergovernmental or nongovernmental character of the main global governors and, overall, of global governance. As a reminder, it is these *changes* that I seek to explain, not as much the *levels* of intergovernmentalism or nongovernmentalism at a point in time. Therefore, I will focus on the question of whether the shifts took place and on their direction, rather than on the more complex question of how great the shifts were. Specifically, I will discuss the establishment of all new major IOs dealing with health, labor, or technical standards; the subsequent changes in these organizations; as well as the increased or reduced use of such organizations. I will consider both formal and informal changes in the rules that are relevant for the three dimensions of the intergovernmental–nongovernmental continuum in each IO: rules regarding voting, financing, and deliberations.

I will then identify the main factors contributing to each individual attempt to shift IOs and global governance across the intergovernmental–nongovernmental continuum. In order to assess the plausibility of the two main hypotheses, I will first establish which states were promoting the changes toward intergovernmentalism or nongovernmentalism and determine whether their domestic preferences were more activist or passive compared to other great powers at that time.[14] I will consider the main states that expressed strong opinions regarding

[14] The level of a country's activism is assessed both through secondary literature and by comparing the ratio of its governmental expenditures and GDP to the ratios of other major powers at that time. The measure is based on data from the Cross-National Time-Series Data Archive (Banks and Wilson 2015). This operationalization of activism has been used by practitioners and academics to illustrate the degree of governmental activism across states (e.g., https://data.oecd.org/gga/general-government-spending.htm; Glenn 2009).

the changes, but will particularly focus on the most powerful states that are expected to have a greater impact on global developments than all other states.[15]

Additionally, to differentiate between the two main hypotheses that connect domestic developments to international ones, I will look for evidence that domestic ideologies and/or institutions contributed to changes in global preferences. Specifically, I will determine whether lower-level officials from narrowly focused domestic institutions or top-level political leaders[16] were involved in the processes leading to shifts toward intergovernmentalism or nongovernmentalism. I will also investigate whether those who promoted one form of governance or another invoked ideological arguments. The information regarding the positions of particular states with regard to the global shifts, the nature of the state representatives involved in debates, and the language used by such officials will be retrieved from primary and secondary sources. I use official minutes of meetings debating the establishment and subsequent changes in IOs or, at minimum, historical accounts of such meetings. Whenever possible, I will highlight the language used by officials supporting intergovernmentalism or nongovernmentalism to identify the ideological or technical nature of their arguments.

When considering system-level explanations for shifts, I will assess the presence of such additional factors and their intensity by referring to secondary literature, but also to well-established existing measures of global conflict, trade, information flows, levels of democracy, economic growth, and number of new IOs established.[17] Additionally, I will highlight instances when other domestic actors played a role in shaping a country's international position with regard to intergovernmentalism or nongovernmentalism. I will pay particular attention to the role of legislatures supporting or opposing the executive's relevant international initiatives. Thus, I will consider not only successful attempts to shift global governance but also unsuccessful ones. This decision is also based on the broader need to avoid selecting on the dependent variable by solely analyzing instances when there were shifts on the intergovernmental–nongovernmental continuum.

Overall, for each of the three issue-areas I seek answers to five questions:

1. What types of changes took place in the intergovernmental–nongovernmental nature of global governance?

For this question, I will seek to determine both whether the changes in global governance took place on the decision-making, financial, or deliberative dimension and whether they represented a shift toward intergovernmentalism

---

[15] The most powerful states are identified using data from the National Material Capabilities dataset (Singer et al. 1972).

[16] Based on the previous discussions of the nature of elites who are likely to engage in ideological arguments, I will focus especially on statements made by heads of state, prime ministers, foreign ministers, or their direct representatives (e.g., ambassadors or top advisors).

[17] For a more in-depth discussion of measures for these system-level factors, see Grigorescu and Baser (2019).

or nongovernmentalism. I will also differentiate between changes that took place through the emergence of new organizations, those due to developments within existing IOs, and yet others that were the result of states' making greater use of one organization rather than others.

2. How strong was governmental activism in the most important countries promoting or opposing changes in the nature of global governance?
3. Did officials promoting intergovernmentalism or nongovernmentalism use arguments that invoked specific ideologies?
4. Which national institutions were represented in the international efforts to shift global governance toward greater intergovernmentalism or nongovernmentalism?
5. Are there any system-level explanations for the shifts?

To summarize: the first question refers to the outcome variable (change in global governance); the second seeks to assess the plausibility of the two main hypotheses (without differentiating between them); the third and fourth help distinguish between the two mechanisms hypothesized to connect the domestic and international realms; and the fifth seeks to assess whether there are other (system-level) explanations for the changes.

Each chapter will summarize the answers to these questions in two different types of graphs and a table. The concluding chapter will bring the graphs and tables together to offer a broad view of the similarities and differences in the shifts across the intergovernmental–nongovernmental continuum and the causes of such shifts in the three issue-areas.

3

Global Governance in the Health Realm

The present chapter follows the evolution of global governance in the health realm starting in the mid-nineteenth century. It begins by noting the first important actions taken by governments and nongovernmental groups to deal with health issues on a national scale. It then shows that activism in the domestic health realm quickly "spilled over" into global governance due to the increased physical interactions that came with a rise in international travel.

The following narrative then highlights the very many changes in the main global governors in the health realm across time as well as numerous changes in the intergovernmental or nongovernmental nature of these organizations. By doing so, it addresses the first main question for this chapter, regarding the types of changes taking place in the intergovernmental–nongovernmental nature of global governance. Additionally, I will identify the main states that supported or opposed each attempt to shift global governance across the intergovernmental–nongovernmental continuum (whether successful or not) and determine whether such states embraced activist or passive domestic approaches to health. That will allow me to assess the plausibility of the linkages between the domestic and international realms and thus address the second main question for the chapter. I also point out instances when in the debates that involved attempts to alter the nature of global governance, officials representing states came from domestic health institutions and/or invoked arguments with ideological undertones. This allows me to respond to the third and fourth main questions, differentiating between the two main mechanisms hypothesized to connect domestic and global developments. Lastly, I will point out several possible system-level explanations for the shifts across the intergovernmental–nongovernmental continuum, in response to the fifth question.

In the last section of this chapter, I offer two possible visualizations of the shifts on the intergovernmental–nongovernmental continuum across time, thus illustrating the main trends of the outcome variable. A comprehensive table (3.1) then summarizes the evidence for the various explanations for such shifts, involving both domestic–international linkages (captured by H_1 and H_2) and system-level factors. As a reminder, I will offer similar figures and tables for the other two empirical chapters in order to compare the three issue-areas in the concluding chapter.

It should be pointed out that, as in all issue-areas, it is often difficult to draw clear-cut lines delineating health from other realms. Following the example of comprehensive studies of global health governance (e.g., Howard-Jones 1978; Weindling 1995; Harman 2012; Youde 2012), I discuss not only the role of the obvious global health IOs, such as the League of Nations Health Organization (LNHO) and the World Health Organization (WHO), but also other organizations such as the Gates Foundation (GF), International Committee of the Red Cross (ICRC), League of Red Cross Societies (LRCS), International Relief Union (IRU), Rockefeller Fund (RF), and World Bank. I do so because all of these organizations, at one time or another, either contributed substantially to the finances of other important actors (as in the case of the RF and GF), sought to expand their focus from their original issue-area to also include health issues (especially the LRCS and World Bank), or were involved in struggles to absorb and not be absorbed by IOs that specifically focused on global health issues (as occurred with the ICRC and IRU). The interactions between such actors are important for understanding the shifts across the intergovernmental–nongovernmental continuum in this issue-area.

GLOBAL GOVERNANCE IN THE HEALTH REALM BEFORE WORLD WAR I

Before the nineteenth century, governments rarely became involved in domestic health issues. Science had not yet developed an understanding of diseases, and both the public and government officials tended to view illnesses with a passive resignation (Institute of Medicine 1988, 56). "The great sanitary awakening" of the early nineteenth century led to increased knowledge of contagion and disease control (Winslow 1923). At that time, public authorities began taking on tasks related to sanitation, immunization, and health education (Chave 1984).

A key moment in the history of public health development came in the late 1830s when a team led by Edwin Chadwick conducted a series of studies of the life and health of the working class in the United Kingdom. The reports made public the terrible conditions in which most people lived at that time and proposed that both a national board of health and local boards of health be established (Chave 1984). Most of these proposals eventually were included in the British Public Health Act of 1848. Other advanced states quickly followed the British lead and by the second half of the nineteenth century, many governments began adopting similar public health laws and establishing at least some incipient forms of public health institutions.

The scientific discoveries of the first half of the nineteenth century also made government officials aware that the spread of diseases was often an international problem, not just a domestic one. The first efforts to take on international health issues therefore came only slightly later than those in the domestic realm.

In the first half of the nineteenth century, there were a number of intergovernmental initiatives intended to stop the spread of contagious diseases across borders by coordinating various forms of quarantine. The fears of such illnesses were often exacerbated by their perceived exotic nature for Europeans as well as by the threat they posed to the militaries that powerful states sent abroad. For instance, the first calls for an international conference to deal with health issues came in 1834, after the spread of cholera from India. In the 1820s, cholera had killed more than a million Indians and about 10,000 British troops stationed there. As the disease spread to Europe, tens of thousands more died (Youde 2012, 14–15).

It was only in 1851 that governments eventually decided to organize a conference to discuss how to deal with the spread of cholera and other infectious diseases. In the conference, each state was represented by two delegates, a diplomat and a physician. In most instances the latter was not affiliated with any government institution. Each delegate had a separate and independent vote (Charnovitz 1997, 5). Despite their representing apparently different domestic groups, historical accounts do not indicate that there were any differences in opinions among such individuals regarding the need for the future international health organization's decision making and deliberations to be purely intergovernmental. The funding for these conferences and for the proposed organization was to be based solely on governmental resources.

This first conference (as well as three more that were organized throughout the second half of the nineteenth century) was unsuccessful because there was little agreement among experts at that time about the causes of such diseases and, implicitly, about the best way of stopping their spread (Staples 2007, 123). Therefore, the meeting did not concentrate on collaborative curative solutions to diseases in the originating countries. Instead, discussions focused on how to set up the most effective quarantines, a topic that allowed for much greater input from government officials than from medical experts. Quarantines faced varied degrees of opposition from major European powers depending on their specific trade interests. Indeed, many governments believed that the efforts to institute quarantines were often nothing more than competitors' attempts to cripple their trade (Youde 2012, 15). This led to clashes between those emphasizing the importance of free trade (especially the British) and those calling for quarantines as a way to stop the international spread of diseases.

The first successful efforts to establish an international organization to deal with health-related issues came a decade later, after Henry Dunant proposed creating the International Committee of the Red Cross. The founding of the ICRC is famously traced to Dunant's emotional reaction upon seeing the aftermath of the bloody battle of Solferino in 1859. The sight of the thousands of wounded lying on the battlefield without any medical care prompted him to write and self-finance the publication in 1862 of a book titled *Un Souvenir de Solférino* (*A Memory of Solferino*). Dunant soon began looking for others to help him promote the idea of private societies for tending to the wounded in wars. He did not feel that governments could be trusted with this task. In the words of David Forsythe, in the founding of the ICRC, "the weakness of the state opened the way for private 'charity'" (2005, 15).

Dunant first found support for his idea among acquaintances in his home-town of Geneva. Then he called for an international conference to discuss the establishment of volunteer relief societies to tend to the wounded on bat-tlefields. His plans were to include only representatives of nongovernmental groups in the conference. The strong nongovernmental networks that emerged across Europe after the 1848 revolutions made it easier to bring such groups together in meetings.

Not all of the initial Geneva-based ICRC founders shared his view that the new organization needed to be nongovernmental. Gustave Moynier, a jurist and eventually the main figure in the Red Cross movement after Dunant, considered that for the ICRC to be successful it needed to be based on an intergovernmental agreement (Hutchinson 1997, 24; Forsythe 2005, 170). Moynier's initial attempts to organize an intergovernmental conference were met with a great degree of reluctance on the part of governments. There was a general understanding in the most powerful states (such as Austria, France, and the United Kingdom) that it was the government's obligation to deal with this issue rather than that of voluntary societies. Interestingly, the purely inter-governmental approach to the question of treating the wounded of war did not only surface in the speeches of government representatives. Well-known activists from outside government circles, such as Florence Nightingale in the United Kingdom and Jean-Charles Chenu in France, also opposed handing this task over to a nongovernmental entity (Hutchinson 1997, 38–40).

In the 1850s, Florence Nightingale had led a group of volunteers to tend to the wounded of the Crimean War. However, her efforts became part of the broader work of the new Royal Sanitary Commission that gave sweeping powers to the government (Maxwell 1956, 6). In fact, after reading Dunant's book, Nightingale wrote to him that his proposal was "objectionable because first, such a Society would take upon itself duties which ought to be performed by the Government of each country and so would relieve them of responsibili-ties which really belong to them and which they can only properly discharge" (cited in Moorehead 1998, 30).

The first international conference to take up Dunant's ideas took place in 1863. Due to the efforts of the pro-governmental Moynier and his supporters, the conference did not only include representatives of nongovernmental groups as initially planned, but also allowed some government experts to attend the meetings, albeit in their individual capacity, not representing their respective governments. These government experts nevertheless presented the greatest opposition to the nongovernmental nature of the proposal before them. A British official argued that his country had already resolved the problems of the wounded on the battlefield with trained personnel and army doctors who are "kings in their own domains" (ICRC 1863a, 57).[1] The physician-in-chief of the French army was even more outspoken, considering the simple existence of a nongovernmental proposal to be a criticism of governments and the military. In fact, the representatives of both the British and French medical establishments appeared to be the most critical of a task that they felt had long been dealt with adequately through their own domestic institutions. However, the opposition to Dunant's nongovernmental proposal from many nongovernmental groups and not just from domestic government institutions suggests that the institution-based mechanism connecting the domestic and international realms did not function (ICRC 1863a, 68–70).

At that time, the only powerful state that appears to have embraced the idea that nongovernmental organizations should complement the work of military medical personnel was the United States. In 1861, the year before the publication of *Un Souvenir de Solférino*, pastor Henry W. Bellows organized a meeting in New York to seek a more formalized way of allowing the already 3,000 volunteers who were tending to the wounded of the Civil War to continue their work. Although Lincoln initially opposed this idea, he eventually accepted the establishment by *federal* legislation of a *private* relief agency, the US Sanitary Commission (Maxwell 1956).

The emergence of a governmental British Sanitary Commission and a nongovernmental American one only a few years apart offers a good reflection of the important differences in the two countries' approaches to this issue. While the British had embraced a governmental, "hands-on" approach (that domestically contributed to the adoption of a first Public Health Act in 1848 and of another in 1866) (Ley 2000, 58), Americans tended to emphasize "voluntarism" in the health realm (Moorehead 1998, 33).

The initial focus of such American nongovernmentalism in the sanitary realm was mainly domestic rather than international, as one would expect of a country experiencing a civil war. The international component of the American Red Cross (ARC) developed only after World War I. Therefore, American support for a nongovernmental solution to the question of the wounded of war did not impact the ICRC's founding. Indeed, the United States was one of the last major powers to even join the ICRC, almost twenty years after the IO's establishment.

From the start, the ICRC was officially considered a private institution, governed by Swiss law. It was primarily composed of members who were Swiss citizens and were not supposed to represent Swiss government interests.

---

[1] Author's translation from French.

To this day, the traditional IGO-INGO dichotomous approach has led to the official labeling of the ICRC as an INGO (as reflected in the organization's official status in the UN).[2] Yet, a closer analysis, based on the understanding adopted in this book that IOs can best be understood as falling on an intergovernmental–nongovernmental continuum, suggests a more complex organization with a strong intergovernmental character.

First, according to the original official statutes of the International Conference, the most important decision-making body of the organization, each nongovernmental national committee and each government had one vote, respectively. Yet, the statutes also stipulated that the governmental and nongovernmental components of the organization were not equal. It was up to governments to set up the nongovernmental national societies. Moreover, according to Article 3 of the statutes, once such a nongovernmental organization was established, it needed to "get in touch with the Government of its country, so that its services *may be accepted* should the occasion arise" (emphasis added). Article 6 also stipulated that nongovernmental organizations could send medical personnel to the battlefield "on the request or with the consent of the military authorities," and once they were there, they were placed under military command (ICRC 1863b).

The strong move toward intergovernmentalism in the ICRC in its early years was reflected in and also spurred by the decision to have Gustave Moynier as president of the organization, starting 1864, rather than Dunant, who was in fact expelled from the organization by 1867. Moynier's leadership quickly moved the organization away from the more nongovernmental views of Dunant and embraced an approach that was "cautious, time tested and respectful of public authority and public law" (Forsythe 2005, 169). This led to the emergence of an organization that was very cooperative in its relations with public authorities. This much more intergovernmental model was accepted by all powerful states at that time, including the United Kingdom and France, which had opposed the more nongovernmental original version of the ICRC promoted by Dunant a few years earlier.

The strong role that governments were given in the ICRC took away a great deal of the influence of the nongovernmental groups that was essential in Dunant's original plans for the organization. By the 1880s, a new "Italian model" in which national societies became de facto auxiliaries of their countries' military establishments, became popular among many of the members. Due to the lack of Red Cross societies' independence, one cannot consider their participation in ICRC meetings to signify that the IO was truly nongovernmental on the deliberative dimension.

---

[2] Some disagree with this classification of the organization. Forsythe, for example, suggests that due to its strong ties with the Swiss government, the ICRC was (and is) very close to being a GONGO (government organized nongovernmental organization) (2005, 169). Willetts considers the ICRC as one of the best examples of a hybrid organization, with equally strong intergovernmental and nongovernmental components (1996, 8; 2000).

During most of its history, the ICRC has also been very intergovernmental across the financial dimension. Although the breakdown of ICRC funding sources prior to World War I is incomplete, the sporadic ICRC reports that were published throughout the nineteenth century show that in the organization's first fifty years of existence more than 90 percent of ICRCs funds came from governments. This practice was interrupted only briefly, during World War I, when the nongovernmental Red Cross Societies took the lead, contributing about 80 percent of the organization's funding (see ICRC, various years). As will be shown, the ICRC experienced a similar shift toward nongovernmentalism on the financial dimension during World War II.

Therefore, although the ICRC included nongovernmental elements, overall I consider it far more intergovernmental on all three dimensions as compared to the initial 1862 proposal. This shift toward intergovernmentalism was the result of internal dissention among the handful of individuals who founded the ICRC but, even more important, it was the result of the preferences of powerful states.

If there is one dent in the strong intergovernmental character of the ICRC, it is primarily induced by the Swiss *government* influence, rather than by any nongovernmental influence. In other words, there may be more questions about the "inter" element of the ICRC's *intergovernmentalism* rather than the "governmental" one.[3]

Indeed, the ICRC has long been considered a very Swiss organization with strong ties to the Swiss government. Not only have the leaders of the ICRC been Swiss citizens, they have generally come from Swiss governmental circles. In fact, in the past, some of them have even held simultaneous government and ICRC positions (Forsythe 2005, 20).

Despite the strong Swiss influence, the independence of this self-proclaimed nongovernmental organization was rarely questioned before World War II. However, throughout its first half-century of existence, the ICRC was often under strong international pressure (both governmental and nongovernmental) to hire truly international staff. This question was particularly salient in the debates of the International Conferences of 1867, 1884, and 1887 (Haug et al. 1993, 52).

The strong intergovernmental nature of global health governance before World War I is also reflected in the emergence of several other IOs in this realm at the beginning of the twentieth century. The many aforementioned unsuccessful attempts to establish an organization to deal with quarantines throughout the second half of the nineteenth century were finally followed by two successes in the first decade of the twentieth century as the International Sanitary Bureau (the precursor of the Pan American Health Organization)

---

[3] Some have, in fact, considered the ICRC to be a "mononational" rather than an international organization. See Haug et al. (1993, 52).

was founded in 1902 and the International Office of Public Health (known by its French acronym OIHP) in 1907.

By the beginning of the twentieth century, physical contacts between individuals traveling across borders had increased considerably. This was partially due to the intense transnational connections that came about through the second wave of colonialism as well as through increased global trade (Osterhammel and Petersson 2009, 15, 98). The greater physical interactions increased the likelihood of diseases spreading across borders. This, in turn, made global health problems more salient for governments. Additionally, the advancement of science allowed for more agreement among experts regarding the causes of diseases and their spread (Staples 2007). Indeed, sanitary experts eventually came together at these conferences, forming an "epistemic community" that made international cooperation possible (Haas 1989). Moreover, by the early twentieth century, many of these experts were part of the new governmental structures that had been established to deal with health issues. They were the ones representing these countries in the meetings setting up the IOs. The main promoters of the OIHP were the representatives of the United Kingdom and France.

Despite the official intergovernmental status of the OIHP, the organization also had a strong nongovernmental character. This character derived in part from the hybrid elements of the sanitary conferences that established the organization. Article 6 of the OIHP's statutes specified that "The Office shall be placed under the authority and control of an International Committee composed of *technical representatives*, designated by the participating States, in the proportion of one representative for every state" (International Office of Public Health 1907; emphasis added). Over the first couple of decades of the IO's existence, the officials of the Permanent Committee were virtually all medical experts from outside government institutions, as many countries had not yet established such official domestic structures.

The presence of public health experts allowed the organization to move beyond its initially narrow focus of overseeing international sanitary and quarantine regulations. They quickly added to such purely intergovernmental tasks the collection and sharing of public health information. In part because of the relatively few cases of quarantines they were faced with, the IO's secretariat found itself primarily occupied with answering queries from various national experts who sought medical advice on dealing with contagious diseases that were rare in their countries but common in other member-states (e.g., OIHP 1918, 8).

Starting in the mid-1920s, however, the fairly nongovernmental nature of the OIHP gave way to a much more intergovernmental one. The purely technical experts from outside government circles who participated in the Permanent Committee began being replaced by individuals who had strong ties to their governments, often being retired heads of their fairly new national public health departments (OIHP 1920). By the late 1930s, officials in the Permanent

Committee came to be considered de facto representatives of their respective governments. This shift on the decision-making dimension was broadly promoted and accepted by all powerful states (Goodman 1952, 82–83).

The OIHP was also very intergovernmental in nature across the financial dimension of the continuum. Its entire funding was based on member-states' contributions without any support from nongovernmental entities (International Office of Public Health 1907). Even though the Rockefeller Fund, which at that time contributed financially to a number of international health organizations, had a very active office in Paris where the OIHP was headquartered, the IO did not receive funding from the foundation.

Lastly, one should point out that the OIHP avoided any official contacts with nongovernmental IOs, whether in its deliberations or in any other aspects of its work. Even in the years immediately after World War I, when there was a strong shift away from intergovernmentalism in global health governance, the OIHP considered only very briefly a collaboration with the nongovernmental League of Red Cross Societies (LRCS) before reverting to its pure intergovernmental relations.

Although the OIHP was very intergovernmental on all three dimensions, when it emerged in 1902, it represented a shift only on the deliberative dimension of the intergovernmental–nongovernmental continuum of global governance in the health realm. Indeed, while the ICRC gave access to the nongovernmental national Red Cross societies in most of its meetings (even if many of these were not truly nongovernmental in nature), the OIHP kept all of its discussion solely among government representatives. Financially, the ICRC received almost 90 percent of its funds from government sources. Therefore, although the OIHP was entirely financed by governments, I do not consider that a significant shift took place at that time on the financial dimension of the global governance continuum. Also, early on, neither one of these two organizations was purely intergovernmental on the decision-making dimension.

As in the case of the ICRC, the main reason that the OIHP may be considered to have strayed from its purely intergovernmental character is the organization's very strong connection to one particular government. In the case of the OIHP this was the French government. The Paris-based OIHP offices were staffed solely with French nationals. The line between the intergovernmental and French nature of OIHP became so blurred that for a long time, the organization had to fight the French Finance Ministry that was taxing its staff's income as it would tax the staff of any French (rather than international) institution (OIHP 1909, 25).

The strong ties between France and the OIHP became obvious in later years, when most states pushed to bring the organization under the patronage of the League of Nations or the UN's World Health Organization, while French officials sought to maintain the OIHP as a separate and independent organization. In one instance, when discussing the League potentially taking over the OIHP's tasks, a French official asked, "Why should we lend a hand to an undertaking which would deprive us of an instrument promoting French influence?" (cited in Farley 2008, 11).

GLOBAL GOVERNANCE IN THE HEALTH REALM
DURING AND IMMEDIATELY AFTER WORLD WAR I

During World War I, the OIHP virtually ceased to function. The ICRC, on the other hand, which saw itself primarily as a wartime organization, was highly active on the front lines and behind them. As governments were too busy to deal with ICRC tasks (even with the deliberations within the organization) and too focused on their individual financial war efforts to fund the organization, the nongovernmental national Red Cross societies became the principal contributors to the IO's work and budget (see ICRC various years). This, of course, led to a shift toward nongovernmentalism on all three dimensions of global governance in the health realm during World War I.

The immediate post–World War I era saw a flurry of global health governance initiatives. The first, and perhaps most influential for later developments, was the result of the enthusiastic efforts of the American Red Cross. ARC had a more tumultuous start than most other national Red Cross societies. For more than three decades it unsuccessfully sought to convince the US government to sign the Geneva Convention. Without such a formal agreement, American voluntary Red Cross societies could be only partially accepted in the ICRC's decisions and work.

The rise of ARC, both through domestic and international institutional recognition and through financial means, came only at the beginning of the twentieth century. This shift reflected the strong progressivist ideology in the United States at that time. Theodore Roosevelt had promoted a greater governmental role in resolving societal problems. While, in his view, it was also important to include nongovernmental actors in dealing with such problems, government institutions nevertheless needed to take the lead (Nugent 2010). As early as 1899, Roosevelt had expressed his views on the government-ARC partnership, when he was still governor of New York. At that time, he argued that "The Red Cross Society should be the right hand of the Medical Department of the Army" (Hutchinson 1997, 230).

The 1904 Charter of ARC stipulated that the US president would appoint the chairman of the organization as well as five other members that had to come from the departments of State, War, Treasury, Justice, and Navy. The first four chairmen were retired high-ranking naval officers. This suggests that during Roosevelt's presidency, ARC, like all other nongovernmental actors, was seen primarily as a tool for achieving the government's goals and was essentially subservient to government institutions.

In time, Roosevelt's brand of progressivism shifted toward one that involved greater equality between governments and nongovernmental actors. The newer form of progressivism involved truly equal partnership roles for governments and nongovernmental actors, especially corporations. In the case of ARC, this shift was reflected in the decision to raise an endowment fund from private sources. These financial flows led to a reduced need for US government contributions to ARC and, implicitly, to a more independent (and nongovernmental) organization. Moreover, the increased wealth of ARC during the war allowed it to make more substantial financial contributions to the ICRC. This, in turn, led the IO to become less reliant on governments for its financing.

When World War I ended, ARC was left with $75 million at a time when most other national Red Cross organizations had empty coffers (Hutchinson 1997, 285). This situation led Henry P. Davison, chairman of the War Council of the Red Cross, and a senior partner at J. P. Morgan and Co., to realize in the first days after the war that ARC could help establish a new, *truly* international, Red Cross organization, rather than one that was primarily Swiss. Moreover, the new organization could deal with relief and health issues during times of peace, not just during wars, as the ICRC had envisioned (Moorehead 1998, 259).

Davison side-stepped virtually all American governmental institutions and sought approval for his idea directly from Woodrow Wilson. He immediately received it, especially after showing the president how the new voluntary organization could work in tandem with the planned very intergovernmental League of Nations. Then, after receiving $2.5 million from the remaining wartime ARC funds, Davison swiftly set out for Europe to sell his ideas to other major powers and to establish the new organization (Davison 1920, 281–282; Towers 1995, 43).

It is relevant that this international nongovernmental initiative originated in the United States, the most powerful country to emerge from the war. The idea that a very nongovernmental organization, working together with a very intergovernmental one, could be at the center of the global health realm was in tune with Wilson's thinking and, more broadly, American elites' political thinking of the time. As mentioned, Wilson had built upon Roosevelt's progressivism, implementing broad domestic activist policies that made use of partnerships between the state and the private sectors. Such initiatives focused not only on industry and trade but also on health and welfare (Kloppenberg 1988).

The emergence of the RF as one of the most important actors in domestic and international health in 1913 reflected this new thinking. In the United States at the beginning of the twentieth century, public health was considered an issue of concern both for the government and for the corporate class. The latter saw the development of a medical system as fulfilling the broader needs of society (Brown 1979). After World War I, wealthy philanthropists were prepared to export the American model of private-public partnerships to other countries and to the international health realm. This domestic shift happened to coincide with the United States abandoning its long-held isolationist views in the international realm, even if only briefly.

The strong domestic progressivist ideology as well as the empowerment of the very nongovernment ARC (that, in part, was due to the application of the ideology) contributed to the United States' promotion of a nongovernmental approach to global governance in the health realm. Davison's vision for the new organization led him to organize a medical conference in Cannes in April 1919, just five months after the end of the war. Only the five major powers of the post–World War I era (France, Italy, Japan, the United Kingdom, and the United States) were represented in what was called at the time the Committee of Red Cross Societies. The Cannes conference brought together some of the leading medical researchers and public health specialists from these five powerful countries. The US delegation was made up of representatives only from nongovernmental institutions. The other four major powers present at the conference included in their delegations at least one individual who had held or was holding an official government position in the public health realm, in addition to their position in the nongovernmental national Red Cross societies (League of Red Cross Societies 1919a). Together, they began discussing Davison's plans for a major organization.

Virtually all participants gave their stamp of approval to Davison's idea that a new "voluntary" (i.e., nongovernmental) organization was needed to deal with health issues during peacetime, thus complementing the wartime work of the ICRC. Even as the conference unfolded at Cannes, Davison was maneuvering to have his future *nongovernmental* League of Red Cross Societies (LRCS) mentioned specifically in the League of Nations Covenant, as part of the postwar international *intergovernmental* system. His direct relationship with Wilson eventually led to the inclusion of Article 25 in the Covenant specifying that:

The members of the League agree to encourage and promote the establishment and cooperation of duly authorized, voluntary, national Red Cross organizations having as their purpose the improvement of health, prevention of disease, and mitigation of suffering throughout the world. (League of Nations 1920a)

This interesting case of an intergovernmental conference "promoting" the establishment of "duly authorized" nongovernmental organizations reflected the broader US approach in the immediate post–World War I era of having governments step back and encourage nongovernmental actors to take the lead in various realms, including the one of global health. Moreover, while the League Covenant suggested that there was a vague role for governments in the new LRCS, in practice the new organization appeared to be fairly independent and very close to the nongovernmental end of the continuum on all three dimensions.

The very nongovernmental US views of global health governance were not shared by most other states. During the Cannes deliberations most speakers argued that despite its clear nongovernmental character, the new organization should complement government initiatives, not replace them. Some suggested that this nongovernmental initiative could only be a temporary one because public health is truly a task for governments and as soon as governments become more active in this realm, voluntary organizations such as the proposed LRCS would become "unnecessary" (LRCS 1919a, 66). Others felt that even though voluntary organizations should not infringe on the role of governments, the two should always find ways to collaborate (LRCS 1919a, 54–56).

The nongovernmental and intergovernmental views were most ardently expressed by the American and British participants at the conference, respectively, although representatives from France and Italy also appeared to support the British approach. The difference between the two sides was clearly expressed by one British expert. He explained the balance between "official work" and "voluntary work" in the health realm by stating that "In England, the official work predominates; in America, I believe I should not be far wrong from saying, it may be the other way around" (LRCS 1919a, 53).

Indeed, as the Cannes conference was unfolding, the contrast between the British approach emphasizing governmental activism in domestic health issues and the American nongovernmental approach was becoming increasingly obvious. Immediately after World War I, the United Kingdom established the Ministry of Health that centralized for the first time in that country all public health functions. Until 1939, when the Federal Security Agency was created, the US federal government played only a minor role in the health realm.

As can be expected, at the Cannes international health conference, each side emphasized what they perceived to be their strength. The argument for the British system was that "The modern public health movement started in England [...] As a result, there developed in England a practice of local public health administration in which this country still leads the world" (LRCS 1919a, 51). According to the British delegates, in such a system, voluntary organizations such as the Red Cross were intended to serve the broader goals and plans of government entities.

In the American system, on the other hand, as Davison himself emphasized in his speech, the initiative belonged to the voluntary organizations, such as ARC. The government's role was simply to support such organizations. Moreover, the American delegates argued that in smaller countries, where the government would not be able to fulfill its role in the health realm, international voluntary organizations (such as the LRCS) should step in and take the lead (LRCS 1919a, 47). In the end, American funds and influence prevailed, leading to the establishment of an IO that was very nongovernmental in nature.

The new organization approved by the Cannes Conference sought no more – and no less – than to have the very nongovernmental IO oversee the implementation of a "world health program" (LRCS 1919a, 13). It was to be named the Red Cross International Council and Bureau of Hygiene and Public Health. The organization was envisioned as having an important research component, a "demonstration laboratory," several publications, and even a museum.

It would be composed of thirteen different "divisions" (including a division of "industrial hygiene," one for "child welfare," and another for "sanitation") and four additional "sections" (LRCS 1919a). While the new organization had some intergovernmental elements (such as a vague connection to the League of Nations and a council of delegates from each state member), it was primarily nongovernmental in nature.

For Davison, it was not sufficient to have the seal of approval for the new organization from health experts and governments. He also sought to gain the support of the public by quickly showing how useful the new LRCS could be in practice (Davison 1920). While still in Cannes, he received a telegram from ARC regarding the spread of typhus fever across Poland, Ukraine, Serbia, Romania, and Macedonia. He presented the news to the conference and requested adding one more emergency session to discuss this issue. That session ended with a joint declaration that included the following wording: "The Committee of the Red Cross Societies of the Allied Nations is, in our opinion, the natural and, at present, only agency available to undertake this work if the required resources are placed at its disposal and it is invested with proper power" (LRCS 1919a, 163). He then contacted the Allied leaders at the Paris Peace Conference and received their approval to send a medical fact-finding mission to central Europe. Soon afterward, as the League of Nations was established and began functioning, it continued in its first years to rely on the LRCS to deal with the health crisis in central Europe.

As soon as the Cannes conference ended, Davison took the proposal for the new LRCS, with the valuable endorsement it had just received from major experts from the five most powerful states, and set out to organize a meeting formally establishing the global IO. Before the meeting, he stopped in Geneva to discuss his plans with the ICRC. He assumed that it would be only a formality to get the "old" Red Cross organization to accept the new LRCS's central role, especially as it was backed by substantial American funds and political influence. It quickly became evident to him that the ICRC opposed the establishment of the new organization both out of principle and, simply, in order to survive.

He nevertheless continued with his plans and in May 1919 the LRCS was formally established. In June 1919 OIHP's outgoing president, Rocco Santoliquido called for his organization to work more closely with the LRCS. He made the call as part of his broader argument that the OIHP should move away from simply focusing on quarantines and begin fighting sources of infectious diseases (something closer to the LRCS's mandate) (Youde 2012, 20–21). All these events suggest that global health governance experienced a shift toward nongovernmentalism in the first years after World War II. However, the following section will show that these changes were short lived.

GLOBAL GOVERNANCE IN THE HEALTH
REALM IN THE INTERWAR ERA

The new LRCS's first General Council meeting was held in March 1920, just ten months after the establishment of the organization. By that time, a dozen national Red Cross societies from smaller countries had gained membership to the organization, joining the original five societies from France, Italy, Japan, the United Kingdom, and the United States.

During that meeting, almost all representatives spoke in very positive terms of the new LRCS and expressed their gratitude for ARC's generosity in funding virtually all costs associated with the organization (LRCS 1920). The Swiss Red Cross Society representative was one of the few to critique the fact that one country contributed almost the entire budget of the LRCS (LRCS 1920, 15). He was also the only one to ask that the organization not allow Red Cross societies to be represented by diplomats or other government officials, as some indeed were at that time (LRCS 1920, 17).

These critiques may appear ironic, considering the strong role of the Swiss government officials in the ICRC. Yet, the demands of the Swiss representative should be viewed as part of the broader clashes between the ICRC and LRCS in the two organizations' attempts to carve out independent roles for themselves. An important distinction at that time was that while the ICRC had accepted a strong governmental component, the LRCS was intended to remain purely nongovernmental in nature.

The LRCS's decision making was in the hands of the national nongovernmental societies. Government representatives did not even take part in the organization's deliberations, except indirectly, through individuals who had strong connections to government circles. In its first decade of existence, the LRCS's funding also came primarily from public contributions, not from governments, continuing the practices from during the war.

At the first LRCS General Council meeting, Davison took the opportunity to present the recommendations of the Cannes conference. When doing so, interestingly, he did not mention his comprehensive plans for the Red Cross International Council and Bureau of Hygiene and Public Health that he had launched at Cannes. This institution had been envisioned by him to transform the LRCS from an important player in global health to the obvious main actor in this realm. Instead, Davison simply suggested that the LRCS include a much smaller General Medical Department. This far less ambitious organization appears to have been the result of ICRC leaders asking US government officials to convince Davison to tone down his plans (Towers 1995). This suggests that even the apparently very nongovernmental LRCS was, in fact, open to government influence, at least to some degree.

In the OIHP, despite Santoliquido's call for closer collaboration with the LRCS, his successor, Oscar Velghe, made it clear that his organization would remain a truly intergovernmental one that would avoid entanglements with nongovernmental entities such as the LRCS (Youde 2012, 20–21). His position reflected the fact that, like the ICRC, the OIHP was becoming concerned with the growing influence and power of the new LRCS and with the prospect that other health IOs, such as theirs, would eventually become obsolete. Moreover, as mentioned, by the mid-1920s, the experts in the OIHP's Permanent Committee began being replaced with government representatives, shifting the organization toward even greater intergovernmentalism.

The movement toward intergovernmentalism in the early 1920s became especially evident when the League of Nations began taking on a greater role in the global health realm. About a year and a half after the League sought the LRCS's help in the central European health crisis, it withdrew its support for the organization. The change in the League's position was primarily due to internal power shifts. By 1921, it was becoming clear that the United States, the main supporter of the LRCS and of the nongovernmental approach to global health governance, would not join the League. Warren Harding, who had won the 1920 elections calling for a "return to normalcy," replaced the leadership of ARC with individuals who were far less supportive of the organization's involvement in the international realm and who therefore cut American contributions to the LRCS. As the IO depended almost entirely on US funding at that time, it quickly found it financially impossible to fulfill its mission in the central European health crisis.

When it became clear that the United States would not join the League (and, more broadly, when it reduced its overall role in international affairs), the two countries that became most influential in the new IO were France and, especially, the United Kingdom. This is relevant because both of these European powers had embraced hands-on approaches to the health realm immediately after World War I. Indeed in 1918–1919, the Lloyd George government adopted a number of major social reform programs through laws such as the Workmen's Compensation Act, the Education Act, and the Housing and Town Planning Act. In 1919, it founded a health ministry. The French established their health ministry in 1921.

The British, as mentioned, had been less supportive of the nongovernmental approach of the LRCS. They refused to take the leading role in funding LRCS efforts in central Europe once the United States retreated from international initiatives. Together with the French, the British began seeking a more intergovernmental solution to the health crisis in central Europe. In fact, their commitment to intergovernmentalism had increased over the past year and a half as it became clear that the tasks in central Europe had shifted from ones that were purely related to health issues to ones with broader implications, such as the management of sanitary cordons. The British felt that such questions could be resolved only by governments (LRCS 1919b, 2).

The first plans for a new and very intergovernmental IO dealing with international health after World War I emerged in July 1919 from the newly founded British Ministry of Health. The leadership of the ministry called an informal meeting to discuss with representatives of the United States, France, the OIHP, and the LRCS the establishment of a new "active and progressive body," under strict government control (League of Nations 1919).

The meeting reflected, once again, differences between participants. The United States still supported a strong role for the nongovernmental LRCS. The French promoted strengthening the Paris-based OIHP. The British preferred a new IO as part of the nascent intergovernmental League of Nations. As a compromise, the three powerful states agreed at that time to support all three organizations and allow them to co-exist (Towers 1987, 147–148). LRCS and OIHP representatives left pleased with the outcome, as they felt that this solution would allow them to remain relevant in the global health realm. At the same time, they were very apprehensive because the British proposal implied that yet another IO would emerge to compete with them.

Immediately after the meeting, the new League Secretariat established an informal health section (Borowy 2009, 46). In February 1920, the League Council, in its second meeting after having been formally established, discussed plans for the future health IO. It considered two proposals: a simpler British one and a more complex Argentinian one. The latter called for a new International Organization for Health and Demography that would "deal with international health in the largest and loftiest sense of the word" (League of Nations 1920b). This second proposal reflected the more activist approach to health of Latin American countries (Borowy 2009, 48).

The United Kingdom, supported by France, led the opposition to the Argentinian proposal. They called for a conference in London in April 1920 to discuss the establishment of the IO. This second conference was more formal and included more states than the informal one of July 1919.

The strong British influence (especially in a conference that the United Kingdom co-chaired in its own capital) led to the acceptance of the proposal that had come from the British Health Ministry. The new organization was to include (1) a General Committee, with representatives of all countries that were members of the League and of the OIHP; (2) a Permanent Committee with representatives solely from the permanent members of the League Council, as well from the ILO and the LRCS; and (3) an International Health Bureau. The addition of the OIHP and LRCS representatives was important because it allowed the United States to become involved through these two organizations in the League's health efforts, even if it did not accept membership in the new IO.

Just as important, the London meeting established a League Epidemic Commission that was intended to begin working immediately to deal with the typhus situation in Poland. The conference thanked the LRCS for its "invaluable aid" in central Europe but concluded that the League had to take direct charge of the situation as "the sole organization sufficiently strong and authoritative to secure that the measures required be taken" (League of Nations 1920c, 8).

The conference called for states to contribute voluntarily to the more than 3 million pounds sterling that were necessary for the work in Poland. By July 1920, the chief commissioner resigned when it became apparent that states had not volunteered to finance even 7 percent of the new Epidemic Commission's work (Borowy 2009, 50). Among the reasons governments did not want to fund the Commission was that they felt they had donated sufficiently through volunteer aid agencies such as the Red Cross and Save the Children (Balinska 1995, 87). Therefore, despite the fairly smooth shift toward greater intergovernmentalism on the decision-making dimension of the continuum, the one on the financial dimension appeared to be more difficult to sustain due to a somewhat expected inertia.

The first Assembly of the League of Nations, which met in December 1920, took on the question of the League of Nations Health Organization (LNHO). It approved the new organization, keeping the proposal from the April 1920 London conference almost intact.

For the proposal to enter into force, the OIHP also had to formally change its status, something that required the approval of all its members. However, the very isolationist American stance delayed the process. League member-states and representatives of the secretariat did not want to give up on finding a formula through which the United States would somehow be included in the League's health work (Howard-Jones 1978, 26). Therefore, in June 1921, the League Council approved the establishment of a Provisional Health Organization with a Provisional Health Committee (that included representatives of member-states, the OIHP, and the LRCS) and a secretariat. This provisional status lasted for two years, until the specific role of the OIHP was clarified and accepted by all of the organization's members, including the United States.

The 1923 move to a "permanent" Health Organization in the League of Nations did not bring about too many actual changes. Its Standing Health Committee comprised the OIHP's president, nine elected OIHP members (including representatives of the states with permanent membership in the League Council as well as a representative of the United States), and six more members selected by the League Council. Lastly, it included a representative of the LRCS and the head of the Industrial Health Section of the ILO.

According the LNHO's founding documents, the members of the Health Committee were supposed to be selected in their individual capacity, not as representatives of their states. Moreover, in yet another nod toward nongovernmentalism, the committee was allowed to include "assessors" (representatives of nongovernmental IOs and individual medical experts) in its deliberations, albeit without a vote. As mentioned, the assessor system had been instituted in many other committees within the League, giving nongovernmental IOs important roles, such as proposing resolutions and amendments, and initiating discussions (League of Nations 1922, i).

American nationals who had worked for the League before it became apparent that the United States would not join the IO (such as Under Secretary General Raymond B. Fosdick and Arthur Sweetser, who worked for the League's Public Information Section) were among the most active supporters of the Wilsonian idea of opening the League to the public and to nongovernmental IOs and doing away with intergovernmental "closed door diplomacy" (Sweetser 1920, 187).

In the end, the intergovernmental character of the organization prevailed. The members of the Committee saw themselves as government representatives from the start. For example, British expert George Buchanan explained that he could not even accept his position on the Committee before receiving clear instructions from the British Health Ministry (Borowy 2009, 62). Virtually all such officials were in direct contact with their governments (usually through health ministries that had recently been established),[4] keeping them informed of the proceedings and seeking advice for their positions. Also, in practice, only very few nongovernmental IOs were ever given assessor positions in the LNHO. The initially strong intergovernmental character of the LNHO was also evident on the financial dimension, as the organization received all of its funding from member-governments. In fact, one can argue that the League's decision in 1923 to establish the LNHO and the immediate replacement of the LRCS as the main actor in the central European health efforts represented one of the greatest shifts across all three dimensions of the intergovernmental–nongovernmental continuum of global health governance over the past century and a half. While the LNHO left the nongovernmental LRCS with a deliberative and even decision-making role in the IO (as a way to ensure at least some American presence in the global health realm), in virtually all other aspects of its work, the new main global governor was very intergovernmental.

The "motor" of the League's Health Organization was, in practice, its secretariat. The position of medical director, which oversaw the work of this office, was held for almost the entire history of the organization by Ludwig Rajchman. Rajchman was a Polish medical expert who had led his country's post–World War I antityphus efforts. In this capacity, he had become well known to officials from all health organizations discussed here. His appointment as the head of the LNHO office was therefore not surprising. However, his very assertive style and his activist views of public health policies made him a controversial figure.

Before the war, Rajchman had been active within the Polish Socialist Party. After being detained by Polish authorities for his activities, he left for France and later the United Kingdom, where he became active in prestigious medical

---

4 Indeed, by that time, such ministries had quickly appeared in many other countries, most notably, in France.

expert circles. After being appointed by Drummond as medical director of the League, he tried to hide his political views behind his scientific persona. Nevertheless, his activist leanings quickly became apparent. Just months after being named medical director, he explained that he saw the role of the LNHO as being much closer to the proactive one that Latin American officials had proposed, rather than the reactive one envisioned by western European great powers. He considered the health secretariat as having "a duty" to initiate actions that individual states could not undertake (Dubin 1995, 67).

Rajchman, however, did not see a place for nongovernmental IOs in the LNHO. In 1921, when he organized a first conference to discuss epidemics in central Europe, he insisted that only government representatives be present and tried, unsuccessfully, to keep all nongovernmental entities out of the meetings (Balinska 1998).

Despite his strong initial intergovernmental preferences, Rajchman quickly realized that to attain even a part of the goals he had set out for the LNHO, he needed to (1) avoid as much as possible interstate politics and (2) secure more funds than governments were willing to offer his organization (Birn 2014a). Therefore, early on in his tenure as medical director of the League, Rajchman found in the RF an essential nongovernmental partner that could help it resolve its financial problems.

Rajchman had first impressed Wickliffe Rose, general director of the RF's International Health Division, in 1921, when he was leading the Polish antityphus efforts. Rose had agreed for the RF to contribute a substantial amount for a new Polish School of Hygiene. After Rajchman took on his position in the League, the relationship between the foundation and the IO flourished. This relationship was viewed as being "symbiotic" (Dubin 1995, 72), with both organizations benefitting substantially. Rajchman's LNHO was able to deal with issues that otherwise would have been left unresolved. In fact, some suggest that the organization would have ceased to function in the 1930s had the RF not supported it financially (Birn 2014a). The RF, in turn, found in the LNHO a global institution that could extend its reach to countries and regions where it otherwise would have been difficult for it to act. Indeed, the nongovernmental foundation had been able to start programs in Latin America but was far less successful in Africa, Asia, and eastern Europe, areas where the League had better connections (Borowy 2009, 140). The need to expand its programs to new regions was especially important for a foundation that was spending close to $25 million on international health programs each year, an astounding amount for that time (Youde 2012).

Some suggest that, in fact, the foundation benefitted more from this relationship than the IO and that, at times, the LNHO did nothing more than act as a surrogate for the RF (Dubin 1995, 72). The RF often helped the LNHO recruit staff, recommend experts for the League's health-related work, fund travel to Geneva for many of these experts, add funding to projects and countries that were already receiving LNHO support, and even help assess states' request for LNHO assistance. Often it was difficult to determine where the work of the RF ended and that of the LNHO began.

The RF's collaboration with the LNHO was viewed in a very positive way by American groups that sought a greater US presence in international relations, now that the government had reverted to its pre–World War I isolationism (Balinska 1998, 119). Such groups felt that the RF's philanthropic efforts were promoting important American ideals and policies. Indeed, by reducing the incidence of diseases worldwide, the RF's work was seen as increasing global productivity and economic development and, implicitly, opening up new spaces for American trade. Moreover, by supporting health programs across the world, especially for the poor, the RF was indirectly weakening support for radical socialist movements (Brown 1979, 116–119). This nongovernmental foundation was thus tackling a global task that the US government had declined to take on.

In 1922, the RF made an initial grant to the LNHO of about half a million dollars, to create an epidemiological intelligence service and for a personnel interchange program. It continued to add to this grant throughout the 1920s. By the early 1930s, it was spending on average more than 500,000 Swiss francs annually on the LNHO. Figure 3.1 illustrates the evolution of the proportion of LNHO funding received from the RF.[5] It shows that throughout the LNHO's existence, the foundation contributed about one-third of the IO's budget.

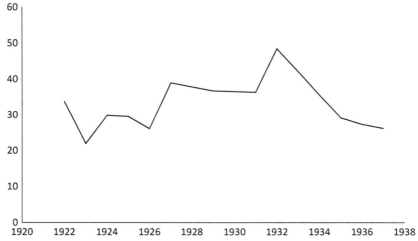

FIGURE 3.1. Proportion (%) of LNHO funding from Rockefeller Foundation.

[5] Graph is based on data from Borowy (2009, 468).

Soon after the 1929 market crash, member-states' funding for the LNHO declined abruptly. This led the RF to increase its contribution, seeking to compensate the governmental losses. By 1932, the RF was contributing 49 percent of the entire LNHO budget. At that point, RF leadership made it clear that it could not contribute half of the IO's the budget (or more). This was not because the RF did not have such funds. Rather, it explained that "there might be a negative reaction if the Health Section were to come to be regarded as an adjunct of the Rockefeller Foundation" (Borowy 2009, 137). Through this extraordinary financial contribution from the RF, the LNHO and, more broadly, global health governance, shifted considerably toward nongovernmentalism on the financial dimension.

The RF's assessment was correct. This external funding source allowed Rajchman to develop programs with very little support from member-states of the Health Committee. Therefore, some governments were especially critical of his activism and, implicitly, that of the LNHO. The British representative felt that the IO had gone too far toward nongovernmentalism, becoming a "super-medical" authority with little government control (League of Nations 1925a).

In 1938, British authorities and Rajchman foes were able to oust the long-standing medical director from his position with the help of Joseph Avenol, the new League Secretary General. This, of course, suggests that even in cases where top IO administrators appear to influence the intergovernmental or nongovernmental nature of the organization (perhaps even as a result of their own ideological leanings), powerful states eventually gain the upper hand and shift the character of the IO closer to those that match their preferences.

Avenol's socially conservative views also clashed with Rajchman's approach to international health (Barros 1969, 14–22). By the time World War II brought a complete stop to the health work of the League of Nations, the LNHO organization had promoted concepts of social medicine as no other IO had done before (Borowy 2009, 323–324). Interestingly, the LNHO was able to promote this very activist approach with the help of a private foundation. At a time when a number of other organizations such as the OIHP, LRCS, and ICRC were vying for primacy and even for survival in the global health realm, the RF offered the LNHO a lifeline without which the IO could not have achieved most of its work. Despite the very intergovernmental decision-making processes in the LNHO, and despite its very strong intergovernmental character on the deliberative dimension of the intergovernmental–nongovernmental continuum, keeping most nongovernmental IOs out of any formal or informal discussions, the organization had a very strong nongovernmental character on the financial dimension of the continuum. It is due to the LNHO's powerful nongovernmental character on this dimension that Rajchman was able to gain considerable independence from governments.

During the interwar era, there is yet another important IO, the International Relief Union (IRU), that competed with some of the previously mentioned organizations in carving out a role for itself. This organization was the brainchild of Giovanni Ciraolo, the president of the Italian Red Cross. As his country was prone to natural disasters such as earthquakes, Ciraolo (who had also been involved with the founding of the first Italian domestic disaster relief agency) sought to establish an IO that would seek to coordinate international relief efforts, including those involving treating those wounded in such emergencies.

Ciraolo felt that in order to be truly successful, both the ICRC and the LRCS needed to be aided (or replaced) by a new organization based on a complex system of mutual insurance. The organization was to be purely intergovernmental in nature, a plan that was very much in line with the dominant statist Italian ideology emerging at that time. The Italian launched his idea in 1921 at the Tenth International Conference of the Red Cross. At that time, as both Red Cross organizations were already engaged in a struggle for supremacy with each other, they did not welcome the proposal to have yet another competitor – moreover a purely intergovernmental one – potentially reduce their roles in the international realm.

During the 1921 conference, ARC and American government representatives were the most adamant opponents of Ciraolo's plan, finding its "statist [...] assumptions ideologically repugnant" (Hutchinson 2001, 253). Due to the strong US influence at that time, as well as the opposition from some other states, Ciraolo initially was not successful in establishing the organization.

Later that year, he took his plan to the Genoa intergovernmental economic conference hoping that government representatives would be more supportive of his proposal. It is noteworthy that none of the other major powers had established domestic disaster relief agencies like the Italian one. Officials at the conference represented domestic economic institutions that had little to no interest in this issue. They therefore encouraged Ciraolo to present his plan in another forum, perhaps at the League of Nations. In 1922, Ciraolo offered a revised version of the IRU proposal to the League. He hoped that without the United States present in the IO, opposition to the IRU would not be as great. Indeed, the plan was generally received positively, but it took states two more years to offer written comments on the IRU proposal. Some of them opposed the idea of "mutual insurance" against disasters, questioning whether an insurance system on such a grand scale was economically and administratively possible (League of Nations 1925b, 16).

The United Kingdom waited longer than other states to respond. By the time it did craft its response, there had been a change in 1922 in its government. When the League Council eventually set out to discuss the proposal for the IRU in December 1924, the British representative expressed his opposition to the plan by arguing that although there were states where "it was the custom to rely on subventions from the State in times of disaster.... [in] other countries – among them Great Britain – reliance was placed on funds voluntarily subscribed for purposes of relief." He continued, pointing out that in the latter group of countries "there was a great reluctance to introduce State action since, action by the State meant the end of action by the individual, who would confine himself to paying his taxes once the State had intervened" (League of Nations 1926a, 146). This position, based on a strong laissez-faire ideological perspective, was very different than the one reflected in the 1919 Cannes conference, where the British representative had had an exchange with the American one suggesting that his country was in fact more accustomed to allowing government intervention in the health realm. Indeed, starting in 1922 and virtually throughout the entire interwar period, conservative British governments moved toward less activist domestic policies. The ideological domestic shift also led to a change in the United Kingdom's stance toward intergovernmentalism.

Despite British critiques, most other states offered lukewarm support for the IRU. The activist French government sided with the Italians. Ciraolo's proposal thus moved forward in the League and, in May 1925, a preparatory commission was formed to begin planning for the future IO. The one victory that the British delegation won in the League debates was to convince others that, as the IRU was intended to become involved in all states, whether they were members of the League or not, the preparatory commission needed to include both members and nonmembers of the League. Of course, that implied that the United Kingdom would have a powerful ally in future negotiations in the United States that, at that time, opposed strongly both domestic and international governmental activist views. In the discussions of the IRU proposal, the United States was represented by Colonel Robert Olds, the president of ARC. Olds used every opportunity he had during those debates to criticize the Ciraolo plan, concluding flatly that "as relief problems in this country are handled by the American Red Cross, a private organization, there seems to be no way in which the Government of the United States can usefully co-operate in the furtherance of Senator Ciraolo's scheme" (League of Nations 1926b, 845).

In an attempt to assuage some of the critiques that had been voiced in the League, Ciraolo sought to improve his IRU plan by proposing that the new IO include the nongovernmental LRCS in its work and deliberations. To use the language introduced in this book, he sought to salvage his original plans for a very intergovernmental IRU on the decision-making and financial dimensions by accepting a shift toward nongovernmentalism on the deliberative dimension. However, his new proposal led to other problems as a number of states questioned the idea that the LRCS should have a monopoly over international relief efforts, while other deserving nongovernmental IOs, such as Save the Children, would be left out.

Others argued that the nature of the IRU now became even less clear. Was it to be a federation of states or of Red Cross Societies? While Ciraolo had envisaged a purely intergovernmental IO, others argued that some states could be represented in the organization by their Red Cross Societies. In the end, the Italian gave in to keep at least part of his plan. For the same reason, he also accepted a modest budget. With these compromises that weakened the organization considerably, the preparatory committee agreed in 1927 on the last details of the IRU. As one historian has noted, "Ciraolo's original intention were diluted almost beyond recognition. Indeed, the conference was as much the funeral of the Ciraolo project as it was the christening for the IRU" (Hutchinson 2001, 286).

For the IRU to actually come into being, it was necessary for twelve countries to ratify the 1927 convention and pay their shares of the organization's budget. The process was slow, as hardly any countries were in a hurry to contribute financially to an organization from which they might not reap benefits in the near or even distant future. The US government made it clear early on that it would not join the IRU. The United Kingdom declared that it would join only after the organization would officially come into being. In other words, it could not be counted as one of the twelve necessary ratifications. The twelfth ratification of the IRU and, implicitly, the official founding of the organization, eventually came in 1932.

Throughout its short history, the IRU was not involved in any substantial relief efforts. Its moment of glory appeared to come in 1936 when a number of states called upon it to deal with humanitarian relief efforts in Spain. Before it could even consider what to do, it discovered that the ICRC and LRCS were already active on the ground. Moreover, the Spanish government declared that it preferred working with the LNHO, rather than the IRU. The organization continued to exist, desperately seeking a role for itself until it was eventually dissolved after World War II.

GLOBAL GOVERNANCE IN THE HEALTH REALM DURING AND IMMEDIATELY AFTER WORLD WAR II

The very intergovernmental LNHO, OIHP, and IRU virtually ceased to function during World War II (Youde 2012, 24). However, during that time, the more nongovernmental actors in the health realm played important roles. In the Red Cross movement, the LRCS, which had primarily been intended to conduct peacetime work, joined the ICRC war efforts.

Both Red Cross organizations sought to compensate the reduced wartime financial government contributions by appealing directly to the public, just as they had during World War I. This pushed them further toward nongovernmentalism on the financial continuum and, implicitly, toward greater independence from governments. Figure 3.2 reflects this trend in the ICRC.[6] It shows that while immediately before and after World War II

---

[6] Based on ICRC annual reports, various years.

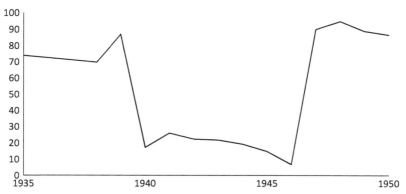

FIGURE 3.2. Proportion (%) of total financial contributions made by governments to ICRC.

governments were the main contributors to the organization, during the war they only provided about 20 percent of its budget.

Despite the ICRC's shift toward greater nongovernmentalism on the financial dimension from the beginning of the war, a couple years later, as the war engulfed the world, the organization became more dependent politically on the Swiss government that had taken a more activist domestic approach after World War II began. The ICRC readily accepted the host country's official "supervision" during the war (Forsythe 2005, 184). Its relative lack of independence was especially visible in the organization's stance on the Holocaust. Although some members of the ICRC called for a public condemnation of the Holocaust, several officials who simultaneously held ICRC and Swiss government positions (including Philippe Etter, president of the Swiss Federal Council and also a member of the ICRC Assembly) blocked the appeal (Independent Commission of Experts 2002).

Soon after the war, a comprehensive ICRC report explained the organization's wartime actions by arguing that it would not have survived the war without the Swiss government's financial and diplomatic aid (International Committee of the Red Cross 1948). Moreover, the organization suggested that there had always been a strong convergence between its interests and those of the Swiss Federation through the fact that "Swiss nationalism and Red Cross humanitarianism are one and the same" (Forsythe 2005, 192).

The problem of the very "Swiss" nature of the ICRC has continued to be raised officially, most poignantly in the 1970s (e.g., ICRC 1977, 87). Indeed, from 1962 to 1971, Swiss financial contributions to the ICRC represented about two thirds of all government contributions and more than half of all contributions (Willemin et al. 1984, 148–149). It was only in the 1990s that, through a series of official agreements, the ICRC eventually gained true independence from the Swiss government (Forsythe 2005, 192).

As soon as the war ended, governments once more began seeking solutions to their collective problems in the health realm. As in the case of the immediate post–World War I era, after World War II, the United States and the United Kingdom took the lead in shaping the global health institutions.

Of course, due to its interwar isolationist stance, the United States had not participated in the LNHO. Even its role in the OIHP had been minimal throughout that period. Indeed, the low levels of US activism at both the domestic and international levels indirectly influenced the nature of global governance in the 1920s. As the government took a more passive approach domestically, it left spaces where nongovernmental actors could become more active. Some of these actors, such as the RF and ARC, then expanded their work from the domestic realm to the international one, thus filling gaps that had been left open in global governance.

However, by the late 1930s, when the Roosevelt administration's New Deal efforts had expanded into a number of social issues, including health, US officials became increasingly interested in the work of the LNHO, especially in its programs for nutrition, rural hygiene, public health in times of depression, and housing. An LNHO official who took part in a conference in Washington in 1938 was surprised to see that US policymakers were very familiar with the League's work in the health realm (Borowy 2009, 422).

As American interests in some of the other League economic and social projects became evident, the IO sought some reforms that would have allowed a greater role for the United States in such work. In December 1939, the League's Assembly approved the Bruce reforms that included the establishment of a Central Committee of Economic and Social Questions that was loose enough to allow room for the United States to become directly involved in its work.

While the reforms came too late to bring about any changes in the American approach to the LNHO, many of the same officials who had sought the rapprochement between the United States and the League were still in positions of power in the Roosevelt administration toward the end of World War II. Immediately after the war, such officials became deeply involved in US social and economic international efforts, including those focusing on health issues.

When the United States convened the Dumbarton Oaks Conference in summer 1944, the four great power victors of World War II agreed that the future intergovernmental structures should include institutions to address economic and social problems and decided to establish ECOSOC as a main organ of the future UN. This decision was in great part driven by Roosevelt's projection of domestic activism to the international realm. The link had been clearly stated in his 1941 speech that presented the broad "freedom from want" as a global freedom, not just a domestic one (Roosevelt 1941).

Although the four great powers did not discuss the possibility of a global health IO early on, American officials eventually raised this issue with the British (Farley 2008, 9). Despite some small differences, at the end of the war, the two great powers had fairly similar (activist) views on the state's role in the health realm. In the United Kingdom, the Labour Party had won the 1945 elections and promised to address what the 1942 Beveridge report called "the five giant evils" of society: want, ignorance, squalor, idleness, and *disease*. The plan had been put on hold in 1943 by Churchill under the promise that it would be discussed after the war as a way to repay society for its wartime sacrifices. In the immediate postwar era, the Beveridge plan led to the adoption of several acts of parliament broadly considered to represent the establishment of the modern welfare state in that country. The National Health Service Act and the National Insurance Act, adopted immediately after the war, introduced a comprehensive state health service and compulsory contributions for unemployment, sickness, maternity, and pensions from employers and employees, as well as significant government funding (Abel-Smith 1992; Timmins 2001).

In the United States, the idea of compulsory universal health insurance was part of Roosevelt's New Deal policies and was introduced in the 1943 Wagner-Murray-Dingell bill that sought to institute a national medical and hospitalization program. The bill did not pass either in 1943 or in 1945. It was opposed by the American Medical Association and the pharmaceutical industry, two powerful domestic nongovernmental actors. After Roosevelt died, Truman sought to wait for the 1946 elections to gain greater support in Congress for the bill. When Republicans won those elections, opponents of the bill quickly made it clear that "voluntarism was the American way" and that they would not support any form of "socialized medicine" and compulsory insurance that "came right out of the Soviet Constitution" (Farley 2008, 66–67).

Perhaps because both the United States and the United Kingdom were awaiting a clearer formulation of domestic health policies, they did not offer any plans for the global governance of health before 1946. Therefore, there was no specific discussion of an international health organization prior to the 1945 San Francisco UN Conference on International Organization. Even there, it was a handful of physicians (rather than top government officials) from the national delegations of Brazil, China, and Norway who happened to be part of their national delegations and sought to place health on the conference agenda. They were somewhat successful, as they at least introduced wording about international health issues in the UN Charter (Farley 2008, 7).

Taking advantage of the lull in setting up an organization to deal with global health, the OIHP moved to organize its first postwar conference in early 1946. The United States, which had originally allowed the OIHP to survive after World War I in order to have through this IO a seat in the League's Health Committee, felt that the Paris-based organization had now outlived its purpose and responded bluntly to the invitation to the conference that it envisioned another organization dealing with international health in the future (US Department of State 1946).

At the first ECOSOC meeting, in February 1946, the United States and the United Kingdom called for the establishment of a preparatory committee to discuss a new health IO. While the British and Americans wanted to keep the committee small (with only representatives from the P5 and, perhaps, one from Brazil), the Soviets, who feared being outvoted in such a small forum, were successful in having all eighteen ECOSOC members included in the talks. The preparatory committee, made up almost entirely of medical experts, met in March 1946, in Paris. Many of the experts knew each other, having worked together in the various interwar organizations mentioned earlier. They hoped that the future health organization would function in a collegial and apolitical fashion, as the older health IOs generally had, at least at some point in their existence (Jackson 1997). The committee was able to include in Article 11 of the organization's constitution the stipulation that "delegates should be chosen from among persons most qualified by their technical competence in the field of health, preferably representing the national health administration of the Member" (WHO 1946).

There was indeed a great deal of agreement among the officials present at the drafting of the new IO, even when it came to the structure of the future organization. Perhaps for that reason, the discussions did not require participants to convince each other of one particular solution or another and, implicitly, nobody invoked any ideological arguments, even at a time when both the United States and the United Kingdom had embraced very activist approaches domestically. The new IO was to have a World Health Assembly where representatives of all member-states would meet once a year, an executive board with twelve to eighteen members that would meet several times a year to direct the organization's activities, and a director general who would run the staff of the organization. Unlike the period after World War I when the United States proposed a very nongovernmental approach to the global governance of health, in the immediate post–World War II period, it did not hesitate in accepting the strong intergovernmental proposal for the future global health IO.

The International Health Conference (IHC) met in New York in July 1946 to discuss the proposal of the preparatory committee. The IHC, however, was much more political in nature than the preparatory committee. The technical experts at the IHC were present alongside government officials, but as representatives of states rather than in their personal capacity, as had been the case in the preparatory committee. The changes in the immediate post–World War II years that led to the establishment or empowerment of domestic government institutions in the health realm determined the very governmental nature of participants in the IHC.

The conference was able to make important decisions on controversial issues that it had inherited from the preparatory committee. Its greatest hurdle was in resolving the question of the IO's universality. As the conference was unfolding in the Western Hemisphere, the Latin American bloc was larger and more influential than usual. The first litmus test of the question of universality referred to fascist Spain, a country that was not going to be a member of the UN for some time. Latin American countries supported the idea that even though it was not a member of the UN, Spain should be allowed to join the WHO if the World Health Assembly would allow it by a majority vote. Delegates argued that "no political inhibitions should intervene in health matters" (Cumming et al. 1946). Despite the opposition from the United States, the Soviet Union, and many European states, the Latin Americans and their allies carried the vote.

The question of universality is relevant for a study of the nongovernmental–intergovernmental nature of global governance. As a reminder, one of the reasons after World War I the nongovernmental LRCS was initially accepted with an important quasi-membership role in the intergovernmental LNHO is that this allowed the United States (which was not a member of the League) to be present in important decisions involving global health. This formula also allowed for German input in the LNHO at a time when some states, especially France, vehemently opposed the idea of universality of intergovernmental IOs. After World War II, by opening the door to non-UN members, the WHO eliminated the practical necessity of giving nongovernmental IOs a role in the formal decision-making process, as the LNHO previously had when seeking ways to give some powerful states at least an indirect role in the organization. The WHO thus emerged as a very intergovernmental actor. It was more intergovernmental across the decision-making and financial dimensions compared to its predecessor, the LNHO. Indeed, it did not give nongovernmental actors any decision-making power, as the LNHO had given the LRCS. It did not rely on nongovernmental actors for funding, as the LNHO had relied on the RF. Despite some initial hesitation, discussed below, the WHO did continue, however, to allow nongovernmental IOs in many of its deliberations just as the LNHO initially had.

Although the WHO constitution was adopted in 1946, it took another two years for the organization to actually begin functioning. The main reason for the delay was the apparent change in the United States' willingness to become involved in intergovernmental initiatives. The change was a result of the Republicans taking control of Congress in the 1946 midterm elections. The isolationist stance of the Senate and the opposition to increasing the role of government, both domestically and internationally, led to a difficult ratification process of the WHO's constitution. In March 1948, Congress killed the bill to ratify the WHO constitution, and it appeared that the United States was going to remain outside the main health IO, yet again. This instance is yet another example (alongside the one of the US Senate refusing to ratify membership in the League of Nations) of intergovernmental initiatives of the executive branch from a powerful state being thwarted by the legislative branch.

GLOBAL GOVERNANCE IN THE HEALTH
REALM DURING THE COLD WAR

The beginning of the Cold War and the realization of the importance of international health for US strategic interests eventually allowed the WHO to gain Congress's support. The most important event leading to this change of heart was the cholera outbreak in Egypt in late 1947. As Egypt was a key strategic partner for the United States in the Middle East, Washington scrambled to come to its ally's aid to avoid instability in the country and region.

However, by the time the United States was able to act in Egypt, it discovered that Brock Chisolm, the new director of the WHO, had already contacted the Egyptian health minister and sent much needed vaccines to the country. This episode and the growing tensions of the Cold War convinced US lawmakers that they could not allow the Soviets to gain any advantages in the newly emerging international system, even in IOs. The United States decided to assert its interests by making its presence felt in virtually all intergovernmental forums. Indeed, the Soviet Union had already joined the WHO and begun using its influence there to promote its own brand of health policies and social reform (Farley 2008, 62).

The United States joined the WHO in June 1948. The new political climate in the United States and abroad, however, led to attempts to control very strictly who would represent the United States in this IO and who would work in its secretariat. The United States required that all Americans working for the WHO sign "loyalty oaths" to their government (Farley 2008, 186). Indeed, the issue of staff independence became an essential issue for all new organizations in the UN system (e.g., Behrstock 1987).

The United States and some of its allies tried to alter the working rules of the WHO by requiring that representatives to the Assembly and the Board act in state capacity, not their own independent capacity, as experts. The Soviet Union and its allies also supported this change. Even though the two superpowers promoted this shift toward intergovernmentalism on the decision-making dimension, they were not successful in getting other states to adopt a formal change in the WHO's rules (WHO 1950a).[7]

Like all other UN agencies, the WHO accepted from the beginning a role for nongovernmental IOs. It was difficult to keep such organizations out of any formal IGO by the end of the World War II era. Indeed, Roosevelt had learned from Wilson's mistakes when the latter unsuccessfully sought to gain domestic support for the United States joining the League of Nations. One such mistake had been that Wilson did not act quickly to gain American public backing for the League. By the time he did seek support, the domestic political process

---

[7] However, a number of states embraced the *practice* of having their nationals in the Assembly and on the Board act as representatives of their respective governments, even though the formal rules were not altered.

for ratification was too advanced. Roosevelt therefore courted domestic and international nongovernmental organizations early on, in the hope that they could contribute to swaying public opinion in support of the country's membership in the UN (Charnovitz 1997, 22). Despite US support for domestic nongovernmental organizations, the Truman administration initially opposed in San Francisco the introduction of any wording in the Charter that would give nongovernmental actors a formal role in the UN. It later accepted their inclusion only in the work of ECOSOC (not other UN organs). Moreover, it gave in only after the wording in the Charter was changed to give nongovernmental IOs a "consultation" role rather than the original "participation without a vote" status proposed by some states.

Although the Charter formalized "consultative" roles for nongovernmental IOs, those who had worked both in the League and the UN noted that, in practice, nongovernmental actors were less influential in the UN throughout the first few decades of the Cold War than they had been in the League in the 1920s (Pickard 1956, 72). Their collaboration with the UN did not go beyond the economic and social realm, as it had in the League. Also, while the UN Charter called simply for "consultations" with nongovernmental IOs, in the League, representatives of such organizations had been allowed to propose resolutions and amendments (Chiang 1981, 35).

The WHO's relations with nongovernmental IOs was first taken up in an April 1946 ECOSOC meeting (ECOSOC 1946, 14, 24). Interestingly, these relations were mentioned immediately after those with intergovernmental IOs. This latter topic was an important one, which was discussed at length, as the WHO was in the long term replacing and in the short term collaborating with major very intergovernmental IOs such as the LNHO, the UN Relief and Rehabilitation Administration, and the OIHP. In this context, one might interpret the brief mention of nongovernmental IOs as an afterthought that came naturally after discussing the more important relations between intergovernmental IOs. The wording describing nongovernmental IOs' work in the WHO was also brief and vague. It appeared in Article 18 of the WHO's constitution stipulating that the World Health Assembly was "empowered to invite any governmental or nongovernmental organization which has responsibilities related to those of the Organization to appoint representatives to participate without right of vote in its meetings or in those of committees and conferences convened under its authority" (WHO 1946).

The United States, however, maintained a cautious tone toward nongovernmental IOs. In a 1947 letter to the WHO director, a US official argued that a "thorough study of the existing non-governmental organizations in the field of health is required as a basis for developing a pattern of relationship with these organizations" (WHO 1947b, 3). WHO leadership often had to explain to American officials and other suspicious government representatives why the organization was collaborating with one specific nongovernmental IO or another (e.g., WHO 1957).

In the first few years of the WHO's existence, while nongovernmental IOs were allowed to take part in the organization's Assembly, there was no similar stipulation for their participation in Board meetings. Moreover, while the first World Health Assembly in 1948 specified that its meetings would be open to the public, it did not refer specifically to nongovernmental IOs' access. At that time, only a dozen such organizations had acquired formal status with the WHO (WHO 1948a, 10).

There were many nongovernmental IOs that sought collaborations with the WHO from the beginning. The secretariat of the organization responded politely but vaguely to such early advances. The fate of one particular proposal from 1949 for a "Grass Roots for UNO" that had originated in nongovernmental circles close to Eleanor Roosevelt was particularly telling. It envisioned the establishment of national health nongovernmental organizations that would make the WHO's work known to the public and, conversely, inform the WHO of proposals generated at the grassroots level (WHO 1949a). This was an important initiative because, while some organizations in the UN system (such as UNESCO and UNICEF [the UN Children's Fund]) developed national nongovernmental committees to help in their work, the WHO did not embrace this idea. The WHO's response to the proposal was that any such grassroots efforts should take place "under the leadership of Health Authorities." It further argued that such committees needed to "please national ministries of health" and "avoid the danger that the national health department would feel that UN or WHO is trespassing in their field of work" (WHO 1949b).

Even the WHO's relationship with the powerful RF reflected the problems the IO faced early on in its collaborations with nongovernmental actors. WHO officials encouraged the RF to cooperate more with them (WHO 1950b). The foundation, however, felt that as the WHO was a more ambitious organization than the LNHO, it could not contribute in the same way to the post–World War II work of the new global health governor (and influence it) as it had to the League's work. Moreover, as McCarthyism affected even the RF's personnel and work, the foundation feared that collaborations with the WHO could be interpreted as supporting a left-wing "social medicine" approach (Birn 2014b, 136). The foundation therefore developed only a lukewarm relationship with the WHO, which eventually ended by the early 1960s. These developments at the WHO contrasted with the strong role given to the RF in the LNHO during the interwar era.

The WHO's slow start to its relations with nongovernmental IOs became noticeable during its interactions with UNESCO, an organization that had been much more active in establishing such relations. When representatives of the two intergovernmental IOs met in 1947 to discuss possible collaborations with each other, as well as with nongovernmental IOs, it became evident that the WHO had not even drafted a formal policy for its relations with nongovernmental IOs, while UNESCO had drafted, implemented, and already altered once its original policy. Moreover, UNESCO had instituted the practice of offering grants to nongovernmental IOs that were relevant to its work. The WHO, however, was not prepared to support nongovernmental IOs financially. The discussions between the WHO and UNESCO over the best approach to dealing with nongovernmental IOs became heated as one UNESCO representative accused WHO officials who did not want to allow nongovernmental actors to participate in their work of "shutting themselves up in an ivory tower" (WHO 1947a, 8).

In 1948 the WHO adopted formal rules for establishing relations with nongovernmental IOs. It created a Committee on Non-Governmental Organizations to consider applications for formal relations. The final decision of who would receive such status was given to the Executive Board. In the first year with a formal policy, the WHO approved the applications of sixteen organizations seeking such formal relations. The first to acquire this status was the LRCS. In time, the number of nongovernmental IOs to gain formal relations with the WHO, as can be expected, increased, but not in a linear fashion. Figure 3.3 illustrates the proportion of nongovernmental IOs that were granted this formal status from all of those that applied that year.[8]

Although WHO's relations with nongovernmental IOs focused primarily on the process of implementing policies, they are also important for assessing the organization's willingness to include nongovernmental entities in its deliberations. The nongovernmental IOs having formal relations with the WHO,

FIGURE 3.3. Proportion (%) of nongovernmental IOs granted formal relations with WHO.

---

[8] Data based on WHO (1971, 9).

which Figure 3.3 refers to, were the ones that had access to the organization's important formal meetings, not just the smaller, informal ones.

The graph shows that in its first year of existence, the WHO admitted about two thirds of the nongovernmental IOs that applied. It needed to show that it had developed such collaborative relations, like other UN agencies that had started forging official ties with nongovernmental IOs a year or two before it did. Moreover, at that time, the first dozen or two nongovernmental IOs that applied included some fairly obvious choices. Many of them, such as the LRCS and Save the Children International Union, had headquarters nearby, in Geneva, and were known for their collaborative work with the League of Nations Health Organization. The WHO also found these organizations to be useful partners.

However, by 1950, the WHO seemed to be more selective, as it turned down eleven of the fifteen organizations applying for this status. In 1952 and 1953, it did not accept any new nongovernmental IOs. This downward trend is a result of government representatives in the WHO considering that only a handful of nongovernmental IOs (those initially admitted) were the ones that truly could be helpful for the global health IO. Later applications were seen as coming from organizations whose work was more trivial and therefore did not warrant having a formal relationship with the WHO.

Moreover, WHO officials realized quickly that working with nongovernmental IOs was time-consuming. Even as late as the mid-1970s, formal meetings with nongovernmental IOs would only include five to six such organizations, and they were often referred to in official documents as "a sample of NGOs" (e.g., WHO 1975a). Additionally, WHO officials did not treat such organizations equally. For instance, in a meeting intended to assess how it could best work with nongovernmental IOs, of the nine representatives of such organizations invited to WHO headquarters, five were in fact from the LRCS and one came from each of the four other organizations (World Medical Association, International Union of Child Welfare, International Dental Federation, and International Council of Nurses) (WHO 1975a).

Indeed, the LRCS's previously strong ties with very intergovernmental IOs transferred to the post–World War II era, in part because many officials working in global health governance felt comfortable dealing with individuals who they had known for some time. The prominence of the LRCS became obvious in 1950 when the UN Security Council requested that the task of providing aid to Korean refugees be handled by several nongovernmental IOs led by the LRCS rather than by any of the UN institutions (Charnovitz 1997). The WHO's attempts to shift from its exclusivist policy for establishing relations with nongovernmental IOs in the early 1950s to a more inclusive policy starting the mid-1950s (reflected in Figure 3.3) was due to financial considerations. Between 1950 and 1952, a number of Eastern European states, starting with the USSR, left the WHO. They had concluded that they did not want to be part of an organization that they perceived as spreading essentially Western health policies (Youde 2012, 81). Soon afterward, Nationalist China also withdrew. With nine countries leaving the organization in a span of just a few years, the WHO found itself missing a little more than $1 million of its expected $7 million budget for 1952. The remaining countries did not want to make up the missing amount (Farley 2008, 84–85).

In a first attempt to deal with its funding problems, the WHO encouraged states to make voluntary contributions. Very few states responded to such encouragements throughout the 1950s.[9] The WHO therefore tried to make up some of its funding deficit by tapping into the resources that came with collaborations with nongovernmental IOs. This need for nongovernmental support is reflected in Figure 3.3. Indeed, by the mid-1950s, WHO was willing to accept virtually any organization that could contribute to its work.

The return of the Soviet Bloc to the WHO in 1958 resolved the most stringent financial problems of the organization, and the WHO went back to being more selective in its relations with nongovernmental IOs. Moreover, with the USSR and its Eastern European allies back in the WHO, and with a growing number of new states that had just broken free from their colonial past embracing very statist approaches to health care, the organization was increasingly under pressure to adopt more activist policies. Additionally, many of these countries did not trust and support nongovernmental IOs, as they saw them as extensions of Western powers.

In 1953, the United States established the Department of Health, Education, and Welfare. Starting in that year, and throughout the rest of the Cold War, the United States never really went back to the strong support for "voluntarism" in the health realm that had shaped its policies in the early interwar era. Although it was sympathetic to the idea of including nongovernmental IOs in WHO's work (compared to the positions of the vast majority of other states), it was not as supportive of nongovernmentalism as it had been in the interwar era.

Overall, in the first years of the WHO's existence, the main pressure to include nongovernmental IOs in the organization's work came from its own staff. Indeed, during the 1950s WHO staff had learned an important lesson regarding the usefulness of the nongovernmental sector, and it therefore continued to seek nongovernmental partners for much of its work. This pragmatic view of relations with nongovernmental IOs is reflected in the fact that, starting in the 1960s, the WHO began requiring "triennial reviews" for all of its partner organizations to assess the "benefit accrued to the [World Health] Organization" from such collaborations (WHO 1971, 5). In a 1975 internal memo, WHO officials concluded that nongovernmental IOs with resources

---

[9] Voluntary contributions increased slowly, reaching about 20 percent of the WHO's budget by 1970, about 50 percent by 1990 (after the regular budget was frozen in the 1980s), and more than 80 percent after 2010 (Youde 2012, 34–35; Legge 2015).

had "much to contribute" to the work of the WHO (WHO 1975b, 1). Implicitly, one of the most important criteria for an organization's admission to special relationship status with the WHO was the degree to which it could help the WHO financially. The organization did not promote a view of such nongovernmental IOs as democratic representatives of "global civil society" (as was the case later, in the post–Cold War era), and it therefore did not engage in arguments with ideological undertones.

Contrary to the financial relationships found in other UN organizations (most obviously UNESCO) where the flow of funds was toward nongovernmental IOs, the WHO made it clear that it could not support such organizations. In 1963, in an official communication for all its partners, it stated: "Most nongovernmental organizations do not have the funds to make the inputs they would desire and look for grants from the WHO, but the WHO itself does not have enough resources to support its own programmes, and the problem is an acute one" (WHO 1963, 4).

The WHO's decision to seek resources from private sources to supplement the ones received from governments was partially due to the LNHO's positive experience with the RF. Indeed, as much of the WHO's original staff came from the LNHO, they thought it would be useful to introduce in the new global health organization's constitution a clause allowing for external donations. Despite this stipulation, in the first years of the WHO's existence there were very few external donors prepared to help the global organization, as they felt that governments were sufficiently capable of funding it (WHO 1948b). In December 1948, the WHO decided to begin making direct appeals for funding to the public, considering that "the WHO is an organization with a philanthropic aspect" (WHO 1948b, 1). By 1963, this practice led nongovernmental IOs to officially complain that intergovernmental IOs, including the WHO, were involved in public fund-raising campaigns and were thus tapping into the few existing funding resources that were available to the nongovernmental sector (WHO 1963). The WHO's failed attempt to gain financial support from nongovernmental actors (and implicitly shift global health governance toward nongovernmentalism on the financial dimension) was greatly due to the high levels of organizational density and the competition between the various IOs in this realm (Abbott et al. 2016).

The relatively strained relations between the WHO and nongovernmental IOs in the 1960s was a reflection of the broader problems in the UN system. By then, Cold War tensions had led both superpowers to think about all actors in international relations, including nongovernmental ones, in a black or white, "us versus them" fashion (Birn 2014a). This became most evident in 1967, when the *New York Times* uncovered evidence that the CIA had financed a number of anti-communist nongovernmental IOs with consultative status in the UN (Willetts 2000, 41). The uproar led that same year to ECOSOC adopting Resolution 1296 that increased the power of the Committee on NGOs to control and limit the participation of nongovernmental IOs in UN activities (Chiang 1981, 161).

Throughout the 1960s and 1970s, despite overall lukewarm relations with nongovernmental IOs, the WHO made it clear that it sought to intensify efforts to involve them in "areas where the resources of the Organization are limited" (WHO 1976, 2). However, when relations with such organizations were not directly beneficial to its work, it preferred acting alone. This pragmatic approach to the WHO's relations with nongovernmental IOs was one of the few that both sides of the Cold War could accept. Thus, despite the failed attempt to convince nongovernmental IOs to contribute financially to the WHO's work, the secretariat's efforts, willfully or not, led to a greater acceptance of these organizations in the deliberative processes (as reflected in Figure 3.3).

The 1970s also saw increased intergovernmental–nongovernmental tensions in other health organizations such as the ICRC and LRCS. After the more intergovernmental ICRC and the more nongovernmental LRCS had been able to resolve most of their differences by 1928, they found a formula through which they would not impede each other's work and, in some instances, even collaborate, as was especially evident during World War II. The same global economic woes that had led to increased competition between the WHO and many nongovernmental IOs in the first half of the Cold War were also responsible for tensions flaring between the nongovernmental elements in the Red Cross movement and the more intergovernmental ones. At that time, although the Red Cross national societies were raising most of the funding for both the ICRC and LRCS, they felt that they were not sufficiently independent from the centralized Geneva-based IOs (Forsythe 2005, 304–305). The crisis led to an evaluation of the Red Cross movement in the comprehensive "Tansley Report." While the report called for a greater role for nongovernmental national societies in decisions of both the ICRC and LRCS, in the end, the organizations did not really adopt any changes (ICRC 1977). This can be viewed as yet another failed attempt to shift global health governance toward greater nongovernmentalism (on the decision-making dimension) in the first half of the Cold War era.

In the late 1970s, a shift in the relations between intergovernmental and nongovernmental organizations began taking place in many realms, including the one of global health. As early as the late 1960s and especially throughout the 1970s, *bilateral* international aid flowing through nongovernmental IOs increased dramatically (Smith 1990). Governments had discovered that nongovernmental IOs were more adept in forging necessary ties with local grassroots organizations and, implicitly, were more effective in delivering foreign aid in developing countries than governmental and intergovernmental actors were. As expected, Western states, with vibrant civil societies, became the members most supportive of giving nongovernmental IOs important roles in intergovernmental IOs. The United States created a specific agency to fund domestic and international nongovernmental organizations in the late 1940s (Cabanes 2014). Virtually all other Western states followed suit, establishing similar structures by the 1970s (Egger 2017, 1).

As most of these very active nongovernmental IOs worked in the development realm, the World Bank was among the first of the very intergovernmental organizations to take note of their usefulness and include them more in its programs (Smith 1990). Other intergovernmental IOs followed, and by the end of the Cold War, nongovernmental IOs were delivering more aid across the world than all UN agencies combined (Chaplowe and Engo-Tjega 2007).

The increased World Bank partnerships with nongovernmental IOs (and its implicit shift toward nongovernmentalism) began about half a decade before the IO became more active in global health. The Bank's interests in health issues can be traced as far back as Robert McNamara's first years as president of the organization, when he emphasized the importance of the "health of man" for a country's overall development (Harman 2009, 31). In the early 1970s, the Bank began financing programs that focused on family planning to control population growth. By the mid-1970s, it was also working on projects to improve sanitation, often together with the WHO, and combat diseases such as river blindness. In 1979, the World Bank created a health department and, in 1980, its *World Development Report* declared malnutrition and ill health to be the worst symptoms of poverty and that they deserved increased attention and finances from the organization. Over the next two decades, the Bank's proportion of health funding increased more than fourfold (Ruger 2005, 61). The greater role given to the World Bank in the health realm, coupled with the fairly strong shift at that time of the organization toward nongovernmentalism, on the deliberative dimension, led to a broader movement of global health governance toward nongovernmentalism.

The World Bank's greater involvement in the health realm was a direct result of the United States finding itself in the 1970s increasingly challenged by the Soviet Union and losing its influence in UN agencies such as the WHO. The decolonization process had led to a rapid increase in the number of UN members. Most of these new members tended to embrace Soviet statist domestic models. IOs such as the WHO and UNESCO, where all states, great and small, had equal votes, began promoting policies in tune with such models.

The tension between the American more nongovernmental preferences in the global health realm and the WHO's more statist approach became evident in the late 1970s, as US policymakers were becoming more active in both domestic and international health issues. By 1979, the United States established for the first time a separate Health and Human Services Department that splintered off from the former Department of Health, Education, and Welfare. At the global level, in the late 1970s, USAID (an agency established in the early 1960s) began looking for the best way to contribute more to health issues. Its leadership set up a series of meetings with top WHO officials. The Americans were, however, underwhelmed by the organization and decided to look for other partners in their global health work (WHO 1975c). They were not prepared to support an IO that was perceived to embrace such a statist ideology.

As neoliberal ideology became more powerful in the United States, the United Kingdom, and some other Western states in the 1980s, the tensions between these countries and the UN system increased. The tensions were best illustrated by the US and the United Kingdom leaving UNESCO in 1984 and 1985, respectively. At that time, the US began pressuring IOs where it had a greater influence, such as the World Bank, to take on more projects. The strong neoliberal views were also reflected in the US decision to have the World Bank and other IOs where it had greater influence, to give greater roles to nongovernmental IOs (Mundy 2010, 340).

In the health realm, the US decision to promote its global policies through the World Bank rather than through the WHO led to important changes in the Bank's approach to this issue-area. The World Bank moved from programs intended to control diseases to others intended to alter national health-care systems (Youde 2012, 48). These new policies reflected the neoliberal ideologies that the United States had embraced (Harman 2009, 228). World Bank programs promoted governments cutting health spending and introducing competition and privatization in health governance. The programs inevitably gave not just nongovernmental IOs but also private corporations a greater role in the World Bank's work.

These developments are a useful reminder of the difficulties in differentiating between laissez-faire ideology, which promotes a greater role for markets, and the democratic pluralist one, which calls for an increased role of the voluntary nonprofit sector. The positions expressed by the United States and the United Kingdom in the 1980s appeared to bring the two ideologies together into one "anti-statist" ideology that can be seen as a reaction to the Soviet authoritarian and statist ideologies.

With the emergence of the World Bank as the dominant actor in global health governance (Youde 2012, 46), the WHO began looking for ways to regain some of its influence. In order to do so, the WHO's members accepted some changes to bring the IO somewhat closer to American preferences for fear of losing the largest contributor to the organization's budget, as UNESCO and the ILO had. One of the relatively small concessions made in order to please the United States was that the WHO opened its doors further to nongovernmental IOs within its deliberations (and in the implementation processes), thus shifting global governance toward nongovernmentalism on the deliberative dimension. The arguments used to bring about this change were clothed in democratic rhetoric (Rau 2006).

GLOBAL GOVERNANCE IN THE HEALTH
REALM IN THE POST–COLD WAR ERA

The number and importance of international health-related nongovernmental IOs increased even more dramatically in the 1990s as the third wave of democracy led to the mushrooming of independent domestic nongovernmental organizations in formerly authoritarian countries (e.g., Sandberg 1994;

Opoku-Mensah 2001). As the number of such domestic organizations grew dramatically, so did their involvement in international health issues and, implicitly, the pressure to include them more in the work of WHO. The US-led initiative favoring a greater role for nongovernmental IOs (often promoted using very pro-democracy language both by older and newer democracies) did not encounter any major opposition in the 1990s. Global health governance thus quickly shifted further toward nongovernmentalism on the deliberative dimension.

More important, throughout the first decade after the end of the Cold War and, especially, during the second decade (when neoliberal ideology gained greater influence on American policies), as the United States became the sole remaining superpower after the end of the Cold War, it began promoting more successfully than before its own "public-private" partnership model to multiple intergovernmental IOs. UN secretary-general Kofi Annan showed that he had accepted such partnerships when he announced in January 1999 the launch of the UN Global Compact.

In the WHO, the rise of the public-private model is associated with the tenure of Gro Harlem Brundtland, director general of the organization between 1998 and 2003. Brundtland was part of the larger "Harvard group" that collectively gained a great deal of influence over many of the more intergovernmental IOs in the late 1990s (Harman 2009).

However, the rise of private sector influence in the WHO was not only (or even primarily) the result of personal preferences of individual leaders of the IO. It was also the result of the growing number and influence of transnational corporations brought about by globalizing processes of the post–Cold War era. Such corporations quickly realized that their increasingly global interests very often were best addressed through major IOs. More important, it was the direct result of the United States and other powerful member-states imposing a "zero nominal growth policy" on assessed member-state contributions starting the early 1990s. The WHO and other major IOs were forced to rely more on voluntary contributions. Over the past few decades, the proportion of WHO funds coming from voluntary contributions increased from around 20 percent to more than 80 percent (Legge 2015). While a large part of the voluntary contributions came from states or other intergovernmental IOs, such as the World Bank and the UN Development Programme (UNDP), starting in the 2000s, an increasing proportion has also come from the private sector, shifting the organization toward greater nongovernmentalism on the financial dimension. Most of the contributions of such corporations to WHO are in-kind (such as pharmaceutical corporations donating drugs) (Harman 2012, 3).

These public-private partnership models and the greater influence of corporations has raised a number of concerns in the global health realm. Most important, the increasing power of global transnational pharmaceutical companies has been seen as diminishing Global South countries' abilities to find affordable solutions to their health problems (Birn 2014a). Not surprisingly, many states have supported their own corporations. The United States has been particularly opposed to WHO initiatives that run counter to American corporate interests, such as the code on marketing breast milk substitutes, the rational use of medicines, and the ethical criteria for drug marketing (Youde 2012; Legge 2015, 10).

Perhaps the most visible change in the WHO's relations with nongovernmental actors in the post–Cold War era has been the emergence of its partnerships with a number of very powerful foundations promoting large-scale health programs, especially the Gates Foundation. In the GF's first ten years of existence (1998–2008), it awarded more than 1,000 grants for global health totaling close to $9 billion. In 2007 alone, the foundation spent almost as much as the WHO on global health (McCoy et al. 2009). Although its funds have been awarded to a large number of organizations, about two thirds of the total amount has gone to only twenty of them. Of course, the WHO itself was one of the major recipients of GF funding. For the period 2012–2013, for example, the GF contributed almost $600 million to the WHO, about 1.5 times the voluntary contribution made by the US government, the second largest voluntary donor to the IO. Considering that Gavi: The Vaccine Alliance, a public-private partnership that was also founded by and receives substantial funding from the GF, was the fourth largest voluntary donor to the WHO (with more than $200 million), the potential influence of this nongovernmental actor becomes evident. Indeed, together, the GF and Gavi alone represented about 20 percent of the entire WHO budget for 2012–2013 (WHO 2013). This shift toward nongovernmentalism on the financial dimension of global governance in the health realm was similar to the strong shift that unfolded in the interwar era when the RF played a similarly powerful role. Once again, the shift was promoted by the United States (often invoking strong liberal ideological arguments) together with some other Western powers.

As expected, when a nongovernmental actor has such great influence, there are a number of critics of its policies. One of the major critiques against the GF is that it overemphasizes technology and new vaccine development in a "clinical" fashion, rather than addressing them as public health problems that need social, economic, and political solutions. Such critics suggest that the GF has too much influence over the WHO and over global health governance (McCoy et al. 2009). Others argue that the rise in the foundation's influence is simply part of a broader trend in which nongovernmental actors have come to be more relevant in the post–Cold War era in global health governance while the WHO has become less relevant – or even irrelevant (Chow 2010). The latter group notes, for example, that while the WHO spends only about $400 million each year on emergency response, nongovernmental and hybrid organizations such as Doctors without Borders and the ICRC spend more than $1 billion each (Legge 2015, 6).

Yet, others feel that the GF and other major foundations are not truly independent because they rely a great deal on governments and on very intergovernmental organizations to promote their policies and therefore are closer to being "hybrids" between governmental and nongovernmental actors. Not surprisingly, the United States was the strongest supporter of allowing such foundations to play an important role in the WHO. Its support was often expressed through liberal ideological arguments (Dodgson et al. 2002). Last, but not least, some point to the alliances between the GF and large corporations. Indeed, the GF is a major investor in corporations such as Coca-Cola, McDonald's, and Nestlé (Harmer 2012).

In 2001, the concerns surrounding the increasing impact of large corporations and foundations on the WHO were raised in the Executive Board by a number of large developing countries, such as China and India (with strong domestic activist traditions), as well as by several Western European states with more activist views in the health realm than those of the United States, such as France and Sweden. These concerns were, as expected, echoed by a large number of Western-based nongovernmental IOs. That same year, the WHO initiated a thorough review of its partnerships with the nongovernmental sector. As a compromise between the various state interests (yet again expressed in many cases using language with strong ideological undertones) (e.g., Raghavan 2001), the review focused not only on private corporations but also on nongovernmental IOs. There was a general agreement, both from those opposing private-public initiatives and those supporting them, that nongovernmental IOs – not just governments – should play a role in controlling the increasing influence of major corporations and foundations (Lee 2010, 3).

The 2001 Civil Society Initiative was launched to review both formal and informal relations between the WHO and civil society organizations. The review found that although the WHO had official relations with 189 nongovernmental IOs, giving them access to deliberations, it actually collaborated on the implementation of projects with more than twice as many organizations. Many of the nongovernmental IOs that worked with the WHO but did not have official relations with the IO complained of the review process that conferred upon organizations such status. They pointed out that to receive official relations status, the rules stipulated that they needed to have had a "working relationship" with the WHO for at least two years and a joint three-year work plan with a WHO technical department. Numerous nongovernmental IOs argued that this was difficult to achieve when their unofficial status precluded them from attending official WHO meetings and did not allow them to have access to important WHO documents to prepare realistic proposals. Many such organizations felt that although they contributed substantially to the implementation stage of projects, they were not given access to the more important deliberative stages of the WHO's work (Lee 2010).

The review of the WHO's relations with civil society slowed down considerably in 2003 when there was a change in the IO's leadership. In the end, the review nevertheless led to some improvements in *informal* relations between nongovernmental IOs and the WHO, especially with regard to access to documents and consultations. Acquiring formal relations with the WHO, however, has remained just as difficult.

The WHO's relations with corporations and with private foundations were not altered after the review process. While private actors certainly had influence over the WHO, it was never clear how much they could impact its policies. Foundations and corporations worked with WHO staff behind closed doors but generally did not have access to the broader deliberative processes in the main bodies, where only member-states and a handful of nongovernmental IOs were admitted. In 2011, the WHO sought to formalize the deliberative role that such private actors had always been assumed to have acquired. At that time Director-General Margaret Chan proposed establishing a World Health Forum, envisioned as a "multi-stakeholder" periodic meeting that would bring together member-states, nongovernmental IOs, other major intergovernmental IOs, global health funds, and representatives of the private sector. Many small states were alarmed by this proposal to "supplement" the intergovernmental WHO forums with a hybrid one. Virtually all nongovernmental IOs working with the WHO also opposed the establishment of the forum. By the end of that year, the proposal was abandoned (Richter 2012).

However, just five years later, in 2016, a revised mechanism, WHO's Framework for Engagement with Non-State Actors, was adopted. While this mechanism formalized private actors' participation in meetings of the Governing Body, consultations, hearings, and a broad set of other types of meetings, it also adopted a series of measures that were intended to "manage conflict of interest and other risks of engagement" with private corporations (WHO 2016). This, of course, contributed to the organization's shift toward even greater nongovernmentalism on the deliberative dimension. It should be noted, though, that the framework made no actual formal changes to the functioning of the WHO. Rather, it adopted a number of informal procedures allowing more nongovernmental actors to participate in the various WHO forums and projects.

ANSWERING THE FIVE MAIN QUESTIONS:
SOME PRELIMINARY CONCLUSIONS

Figure 3.4 summarizes the above discussion of the evolution of the global health realm with regard to its intergovernmental versus nongovernmental nature. It was developed in an analogous way to Figure 1.1, which represents the evolution of the global education realm. Figure 3.4 includes in parentheses the main global governors for each time period. The dashed arrows represent failed attempts to bring about change, and the full arrows reflect

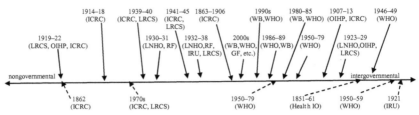

FIGURE 3.4. The intergovernmental–nongovernmental continuum in global health governance.

successful ones. Just as in Figure 1.1, the placement of these time periods on the continuum in Figure 3.4 is approximate (often dictated by the need to distinguish visually between different moments when global governance was in very similar places on the continuum). The figure should therefore be seen primarily as reflecting how global governance in the health realm during a time period was more intergovernmental or nongovernmental *relative* to other periods immediately before or after it. The main benefit of illustrating where global governance falls on this continuum is that it helps us visualize the direction of the shifts across this continuum. After all, it is these shifts that I seek to explain.

To help visualize such shifts further, I include Figure 3.5, which offers a better illustration of the intensity of such shifts. While Figure 3.4 simply indicated that a change occurred from one time period to another (illustrated with full arrows in different places on the continuum), Figure 3.5 also considers *how many* shifts (on the decision-making, financial, and deliberative dimensions) took place. Specifically, the level of intergovernmentalism on the vertical axis begins at 0 in 1850, the year before the first efforts to develop a form of global health governance. Then for each subsequent time period, I add or subtract one unit on the vertical axis for each shift toward intergovernmentalism or nongovernmentalism, respectively.[10]

The line in Figure 3.5, like the continuum in Figure 3.4, shows that the nature of global health governance has indeed experienced significant movements across the intergovernmental–nongovernmental continuum over the past century and a half. However, as mentioned in the introductory chapter, unless a measure of the actual degree of intergovernmentalism versus nongovernmentalism is developed, neither Figure 3.5 nor any other visual representation of such shifts should be interpreted as accurate depictions of the *levels* of intergovernmentalism or nongovernmentalism. Rather, the figure shows that changes have taken place, sometimes simultaneously across different dimensions, and other times only across one dimension.

---

[10] The unit increases and decreases used for this graph are specified in column two of Table 3.1 that I discuss in detail below.

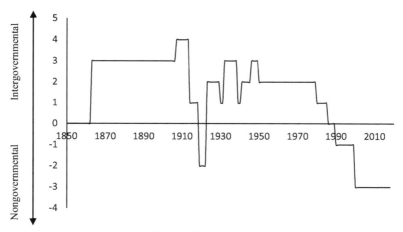

FIGURE 3.5. Shifts in the nature of global health governance.

As I acknowledge that neither figure offers a completely accurate reflection of the changes in global governance, I complement them with Table 3.1. This comprehensive table summarizes developments in the global health realm over the past century and a half by capturing the answers to all five main questions for this section. The first column identifies the various moments (or in some cases, longer time periods) when there were attempts to shift global health governance across the intergovernmental–nongovernmental continuum. I use italic letters to signal the unsuccessful attempts to alter global governance. The second column identifies the IOs where the changes were attempted.

In the third column (with its three subcolumns) I respond to the first of the five questions: *What types of changes took place in the intergovernmental–nongovernmental nature of global governance?* The column notes each shift across the intergovernmental–nongovernmental continuum on each of the three dimensions and offers detailed information regarding the changes in global governance (my outcome variable) that Figures 3.4 and 3.5 cannot entirely capture. It notes whether the shifts were toward intergovernmentalism (+) or nongovernmentalism (–). It also indicates when shifts took place due to the emergence of a *new* organization (NO), changes *within* existing organizations (WO), or changes in relative importance *among* organizations (AO). In the last row I include the total number of instances for each type of successful change. There are almost exactly as many shifts on the decision-making (nine), financial (nine), and deliberative dimensions (ten).

All subsequent columns in Table 3.1 refer to the possible explanations for the global governance shifts. Column 4 summarizes the answers to the second main question: *How strong was governmental activism in the most important countries promoting or opposing changes in the nature of global governance?*

TABLE 3.1. *Summary of shifts on the intergovernmental–nongovernmental continuum in global health realm (failed attempts in italic)*

Year(s)	IO(s) where change was attempted	(Q1) Type of change			(Q2) Major states supporting or opposing change and their ideology		(Q3) Evidence of ideology-based mechanism	(Q4) Evidence of institutional mechanism	(Q5) Evidence of system-level explanations
		(a) Decision-making	(b) Financial	(c) Deliberative	Support change	Oppose change			
1851–1861	*New IO*	*+ (NO)*	*+ (NO)*	*+ (NO)*		*UK (–), and other states*	*no*	*no*	*no*
1862	ICRC	– (NO)	– (NO)	– (NO)		UK (+), France (+)	no	no	yes
1863	ICRC	+ (NO)	+ (NO)	+ (NO)	UK (+), France (+)		no	yes	no
1907	OIHP		+ (NO)	+ (NO)	UK (+), France (+)		no	yes	no
1914	ICRC	– (WO)	– (WO)	– (WO)			no	no	yes
1919	LRCS	– (NO)	– (NO)	– (NO)	US (–)	UK (+), France (+)	yes	yes	no
1921	*IRU*	*+ (NO)*	*+ (NO)*	*+ (NO)*	*Italy (+)*	*US (–), UK (–)*	*yes*	*yes*	*no*
1923	LNHO	+ (NO)	+ (NO)	+ (NO)	UK (+), France (+)		no	yes	no

Year(s)	IO(s) where change was attempted	(Q1) Type of change			(Q2) Major states supporting or opposing change and their ideology		(Q3) Evidence of ideology-based mechanism	(Q4) Evidence of institutional mechanism	(Q5) Evidence of system-level explanations
		(a) Decision-making	(b) Financial	(c) Deliberative	Support change	Oppose change			
1923–1929	OIHP	+ (WO)			UK (+), France (+)		no	yes	no
1930	LNHO, RF		– (WO)				no	no	yes
1932	IRU	+ (NO)	+ (NO)		Italy (+)	UK (–)	yes	no	no
1939	ICRC, LRCS, LNHO	– (AO)	– (WO)				no	no	yes
1941	ICRC	+ (WO)			Switzerland (+)		yes	no	no
1946	WHO	+ (NO)	+ (NO)		US (+), UK (+), USSR (+)		no	yes	yes
1950–1959	WHO	+ (WO)			US (–), USSR (+)		no	no	no
1950–1969	WHO		– (WO)				no	no	yes
1950–1979	WHO			– (WO)			no	no	yes
1970s	ICRC, LRCS	– (WO)					no	no	yes

(continued)

TABLE 3.1 (continued)

Year(s)	IO(s) where change was attempted	(Q1) Type of change			(Q2) Major states supporting or opposing change and their ideology		(Q3) Evidence of ideology-based mechanism	(Q4) Evidence of institutional mechanism	(Q5) Evidence of system-level explanations
		(a) Decision-making	(b) Financial	(c) Deliberative	Support change	Oppose change			
1980–1985	World Bank, WHO			– (AO)	US (–), UK (–)		yes	no	no
1986–1989	WHO			– (WO)	US (–)		yes	no	no
1990s	WHO, World Bank			– (WO)	Old and new democracies (–)		yes	yes	yes
2000s	WHO		– (WO)	– (WO)	US (–)	France (+), China (+), India (+)	yes	yes	yes
TOTAL		9	9	10	12		7	9	7

Key: NO: new organization; WO: change within existing organization; AO: change in relative importance among organizations; +: domestic activism or inter-governmentalism when referring to state or global governance, respectively; –: domestic passivism or nongovernmentalism when referring to state or global governance, respectively.

104

Specifically, the column (and its two subcolumns) identifies instances in which major states supported or opposed the changes to global governance and also notes whether those states embraced government activism (+) or passivism (–) domestically.[11] Taken together, columns 3 and 4 show that, with few exceptions, support for intergovernmentalism and nongovernmentalism went hand in hand with domestic activism or passivism, respectively, as H_1 and H_2 suggest. The bottom row indicates that there were overall twelve instances (of the sixteen successful attempts)[12] where there is evidence of the domestic–international linkage.

Columns 5 and 6 summarize answers to the third and fourth questions: *Did officials promoting intergovernmentalism or nongovernmentalism use arguments that invoked specific ideologies?* and *Which national institutions were represented in the international efforts to shift global governance toward greater intergovernmentalism or nongovernmentalism?* Specifically, column 5 indicates whether those promoting or opposing changes used arguments with ideological undertones. Column 6 notes whether bureaucrats from domestic institutions promoted the intergovernmental shift at the international level (or whether representatives from domestic nongovernmental institutions supported shifts toward nongovernmentalism). The two columns show that there were instances where there is evidence of both mechanisms functioning simultaneously, others where there is evidence of only one mechanism, and yet others where there is no evidence of either one of the two mechanisms. The bottom row shows that there are slightly fewer instances where there is support for the ideological argument (seven) than for the institutional one (nine).

Lastly, column 7 summarizes the answer to the fifth question: *Are there any system-level explanations for the shifts?* The column notes the instances where there are plausible explanations for the shifts (and for the directions of those shifts) that operate at the global rather than state level. The bottom cell in the column indicates that I found seven such instances.

In four of these seven instances, system-level factors appear to have led single-handedly to changes in global governance (i.e., there is no evidence of institution-based or ideology-based mechanisms). The periods during the two world wars are expected exceptions, as intergovernmental collaboration broke down and nongovernmental actors stepped in wherever possible. The third exception is during the interwar era, when the economic global crisis led to the LNHO becoming more nongovernmental on the financial dimension. Similarly, in the first half of the Cold War, economic downturn led the WHO to improve relations with nongovernmental IOs for pragmatic reasons, even

---

[11] The indication that a certain country had a more (+) or less (–) activist approach reflects the relative degree of activism compared to other major powers at that specific moment in time.

[12] The unsuccessful attempts to alter global governance also offer strong support for H_1 and H_2. Indeed, they include many instances when powerful states opposed changes that ran counter to their domestic preferences.

though in the end, the acceptance of nongovernmental actors led to a shift on the deliberative dimension rather than on the financial one, as initially planned.

However, in all other periods, even when there were system-level factors contributing to the shifts in global governance, their impact appears to have been secondary compared to the one involving the projection of powerful states' preferences to the international realm. For instance, although the need to establish health IOs after two devastating wars was not truly in question, the nongovernmental nature of the LRCS and the intergovernmental nature of the WHO were the result of great power preferences after these wars, rather than simply of the end of the conflicts.

Similarly, system-level factors do not appear to explain the World Bank's (rather than the WHO's) emergence as an important global governor in the health realm, nor the organization's shift toward nongovernmentalism in the early 1980s at a time when the WHO was moving toward greater intergovernmentalism. These explanations need to be complemented by arguments taking into account the differences between US and Soviet preferences and the degree of influence each of these superpowers had in the two IOs.

System-level arguments appear to be more convincing when used to explain the shifts toward nongovernmentalism in the post–Cold War era. Indeed, the third wave of democracy empowered nongovernmental actors worldwide and led to pressures for IOs such as the World Bank and WHO to include them more in their work starting in the late 1980s. Similarly, the global rise in influence of powerful corporations and of private foundations in the WHO, as well as in other IOs, can be in part attributed to the massive wave of globalization that began in the 1990s and that brought about a shift toward nongovernmentalism. Both such explanations are in tune with the system-level arguments derived from existing literature in Chapter 2. However, even in these two cases, domestic preferences played crucial roles. After all, the democratization processes of the post–Cold War era were made possible in part because of domestic shifts in the Soviet Union. Similarly, the eventual acceptance of powerful corporate actors as stakeholders in major IOs was championed by American leaders who embraced neoliberal ideologies.

Overall, this chapter offers important evidence in support of H_1 and H_2. Indeed, shifts in the dominant ideologies and domestic institutions within powerful states have either alone or together with system-level factors triggered changes in global health governance.

4

Global Governance in the Labor Realm

The present chapter follows the evolution of global governance in the labor realm from the mid-nineteenth century to present. It first notes how governments and nongovernmental actors became involved in domestic labor issues throughout the nineteenth century. It then explains how competitive economic pressures led governments and workers' groups to deal with labor issues at the international level. The chapter adopts a structure similar to that of Chapter 3, which discussed global health governance by highlighting the multiple changes in the main global governors and in their intergovernmental versus nongovernmental nature.

As in the health realm, global labor governance has involved many different international actors such as the Second International, the International Association for Labour Legislation (ILL), the International Labour Organization (ILO), and the International Labor Rights Fund (ILRF). I discuss all such global governors, following the example of previous historical accounts of this realm (e.g., Follows 1951; Alcock 1971; Rodgers et al. 2009). More important, I follow the shifts toward intergovernmentalism and nongovernmentalism in these IOs and, more broadly, in global governance

The narrative identifies the main states supporting or opposing shifts across the intergovernmental–nongovernmental continuum and notes their activist or passive domestic approaches to labor at that time. Throughout the chapter, I also note whether individuals involved in the establishment of IOs represented top-level government institutions, specialized lower-level institutions, or nongovernmental groups. Additionally, I highlight instances when such individuals invoked arguments with ideological undertones. This allows me to assess whether the two hypothesized processes connecting domestic preferences to global changes indeed unfolded. Lastly, I identify possible system-level explanations for the shifts in global governance.

In the last section of this chapter, I summarize the evolution of global labor governance using forms of visualization of the shifts similar to those presented in Chapter 3. This allows me to show that even if global governance in the labor realm appears at first sight to have been more nongovernmental than in the global health realm, the two issue-areas experienced about the same number of shifts toward both intergovernmentalism and nongovernmentalism. I conclude the chapter with several general observations regarding the value of domestic–international linkage explanations versus system-level ones.

GLOBAL GOVERNANCE IN THE LABOR
REALM BEFORE WORLD WAR I

With the coming of the Industrial Revolution, the pressure for governments to intervene in domestic labor issues increased substantially. Despite the strong laisse-faire ideology in the United Kingdom at that time, the fact that it was the first country to experience such a revolution led it to also become the first to adopt significant domestic labor legislation, starting with the 1819 law limiting the number of working hours in cotton factories (Follows 1951, 2). Other industries and other countries soon followed with similar working hour limitations.

By the end of the nineteenth century, in addition to the many national laws regarding the number of working hours and necessary working conditions in various industries, governments also began considering numerous forms of social insurance legislation. In some cases, the insurance was compulsory. It covered different categories of workers; it involved various benefits along with various proportions to be paid by employers, employees, and government. Germany took the lead in adopting such insurance laws in the early 1880s, when the country had risen to become a major industrial power. The movement began in 1881, when Wilhelm I sent a letter to Parliament stating that "those who are disabled from work by age and invalidity have a well-grounded claim to care from the state" (Botz n.d.). By 1883, Chancellor Otto von Bismarck pushed through a compulsory sickness insurance law and, in 1884, a worker's compensation law. Similar sickness insurance legislation followed in Austria in 1888, Hungary in 1891, and then in other countries. Although the United Kingdom adopted worker's compensation legislation in 1880, it instituted sickness insurance only in 1911. France adopted in 1905 voluntary unemployment insurance but enacted compulsory sickness insurance legislation only in 1930. In contrast, Germany enacted compulsory old-age insurance in 1889 but did not pass unemployment insurance until 1927. The differences in labor conditions across states increased across the nineteenth and early twentieth centuries.

The international dimension of labor became evident almost immediately after the first domestic laws in this realm emerged. Social reformers realized early on that even when individual employers and governments were sympathetic to improving labor standards, international competitive pressures made it difficult for them to do so unilaterally. When adopting labor laws, governments therefore soon began seeking ways to coordinate or at least to be aware of each other's actions in this realm (Maday 1935, xv). Labor groups also understood the need to organize themselves internationally. These international workers' organizations were not only the result of broad Marxist calls for class solidarity in overthrowing the capitalist system. Very often, they were simply the result of short-term labor unions' need for access to the same comparable cross-country information that employers and governments possessed. Indeed, information regarding working conditions in other countries became essential in domestic employer-labor union negotiations (Schevenels 1956, 14).

The initial (unsuccessful) efforts to place labor issues on the international agenda were very intergovernmental in nature on all three dimensions. These proposals are generally associated with individuals who did not represent any significant domestic labor, employer, or government groups. The first such initiative belonged to Robert Owen who, at the 1833 Aix-la-Chapelle Congress of the Holy Alliance, called on governments to establish a commission to consider his theoretical and practical models of *domestic* labor legislation. The Congress quickly dismissed this proposal (Mahaim 1913, 183).

The idea of adopting *international* treaties for harmonizing labor legislation across states was first promoted in 1836 by Arthur Hindley, a British member of Parliament. Interestingly, his support for international labor legislation was not based, as in later cases, on the argument that international treaties would help states that have already adopted domestic labor laws remain competitive. Hindley believed that his country was sufficiently competitive in world markets to withstand the small setbacks that came with restrictions on labor practices. His argument was rather that international labor treaties were useful to *other states* that would be forced to follow the British example and improve conditions for their workers (Follows 1951, 18).

The normative aspects of the arguments promoting international cooperation in the labor realm were present even in cases where they combined with the more practical ones, referring to the need to level the playing field in trade competition. For example, in 1837, Jerome Blanqui argued, "There is only one way of accomplishing [reform] while avoiding its disastrous consequences; this would be to get it adopted simultaneously by industrial nations which compete in the foreign market" (1880, 119).

Normative arguments for international coordination in the labor realm became even more common by 1847, when Daniel Legrand appealed to the British, French, Prussian, and Swiss governments to adopt international legislation so that "humanitarian ideals [would be] given precedence over considerations of economic profit" (cited in Mahaim 1934, 5). These early unsuccessful efforts to establish an international labor organization or, at minimum, some international agreements, reflected the fact that major powers were not yet prepared to take on this issue.

The first successful international initiatives to focus on labor came at the midpoint of the nineteenth century and were very nongovernmental in nature. Immediately after the failed 1848 revolutions, domestic nongovernmental groups that had recently emerged in many European countries offered numerous international labor legislation proposals (Follows 1951, 49). Perhaps most significant, Karl Marx's *Communist Manifesto* was published the same year as the revolutions. As Marx's ideas spread across Europe over the next few decades, together with those of Friedrich Engels, he established in 1864 the First International, based on the understanding that the only way workers could achieve their goals was to organize themselves internationally. While the arguments for establishing an organization to bring together workers' representatives had strong ideological roots, they were officially presented in pragmatic terms. The practical need for the First International was perhaps best expressed by its president, George Odger at the opening meeting of the organization:

We find that whenever we attempt to better our social condition by reducing the hours of toil, or by raising the price of labour, our employers threaten us with bringing Frenchmen, Germans, Belgians and others to do our work with a reduced rate of wages and we are sorry to say this has been done, not from any desire of our Continental brethren to injure us but through a want of regular and systematic communication between the industrial classes of all countries. (cited in Milner 1991, 22)

The 1866 Geneva Conference of the First International passed a resolution calling for the adoption of international labor legislation (Mahaim 1934, 5). The text of that resolution, drawn up by Marx, stipulated that "The emancipation of labour is neither a local nor a national, but a social problem embracing all countries in which modern society exists" (cited in Follows 1951, 60). The First International emerged as very nongovernmental on all dimensions, avoiding virtually all government participation and influence. It was composed of representatives of domestic nongovernmental groups that had been established recently in numerous states.

Despite the rapid rise of the First International, the tumultuous events surrounding the 1871 Paris Commune weakened it, creating a deep division between anarchists and socialists. It held its last congress in 1873.

The lack of intergovernmental action in this realm at that time is considered to be due to the fact that international economic competition had not yet reached critical levels. Powerful states such as the United Kingdom, France, and Germany did not find that domestic changes to labor legislation impinged substantially on their competitiveness (Delevingne 1934, 12).

The international nongovernmental initiatives continued to suffer well into the late nineteenth century due to the division between anarchists, who sought to pursue their goals outside of state structures, and socialists, who pursued goals primarily through existing government structures. This division led to a number of failed attempts to organize workers' groups throughout the 1870s and 1880s. For example, despite adopting a manifesto for future actions, the 1877 International Workers Congress in Ghent was not followed by any further contacts between participants. The conferences in Coire, Switzerland, in 1881 and in Paris in 1883 had somewhat different participants and agendas but were also unsuccessful in forging long-term contacts and establishing international workers' organizations. In fact, the debates between the British and French representatives at the Paris conference offered a glimpse of the very different approaches labor groups took in these two important states. While the French emphasized political solutions to workers' problems, especially by adopting labor laws, the British sought to empower trade unions in their negotiations with employers and criticized the French for their "statist" approach (Parliamentary Committee 1883, 4).

The international situation began to change in the late 1880s when Europe saw a flurry of activity in the advancement of domestic labor legislation. In part, the impetus came from stronger domestic trade unions that broadened their base by admitting not only skilled workers but also unskilled ones. The increasingly powerful unions started organizing themselves internationally in trade secretariats for various industries. While the first such international secretariats represented smaller groups such as the hatters, cigar makers, and shoemakers (all established in 1889), they were soon followed by larger ones, such as the miners in 1890, metalworkers in 1893, textile workers in 1894, and transport workers in 1897 (Schevenels 1956).

However, broader efforts to establish international ties between national federations of trade unions were not successful at that time. The first comprehensive attempt to bring together representatives of most national trade unions in an international forum took place in 1888 and was initiated by the British Trade Union Committee. However, the Committee sought to keep some types of foreign participants out of the meeting. The conference therefore ended up bringing together British trade union delegations representing 850,000 members and delegations from the other countries representing only 250,000 members. The strong British control of meetings and the promotion of primarily British issues led the conference to end without any international agreement (Schevenels 1956, 17).

In 1889, British unions tried yet again to organize an international meeting. This time, they broadened the list of participants. Most important, they included French trade union representatives who had not been present at the 1888 conference. The French at that time were even more divided than were other national groups. Once again, the international meeting did not lead to any agreements between the national groups. Additionally, with the establishment of the Second International that year, many participants in the 1889 meeting questioned the usefulness of creating an international trade union organization.

The problems of establishing an international organization of trade union federations did not stem only from disagreements between national and subnational groups but also from their lack of material resources for travel, hotel accommodations, and translation for such conferences. Perhaps for this reason, the first major successful international trade union federation, in 1886, brought together representatives from Denmark, Norway, and Sweden, three neighboring countries with similar approaches to labor issues and fairly low language barriers. The experience these countries developed in working together led the Danes to push for a broader organization of trade unions. In 1901, when the Scandinavian Trade Union Conference was held in Copenhagen, delegations from Belgium, Finland, France, Germany, and the United Kingdom were also invited.

The Copenhagen Conference led to the establishment of the International Federation of Trade Unions (IFTU). The arguments used by those pushing for the establishment of the organization were pragmatic, rather than ideological, emphasizing the need for information exchange among trade unions from different countries and for concerted action, similar to the ones used by the founders of the First International. The lingering divisions between trade unions were somewhat resolved during this conference by establishing a clear distinction between IFTU's tasks and those of the Second International that had been in existence for more than a decade by that time (International Labour Office 1920, 2–3).

This Second International, also known as the Socialist International, brought together representatives of socialist and labor parties from most European countries. The move from the First to the Second International can be viewed as a victory for those groups that sought to achieve workers' goals through official government channels rather than outside them. The change thus resulted in a shift in global governance toward intergovernmentalism on the decision-making dimension of the intergovernmental–nongovernmental continuum.

The founding of the Second International in 1889 was possible due to two important factors. First, by the late nineteenth century, the powerful European states had accepted fairly universal male suffrage. By 1884, the United Kingdom completed the process of extending male suffrage that it had begun in 1832. France adopted universal male suffrage in 1848. Germany introduced it when establishing the Imperial Parliament in 1871. These developments allowed vibrant socialist and labor parties to emerge in these countries by the late 1880s and to come together in the Second International (Joll 1955, 5). Second, the new organization took the decision early on to exclude anarchist groups, thus reducing the tensions that had split the First International.

The Second International sought to promote legal and social protection of workers through political means, within the existing systems. The United Kingdom, still the most powerful industrialized economy in the world, was rarely represented in this organization. The British government had adopted some social reforms early, thus mitigating the class struggle that Marx famously predicted. Labor unions, rather than political parties, therefore emerged as the driving forces for labor legislation in that country. The unions avoided participating in the Second International because they considered it too political for their purposes (Milner 1991, 7). The British influence was therefore felt primarily in the establishment and workings of the IFTU, rather than in the Second International. The latter organization was dominated by the Germans. The German Social Democratic Party, in particular, emerged as a key player both domestically, where in 1890 it held 35 seats in the Reichstag, and internationally, where it became a model for labor movements in other European countries. It eventually became the driving force behind the Second International (Joll 1955, 11). In fact, both the founding of the Second International in the late nineteenth century and its demise in 1914 are associated with actions of this powerful German party. While the French were also very active in the Second International, they did not match the German influence, which was primarily the result of a weak working class movement in France due to the splintering of French socialists after the 1871 Paris Commune.

The IFTU also reflected a strong German presence. Indeed, German labor groups adopted both domestically and internationally a "two-arm" strategy, with the Social Democratic Party working in the political sphere while the trade unions worked in the economic one (Milner 1991, 6). The British were initially just as influential as the Germans in IFTU, if not more so. In the first few years, the organization's funding came almost entirely from these two countries. By 1901, almost three quarters of the workers represented in the organization came from Germany and the United Kingdom. However, by the beginning of World War I, the US presence in IFTU (2 million workers represented) surpassed the British presence (1 million workers represented) and almost equaled the German presence (2.5 million workers represented[1]) (Schevenels 1956, 63). US labor groups were usually represented in discussions with the Europeans by Samuel Gompers, the first and longest tenured president of the American Federation of Labor (AFL), from 1886 to 1894 and 1895 to 1924. While Gompers accepted having the AFL join IFTU a few years before the war, he never truly embraced the organization. He and other American labor leaders felt that the AFL was sufficiently strong and that its affiliation with IFTU was not very useful.

German dominance of IFTU was also reflected in the organization's selection of Berlin for the secretariat's headquarters. German Carl Leigen became the first president and secretary of the organization. He remained in that position until 1919.

IFTU's relative success was in great part due to its modest goals. Soon after it was established, it decided to leave the political fights to the Second International and chose to focus on simple exchanges of information between

---

[1] This number was fifty times higher than that of union members in Germany in the late 1870s (Milner 1991, 70).

national trade unions. These trade unions were particularly interested in information related to salaries and the unions' daily activities. IFTU proved its usefulness on numerous occasions. When workers in one country were on strike, it helped them coordinate so that unions from other countries refused to have work transferred to them. Additionally, IFTU financially supported national labor groups that were on strike (Schevenels 1953, 50–51).

IFTU remained very nongovernmental across all three dimensions during virtually its entire existence. All its decisions were adopted by representatives of national (nongovernmental) trade unions. These domestic organizations also funded all of the IO's activities. Lastly, government representatives were rarely allowed in any of IFTU's deliberations.

However, the organization's decision soon after it was founded to play only a small role and allow the Second International to take the lead on important political issues resulted in an overall shift away from nongovernmentalism on the decision-making dimensions of the continuum in global labor governance. The rhetoric surrounding this shift never involved ideological arguments. The decision was simply presented as a result of the strong interest of domestic labor parties in playing an important international role and of IFTU allowing them to take on such a role.

The increasingly powerful domestic and international labor structures that emerged in the last two decades of the nineteenth century also led governments, not just labor groups, to seek international collaboration in the labor realm. Indeed, by the 1880s, many governments feared the empowerment of the radical socialists more than they feared labor unions. Therefore, some governments introduced domestic labor legislation to stave off calls for more drastic alternatives promoted by socialist groups (Alcock 1971, 8). Most famously, in Germany, Chancellor Bismarck decided to deal with the mounting dangers from socialists by "fighting fire with fire" (Follows 1951, 110). He pushed for the adoption of a series of social insurance laws in 1883, 1884, and 1889, arguing: "Give the healthy workman the right to employment, assure him care when he is sick and maintenance when he is old... then these [socialists] will sound their bird call in vain" (cited in Schapiro 1923, 295). Indeed, after the adoption of such laws, socialists garnered far fewer votes in the Reichstag elections than in previous years.

Similar pressures and changes related to labor legislation were visible in other European states. In Switzerland, in particular, the presence of foreign socialist leaders in major cities led to an even greater recognition of the need for reform. The first significant labor laws in that country were associated with the efforts of Colonel Carl Frey. As a politician, he was first, in 1870, to push for the adoption of child labor legislation in his own canton of Basseland. In 1875, when he became president of the Swiss National Council, he successfully fought for similar laws at the federal level, despite Swiss employers' objections that such legislation eroded their international competitiveness (Follows 1951, 98–100).

In 1876, therefore, while still president of the Swiss National Council, Frey called for an international conference to establish similar labor regulations across states. In 1881, Switzerland approached major powers to propose such a conference. It envisioned a very intergovernmental IO similar in structure to the Universal Postal Union and the International Telegraphic Union, two organizations already functioning in Berne (Mahaim 1904, 31). Most other states were, however, reluctant to embrace this cause (Ayusawa 1920, 398). The British government, in particular, opposed the initiative, arguing that the time was "not ripe" (Stewart 1969, 2).

In 1888, the Swiss called yet again for an international labor legislation conference. This time there were some positive replies, most important from the United Kingdom and France. By the 1880s, the industrial competition among European states had increased and, as the wealthiest countries had already adopted some domestic labor laws, they felt they needed to push other states, such as Belgium and Italy, to adopt similar standards and level the playing field. However, the British acceptance of international standards was very guarded, as the Foreign Office made it clear it was "not of opinion that the function to which an International Conference usually addresses itself of framing Resolutions or Conventions by which all the Signatories are bound would be suitable to the subject matter of the contemplated inquiry" (cited in Delevingne 1934, 19). Despite initial support for the conference, it quickly became apparent that most governments were still not prepared to discuss labor legislation in an international forum.

While the Germans at first did not reply to the Swiss call for a conference, domestic power shifts led them to become the champions of government activism in the labor realm. Bismarck, a staunch conservative, had indeed been willing to accept some labor laws in order to reduce the influence of socialists in the country. Yet, he was not willing to go much further, arguing that it would hurt Germany's competitiveness. More important, he was convinced that other states would never agree to a set of common labor standards; therefore, he opposed any kind of international initiative. In 1885, when there had appeared to be strong support in the Reichstag for international labor legislation prohibiting Sunday and holiday labor as well as for limiting women's and children's work, Bismarck intervened by declaring that any international agreement on these topics would clearly be "impossible in the world in which we live" (Follows 1951, 91). Not surprisingly, Bismarck also opposed the Swiss initiative in 1889.

The most important factor leading to Germany's shift in its position on international labor legislation was the emergence on the political scene of the young emperor, Wilhelm II. Wilhelm's entourage had come to include a number of individuals preaching Christian Socialism, the most influential of whom was his childhood tutor Dr. Georg Hinzpeter, who had now become an advisor. Hinzpeter convinced the young kaiser that the promotion of improved conditions for the working classes would make him very popular.

Wilhelm therefore pounced on the opportunity presented to him by the Swiss invitation. In February 1890, he instructed his chancellor not only to convey Germany's acceptance to participate in the international labor legislation conference but, in fact, to host it in Berlin. He argued that "the obstacles to an improvement of the situation of our workers and which lie in international competition can be, if not overcome, at least lessened, in no other way than by international agreements between the countries that dominate the world market" (cited in Delevingne 1934, 23, fn 10). Moreover, the emperor declared that such conferences should be repeated in the future.

Although, as mentioned, Bismarck saw some advantages in a successful conference (the most important of which was helping Germany maintain its economic competitiveness after it had adopted a number of labor laws), he was pessimistic about the possibility of having all major states actually agree on the issues at hand (Bauer 1905, 4). He tried to dissuade Wilhelm from hosting the conference and, after seeing that he could not, he tried to limit its scope. He was able to stipulate in the conference invitations that the meetings would be technical, not diplomatic, thus excluding the possibility of them reaching binding agreements. This stipulation, in fact, was instrumental in getting other states, in particular the United Kingdom, to accept the invitation (Stewart 1969, 2).

The disagreements between Germany's emperor and chancellor over the benefits of hosting the conference as well as of the scope and substance of the proposed discussions and, more broadly, over labor legislation, were the beginning of a major rift between them that led one month later to Bismarck's dismissal. The emperor had his way and the Swiss withdrew their proposal for a conference in Berne, clearing the way for it to be held in Germany.

The instincts of the German chancellor appeared to be correct because the 1890 Berlin Conference did not lead to any agreements among states. One reason for the conference's failure was the extraordinarily broad and ambitious agenda. It included questions related to work in mines, work on Sundays and holidays, child labor, and women's labor. There was also very little support for Germany's proposal to establish a permanent (and very intergovernmental) organization to oversee the implementation of international labor agreements (Delevingne 1934, 25). The United Kingdom was the most vocal opponent of such an organization, arguing with an interesting mix of laissez-faire ideology and pragmatism that the government, even if it wanted, did not have the power to contract international agreements regulating work in the private sector (Follows 1951, 136). France also came out officially against the proposal (Mahaim 1904, 6) and, in the end, abstained even on the watered-down and guarded final conference resolutions, which simply declared that "it is desirable" to have more collaboration between states in harmonizing labor legislation. In fact, there were no decisions taken even in the apparently innocuous proposal to exchange information between states on their labor laws (Mahaim 1934, 6).

During the debates, Belgium and Italy argued that agreements between governments should also leave room for nongovernmental initiatives (Delevingne 1934, 25). In fact, this position was embraced by virtually all states that supported the adoption of common international labor standards, most of them medium or small powers. They realized that as long as governments were not willing to act, only nongovernmental actors could move the process ahead. This conviction was voiced by the Swiss government in January 1891, just months after the end of the unsuccessful Berlin conference (Delevingne 1934, 27, fn 15). The Swiss called for the establishment of unofficial committees made up of individuals acting in their own capacity, rather than representing their governments, that would discuss possible collaborations and organize yet another international conference to continue the debates, also unofficial in character. This proposal was supported by Germany and a handful of smaller states but was opposed by the British and French (Mahaim 1904, 8; Delevingne 1934, 27).

In 1897, in a mixed governmental-nongovernmental conference of "civil social reformers" organized by the Belgian government, there were serious disagreements regarding the establishment of an official forum to adopt international labor regulations. In the end, the conference adopted a resolution calling for the establishment of an International Bureau for the Protection of Labor made up of private individuals (Delevingne 1934, 29).

Another conference, this time purely nongovernmental in nature, took place in Paris in 1900 and included many of the same individuals who had pushed for the establishment of the International Bureau for the Protection of Labor in 1897. Countries that had supported the establishment of an intergovernmental IO at the 1890 Berlin conference, such as Germany, also supported the creation of a labor IO, even if it was to be more nongovernmental. The arguments at the meeting were often ideological in nature, emphasizing the obligation of governments to become involved in this important issue.

The Paris conference established the International Association for Labor Legislation (ILL), an organization that reflected, in the words of one of its founders, a compromise between states that were willing to engage in negotiations on common labor standards at the governmental level and those that would accept an organization only if academic experts would discuss such standards (Mahaim 1904, 15). Although the ILL was formally nongovernmental in character, it included on its permanent staff many individuals who simultaneously held government positions. More important, the ILL invited governments to appoint representatives to the Committee, its main body (Delevingne 1934, 30).

The strong intergovernmental elements in this organization were reflected in the fact that at the 1901 ILL conference, of the 42 delegates present in the proceedings, 22 were government representatives while 20 were not government officials. The French and British delegations did not include any government representatives (ILL 1901, 27–29; Mahaim 1904, 25). Some viewed the British refusal to have government officials represent the country in the ILL conference as proof that the government was "still firmly wedded to laissez-faire" (Stewart 1969, 3).

The ILL's work was conducted primarily by legal scholars who usually came from government circles. Trade unions and other organizations representing workers or employers were not present in the ILL, either during its conferences or between them (Mahaim 1934, 8).

Most funding for the new organization was supplied through government contributions (ILL 1901, 198–199). Although the British government did not contribute financially to the organization, almost every other government involved in the ILL did. It is especially noteworthy that many countries that had not supported the establishment of a very intergovernmental organization in the 1890 Berlin Conference now became important donors to the ILL. Not surprising, the largest amounts came from the Swiss (which hosted the organization's headquarters in Basel) and the Germans (ILL 1901, 94–95). The two governments remained the ILL's main financial contributors through most of its existence (ILL 1910, 166–167). Thus, even though the ILL continued to involve many nongovernmental representatives in deliberations and decisions, its emergence reflected a move toward intergovernmentalism on all three dimensions compared to previous global governance structures in this realm, as governments were directly represented for the first time in decision making and deliberations in an international labor organization and as they were the principal contributors to the IO's budget.

According to its statutes, the ILL's main goal was to serve as a link between national experts of labor legislation. To achieve this goal, it set out to publish a periodical of labor legislation and statistics from the major industrialized states. It also published studies about the "concordance of the various protective labor laws" (ILL 1901, 195). Most important, it organized conferences to discuss the harmonization of labor legislation.

Understanding that it was already very difficult to get all states, especially powerful ones, to agree to common labor regulations, the ILL decided to begin with a very small number of issues and, just as important, ones where there was already a great degree of agreement. The ILL's 1901 Basel conference chose to focus on two international conventions: one prohibiting the use of white phosphorous in the production of matches and a second prohibiting women from working at night (Stewart 1969, 3). The question of night work for women was less controversial because, at that time, powerful states, including France, Germany, and the United Kingdom, had already adopted the necessary legislation. A convention would therefore primarily allow the big three to level the playing field by pushing for similar legislation in smaller countries such as Belgium, Hungary, and Portugal (Mahaim 1934, 10). The proposed convention also gave fairly long periods of time for states to implement the new legislation.

Similarly, the issue of white phosphorous was not very controversial because it applied to a very narrow part of national economies. Moreover, there was a general agreement among states with regard to the effects of white phosphorous and, therefore, the industry was already under government supervision in virtually all states.

In 1905, the Swiss federal government invited other governments to send experts to a first international conference in Berne to discuss the two conventions. It was understood that a second, diplomatic, conference was to be organized later at which governments could actually decide whether they would back these conventions.

While both issues appeared to have been chosen wisely because they reflected a great deal of agreement among states, the debates at the 1905 conference showed that, in fact, there were still considerable differences. For instance, in the discussion of the night-work convention, while some states did not want any exceptions, others called for establishments with fewer workers to be exempt from such limitations. Similarly, there were disagreements regarding the applicability of the convention beyond industry, to agriculture and commerce. In the case of the white phosphorus convention, some states were willing to prohibit the substance only if other important non-European states, particularly Japan, would adopt similar legislation, while others did not seek such assurances. In the end, both conventions were accepted by the vast majority of states. This was surprising, considering that just a few years earlier, there had still been strong opposition to any international labor agreements, which were seen by most governments as an intrusion of "state socialism" in their work (Mahaim 1934, 10).

Despite the final agreement on the two conventions, the *process* that led to their consideration was criticized by a number of states. While the British government accepted the prohibition of night employment for women (but not the ban on white phosphorous), it made clear that it did not want future labor issues to be dealt with in nongovernmental or even quasi-governmental forums (ILL 1906b, 1; Stewart 1969, 3). Although not as drastic as the British, the French, Portuguese, and Swedish delegations also criticized the nongovernmental nature of the process leading to these conventions (ILL 1906a, 8–9; 1906b, 17–18).

A year later, in the diplomatic conference involving the official acceptance of the two conventions, the United Kingdom sought to kill the entire initiative. However, the French government introduced softer language and managed to garner sufficient government support for the two conventions (Mahaim 1904, 10–17).

The British opposition to the ILL began to wane over the following decade as its government introduced more advanced labor policies. The greatest supporter of the ILL in the British government was Winston Churchill. In 1908, as president of the Board of Trade, Churchill introduced the Trade Boards Bill that set up a system of minimum wages in the United Kingdom. In 1909, he was instrumental in establishing "labour exchanges" through which the unemployed could find work (Jenkins 2001). Last, but not least, he contributed to the drafting of the National Insurance Act of 1911, a piece of legislation considered revolutionary at the time.

Therefore, it should not be surprising that in 1910, Churchill was the first British official to call for his country's formal representation in the ILL (Churchill 1910). That year all states, including the United Kingdom, were represented in the organization's conferences by at least some government officials (ILL 1910, 13–20). Virtually all of these government representatives came from fairly new domestic labor institutions (Delevingne 1934, 47).

By 1913, the ILL had become very intergovernmental on the decision-making dimension, with government representation in all its bodies and meetings. However, the organization also continued to have a strong nongovernmental character, as the government representatives in ILL meetings often found themselves faced with proposals that the legal experts had worked on without any real government input.

The ILL's 1913 Berne technical conference adopted two more important conventions: barring night work for children and limiting daily work hours for women and children. The war, however, delayed the diplomatic meeting that was to give the conventions the necessary legal backing and put on hold all efforts to further develop international collaboration in the labor realm. It is not clear whether governments actually would have accepted the two conventions, as the 1913 debates revealed important divisions between states. More important, they reflected the problems the ILL faced in seeking to harmonize legislation when it did not always have access to official government information channels. Also, the issues discussed in the 1913 conference highlighted that the organization did not allow for any real input from labor or employer organizations (Delevingne 1934, 50–51). It is possible, therefore, that the ILL would have ceased to exist in its original form even if the war had not disrupted its work.

GLOBAL GOVERNANCE IN THE LABOR REALM DURING AND IMMEDIATELY AFTER WORLD WAR I

The strength of the labor movement in the most powerful countries continued to grow in the years just before World War I. The establishment of a labor ministry in France in 1906 (during a Radical–Socialist Party government) and of a department of labor in the United States in 1913 (during Wilson's presidency) reflect the growing understanding that governments needed to deal with increasingly important labor issues.

This hands-on governmental approach became even more important during World War I. First, the war underscored how dependent the national defenses of states had become on industry and, implicitly, on governments' relations with labor and employers (Delevingne 1934, 52–53). The military draft led governments and employers to value the remaining workforce even more than before. For example, France, the country perhaps most affected at that time by the loss of workers to the battlefields, sought the assistance of foreign workers, especially from Italy (Picquenard 1934, 184). Workers, many of them women, were also under great strain as the war led to longer work hours, more repetitive and dangerous work involved in producing ammunition, prohibition of strikes, and increases in food prices.

Despite the strains on governments, labor, and employers, the war appeared to bring these three groups closer together in support of national causes (Riegelman 1934). Governments realized they needed to include workers' representatives in important decisions involving their economies. In 1916, the United Kingdom followed the French and American examples and established a ministry of labor. George Barnes, a former trade unionist and one of the first Labour Party members of parliament, was named minister. The ministry quickly began establishing Whitley Councils that included representatives of labor and employers in every industry. Similarly, in France the national defense industries set up workers' delegations in its factories (Alcock 1971, 14–15).

As early as its 1914 Convention, the AFL called for a world labor congress at the same time as the peace conference. Other national labor organizations, such as the French Confederation Generale de Travail, endorsed this idea (Riegelman 1934, 58). The 1916 Leeds Trades Union Congress, attended by representatives from Belgium, Britain, France, and Italy, adopted a list of workers' rights to be discussed in the peace treaty (Alcock 1971, 16).

During the war, the very nongovernmental IFTU and other major labor groups remained organized and relatively active, both domestically and internationally. In contrast, the now fairly intergovernmental ILL virtually ceased to function. Together, these two developments led to an overall shift toward greater nongovernmentalism during World War I on all three dimensions of the intergovernmental–nongovernmental continuum.

Such nongovernmental activism allowed trade unions to reconstitute very soon after the war and hold a conference in August 1919. The postwar IFTU became much more political, making up for the disappearance of the Second International that had acted through political parties and government channels before the war. One of the most important demands of the first IFTU conference referred to the question of German and Austrian membership in the new League of Nations. Especially as it was clear that the League would also deal with labor issues, IFTU sought to pressure great powers early on to allow for labor representation in future official international meetings. Perhaps even more controversial, and a stronger reflection of the degree to which IFTU had become a political organization, was its demand that the new League of Nations Assembly be directly elected by the peoples of member-states themselves, rather than be selected by governments (Schevenels 1956, 95).

The nongovernmental plans for the new postwar international labor organization supported by IFTU and other labor groups quickly fell through as governments took the lead in forging the new IO. The 1917 Soviet Revolution added a greater sense of urgency to their efforts toward easing potential labor tensions. In July 1917, the French government set up under its Ministry of Labor a committee to identify the kinds of labor conditions that should be considered for international agreements (Picquenard 1934, 85). In September 1918, the British Labor Ministry's Intelligence Department also began drawing up plans for international negotiations on labor issues (Alcock 1971, 18). Interestingly, the United States, where the calls for a parallel postwar labor conference and peace conference had originated in 1914, was less prepared for the substance of such talks. In part, this was due to the fact that Samuel Gompers, the leader of the AFL, concentrated his efforts solely on convincing the US government, especially Wilson, to organize an international labor conference at the same time as the peace conference and to include a labor commission in the US delegation sent to Paris. Gompers and the AFL had never been particularly pleased with the work of IFTU and, of course, had not been involved in the Second International (Schevenels 1956, 63). The AFL thus did not attend IFTU meetings after the war and, in 1921, officially left the organization. It returned in 1927.

Wilson agreed to Gompers's proposal for establishing a Peace Conference Labor Commission. The commission would work at the same time that the main conference was unfolding (Riegelman 1934, 74).

As the French were the first to begin preparations for the postwar labor conference, they were also the first to shape the debates. As early as November 25, 1918, exactly two weeks after the end of the war, the nongovernmental French Association for Labor Legislation, the national branch of the ILL, adopted a resolution urging the peace treaty to include clauses guaranteeing the enforcement of humane labor conditions. Just a few days later, the French government's Committee on Labor, established by the Labor Ministry to consider the future international labor conference (and which included a number of experts who had worked in the ILL), adopted a very similar draft resolution for the peace treaty (Picquenard 1934, 88).

Although British plans for the labor conference were laid out after the French plans were proposed, they went into much greater depth. The Intelligence Division of the Ministry of Labour produced a first internal memorandum on the topic in early October 1918. The document argued that because other governments had already called for the establishment of an international organization to deal with labor (most notably, the German government), because trade unions were pushing for international labor standards, and because it was apparent that a League of Nations was to be established after the war to deal with political problems, it was best to have governments take the leading role in shaping the new international labor "committee." Moreover, the memorandum argued that because the United Kingdom had become one of the most advanced countries in terms of labor legislation, it was to its advantage to establish an organization that would promote similar standards in other states (cited in Alcock 1971, 18–19).

The first plans of the ministry's Intelligence Department favored having international labor issues continue to be dealt with by the ILL. However, as discussions evolved, it became clear that the expectations governments now faced involved a broader set of issues than the ILL had focused on and, therefore, the new organization needed to have a more active permanent secretariat. Additionally, there was a consensus that, unlike the ILL, the new organization needed to include both government and labor representatives (Phelan 2009, 17, 137–139, 171).

Indeed, when Lloyd George came into office in 1916 as prime minister of the Wartime Coalition, he had made a number of promises to labor. The establishment of the Labor Ministry in 1916 fulfilled one of those promises. He had also agreed that labor groups could be represented at the peace conference. On the other hand, the British felt that the new organization needed to allow for a stronger role for governments to ensure that international agreements would actually be transformed into national legislation (Phelan 2009, 141–144).

In December 1918, Edward Phelan, the head of the British Labour Ministry's Intelligence Section, presented some first thoughts on the future international labor organization to Harold Butler, assistant secretary in the ministry; Harold Delevingne, a senior official in the Home Office and a very active member of the ILL; and minister George Barnes (British Delegation 1934). Through Delevingne, this group kept in touch during the drafting process with Arthur Fontaine, then labor minister of France, yet another very active ILL member in the previous decade. The British officials from the new Labour Ministry became the most active proponents of establishing the ILO.

The most original aspect of Phelan's plan was the "tripartite structure" of the organization that allowed for direct participation and decision making not only by government representatives but also by representatives of labor and employers from member-states. The model for this structure was the employer-labor councils for improving industrial relations that had been introduced in Britain in 1917 (Phelan 2009, 18).

Butler and Barnes were initially apprehensive about a tripartite structure, as it would put labor and employers on the same footing. This was seen as a dangerous plan because it ran counter to the increasingly powerful trade union demands. The more senior British officials felt, therefore, that the tripartite proposal would offend the unions, which would then take international regulations into their own hands. Moreover, it would push workers closer to communism, precisely what governments were trying to avoid. Phelan was nevertheless successful in convincing the others that if the organization would not allow representation for all interested parties, it would not succeed. Moreover, he felt that even though in terms of representation the three groups could be equal, when it came to the final decision-making process, any such organization would have to give a greater say to governments than to labor and employers. Governments were, after all, the ones that needed to accept and implement domestically all decisions made by the organization. He therefore proposed giving government representatives from each state two votes and labor and employer representatives each only one vote. In January 1919, the leadership of the Labour Ministry and British Cabinet gave their support to this proposal (Phelan 2009, 18).

The French adopted a very similar proposal. The only important difference between the drafts was that the French requested the treaty establishing the organization also mention several new international labor conventions, some of which had already been accepted by the 1913 ILL conference, but not by governments. The British, on the other hand, sought only to have the peace conference come up with a constitution for the new IO. The organization, in turn, could later decide on the conventions it wanted to take up (Picquenard 1934, 91–93).

The American, Belgian, and Italian governments also offered proposals for the future organization. However, all such plans were far less developed than the British and French ones. In the case of the United States, one of the problems was that most labor legislation lay at the state, not federal, level. Therefore, although the United States had established a labor department before the war, the institution was weak and was not in a position to negotiate with representatives of other countries. In the end, the British text became the basis for the negotiations.

On January 31, 1919, the peace conference established a labor commission to discuss the founding of an international organization for labor issues. The commission was to be made up of fifteen individuals: two from each of the five great powers and five more from other states. On February 1, the commission met for the first time. Virtually all representatives present in the commission were from government institutions. The exceptions were an academic from Belgium and one from Cuba (both with strong ties to government circles): Samuel Gompers, president of the American Federation of Labor, and Edward N. Hurley, president of the American Shipping Board. Other nongovernmental representatives, most important France's Léon Jouhaux, took part in only some of the commission's meeting (NICB 1922, 21).

Wilson's support for nongovernmentalism in global governance (reflected also in his backing of the LRCS in the health realm discussed in Chapter 3) led him to not include in the commission any American government representatives. This decision surprised everyone and influenced the outcome of the meetings, as it allowed labor's perspective to be represented forcefully. This was especially due to the election of Gompers as president of the commission. Although the British had expected Barnes to head the commission, the French delegation and several others preferred Gompers, who they felt could keep in check the already powerful British influence in the forum. Moreover, at that time, Wilson's preferences, including having Gompers chair the commission, were generally accepted by those at the Paris peace talks.

In his opening speech as president of the commission, even before the actual debates on the British proposal began, Gompers immediately attacked the principle underlying the proposed voting system where governments received two votes while representatives of employers and workers were given only one vote. Later, when the specific article of the future International Labor Organization's constitution came up for discussion, several other speakers criticized the "2:1:1" voting system, calling it undemocratic because one national representative would carry more votes than the other two (Phelan 1934, 134). Belgium's Vandervelde suggested resolving this problem by allowing governments be represented by two individuals, each with one vote, while employers and labor (considered together as "producers") would be represented each by one individual, also with one vote each. Gompers objected, arguing that governments should not have a veto over labor issues because parliaments, which had very strong connections to governments, were already the gatekeepers of labor legislation. Moreover, he argued that the division between governments and "producers" was a false one because virtually the entire population of a country was made up of such producers (Commission 1919b, 10).

The first British response to these critiques was that governments should have a greater say because, after all, they are the ones who are paying for the organization. More important, they argued that governments will not accept more votes from nongovernmental representatives, as they are already giving up a great deal of their sovereignty as it is. Third, the British explained that a system with more votes for employers and workers might lead to collusion between these two groups, as has sometimes happened at the national level. Lastly, they suggested that, in fact, governments will not be able to veto labor legislation in the parliamentary ratification process because the ILO decisions will be too powerful (Commission 1919c, 8).

The Belgian representative, who supported the British proposal, once more offered a compromise. He suggested that the voting system be 1:1:1 in all ILO meetings except for the ones for the adoption of international treaties, that is, in the international labor conference, where it should remain 2:1:1 (Commission 1919c, 12). The American, French, and Italian representatives continued to oppose the 2:1:1 system even in this form. When the commission eventually voted on this point, the 2:1:1 voting system was chosen over the 1:1:1, with eight commission members supporting it and six opposing it. The British were successful on this point only after they convinced some smaller states to change their original positions.

The debate over the *degree* of governmental and nongovernmental voting power in the organization unfolded primarily between the United States and the United Kingdom. One observer noted:

One can hardly imagine any more marked contrast to the American attitude toward labor legislation than that presented by public opinion generally, and workers in particular, in Europe and especially in England [...]. Since the middle of the nineteenth century on the Continent and since the early thirties of that century in England, the forces of social and labor reform had looked to their respective governments and to the agencies of legislation and administration as their most effective instrument of social welfare. (McCune Lindsay 1934, 337)

In sum, while Americans were "dominated by the theory of voluntarism,"[2] the British "accepted a positive theory of labor legislation as the only effective means of securing international action" (McCune Lindsay 1934, 339).

The discussions of the voting system, invoking both ideological and pragmatic arguments, were much lengthier and heated than those of any other aspect of the ILO's constitution. Nevertheless, several other deliberations in the commission had an important impact on the intergovernmental–nongovernmental balance in the organization. First, there was an important debate involving the proposal to also bring representatives of agricultural workers into the ILO. Indeed, virtually all labor representatives at the conference came from industry. The delegates from Italy and several smaller states whose economies were very dependent on agriculture pursued this issue vigorously. The different degree of relevance of agriculture in each country, the fact that in some countries those who worked the land were likely to also own it while in others this was not the case, and the differences between the sizes of land plots and the structure of the agricultural systems (especially when comparing the United States with Europe) led to a great deal of disagreement on this topic. As a compromise, the commission decided to allow for experts (from agriculture or other sectors of the economy) to participate in meetings as consultants to the formal representatives. These experts were allowed to participate in debates but did not vote. Each formal representative could bring up to two experts in ILO meetings. Article 3 of the ILO's Constitution formalized this procedure.

Another question that later had implications for the nongovernmental nature of the ILO involved countries that did not yet have institutionalized structures for representation of workers or employers. When Japan raised this issue, the British dismissed it quickly to avoid more delays in adopting the organization's constitution. They suggested that governments should simply encourage the emergence of labor and employer organizations and be responsible for selecting the organizations that were to represent all workers and employers (Commission 1919d, 8). This, of course, tilted the balance in the future ILO toward governments, even though the advantage appeared to be a minor one at the time. It is noteworthy that a decade and a half later, Japan was to be chastised by other members of the ILO, including the United Kingdom, for the lack of independence of its nongovernmental representatives in the organization.

---

[2] Gompers used the term "voluntarism" to describe his philosophy underlying the labor movement (McCune Lindsay 1934, 332).

Lastly, the question of how to deal with federal systems where labor legislation was not taken up by the national assemblies revealed more than any other debate the difference between the United States and other countries. The problems involved in adopting ILO decisions in the US system suggested that the United States could not even join the organization. This led the US representatives in the commission to be less influential in the final decisions regarding the structure and work of the ILO (Commission 1919a, 11).

It is also important to note what was *not* mentioned in discussions. For instance, none of the delegates raised the question of participation of nongovernmental IOs in the ILO. This omission is particularly important considering that the question of nongovernmental IOs' access to League meetings and to its work was discussed in great depth. Not only did the ILO framers avoid this question during the adoption of the organization's constitution, but it was never really discussed in the ILO later, throughout the interwar era. The outside experts that, according to Article 3 of the constitution, were allowed to take part in the organization's proceedings, were called "assessors," the same term used in the League for nongovernmental IO representatives. Yet, in the ILO such experts were virtually always from governmental structures, or representatives of labor or employers from specific economic fields, rather than from nongovernmental IOs, as they were in the League.

The battles over the voting formula at the founding of the ILO can be seen as attempts to move the organization in opposite directions on the decision-making dimension of the intergovernmental–nongovernmental continuum. The final decision to have equal votes for governmental and nongovernmental representatives suggests that the organization formally fell close to the middle of the decision-making continuum. It has also fallen close to the middle of the deliberative end of the continuum even though, as I will show, it has often shifted toward intergovernmentalism on both of these dimensions. The ILO has remained very intergovernmental on the financial dimension because only governments contribute to the organization's budget.

Although we tend to view the ILO as a hybrid organization, when it was founded, it represented the most intergovernmental successful initiative in global labor governance up to that point in terms of decision making and deliberations. Once the ILO was established, its predecessor, the ILL, officially a nongovernmental entity that some sought to transform into a more intergovernmental one, ceased to be relevant for the most powerful states. In 1921, at the ILL's first meeting after the war, many countries, most notably the United Kingdom and France, were not represented at all, not even by individual experts in their personal capacity. Additionally, the top leadership of the ILL had been hired by the ILO and by the new labor ministries. Germany, which initially was not included in the ILO, tried in vain to make the ILL relevant once more. It sought ways to develop legislative initiatives that the ILO neglected, such as those related to the agricultural realm (ILL 1921, 10–14). However, it was not successful. The vacuum in the ILL's leadership, its inability to perform even the informational functions it had dealt with before the war, especially as it did not have access to statistics and legislation from countries that had left the organization, and the increasing sense that there would be duplication between its work and that of the new and ever-growing ILO, eventually led to its formal dismantling in 1925.[3]

While the disappearance of the ILL after World War I was slow, the demise of the Second International, the most prominent international initiative dealing with labor issues before the war, was swift. Indeed, much has been written about how the professed workers' solidarity that was the basis of the Second International crumbled in the summer of 1914 due to rising nationalism. Most important, as the German government was preparing for war, it turned to the Reichstag to fund the effort. Despite its assurances that it would promote a peaceful solution to the crisis, the German Free Trade Union backed government efforts declaring a "class truce," and the Social-Democratic Party voted unanimously in support of war credits (Milner 1991). The Second International dissolved in 1916, not able to withstand the deep cleavages brought about by the pro-governmental positions taken by socialist parties right before and during the war.

The Soviet Revolution exacerbated the divisions among socialists even further, making it more difficult for them to organize themselves. Understandably, the new Soviet government wanted to control the postwar international workers' movement. As early as January 1919, it invited workers' organizations from around the world to a conference establishing the Third International and refused to attend the postwar meetings intended to relaunch IFTU's work. Additionally, the Soviets held a first World Congress of "Red Trade Unions" in 1921, excluding organizations associated with IFTU and explaining that decision through ideological arguments (Schevenels 1956, 140). That year, the Red Trade Union International (RTUI) was founded.[4] Although the Third International and RTUI appeared nongovernmental in nature, in practice they were controlled by the Soviet government. The financing of the two organizations remained only in the hands of governments, just as in the case of the ILL and ILO. Similarly, both governmental and nongovernmental representatives (especially those from the Soviet Union, where the line between governmental and nongovernmental labor organizations was blurred) participated in the IOs' meetings as in the ILL and ILO. Thus, the emergence of the Third International and RTUI, along with the weakening of the older international trade unions, shifted global labor governance toward greater intergovernmentalism only on the decision-making dimension.

[3] This case of a formally nongovernmental IO being crowded out by a more intergovernmental one appears to run counter to expectations based on the organizational density argument discussed in Chapter 2.
[4] The organization was dissolved by 1937.

GLOBAL GOVERNANCE IN THE LABOR
REALM IN THE INTERWAR ERA

The formal rules setting up the ILO's original tripartite structure and, implic-itly, giving it both an intergovernmental and nongovernmental character, have remained virtually intact since 1919. Labor and employer representatives con-tinue to participate in all ILO forums and vote on all matters. Funding for the organization continues to come almost entirely from governments. Very few nongovernmental actors, other than those directly representing labor and employer groups, have been allowed to participate in the organization's work, at least before World War II.

Despite this apparent constancy in the ILO's intergovernmental–nongovernmental balance, there have been important changes and fiery debates across time with regard to the relative independence of the nongov-ernmental representatives and, implicitly, to the ability of groups outside of governments to influence the work of the organization. The battles over employer and labor representatives' independence vis-à-vis their govern-ments has led to important shifts in the ILO's character in terms of the actual role nongovernmental groups play in decision making and deliberations.

These battles emerged at the first ILO annual conference in Washington, in October 1919. At the opening of the conference, labor delegates challenged the credentials of the designated labor representatives of Argentina, Cuba, France, Japan, and South Africa because they were not deemed to come from the most rep-resentative organizations in their respective countries (ILO 1934). Government and employer representatives did not support the challenges. Governments pre-ferred leaving the controversies to labor groups. Employers did not want to open the door to future challenges of their own representatives (Galenson 1981, 34).

As this first conference had so many important issues to deal with, the question of nongovernmental representation was not allotted much time. This was also the case at the 1920 and 1921 ILO conferences. However, by 1922, when Mussolini came to power in Italy, the challenges of labor representa-tives took on a new dimension. Workers' representation did not revolve any longer simply around the question of which domestic labor group was best suited to participate in the ILO's work but, rather, whether such groups were truly independent of governments and employers. Indeed, the Italian labor delegate came from a mixed employer-worker organization. With the rise of Fascism in that country, and the increased government control over labor and employers, the debates concerning the Italian labor representative continued at every ILO Labor Conference up to the outbreak of World War II.

The Italian representatives in the ILO based their arguments regarding the representative nature of their labor delegates on Fascist ideology, espousing the idea that the nation (and the state, which was the legal affirmation of the nation) was the only natural collectivity of individuals. Therefore, the interests of any other groups, including labor and employers, were subordinated to those of the state. Fascism thus promoted the conciliation of worker-employer relations for the broader national interest of increased production and power (Alcock 1971, 67).

At the 1922 International Labour Conference, debates over the lack of independence of Italian labor representatives played out across labor versus government and employee lines, rather than across national lines. While virtually all labor representatives sought to oust the Italian labor delegate, governments and employers were not willing to take such a drastic measure. Therefore, the challenge was not successful. Similarly, at the 1923 International Labour Conference, all government and all employer representatives voted to accept the Italian government's choice for its labor representative, while all worker representatives voted against him (ILO 1923, 191).

The strong national interests in maintaining good relations with the Italian government, especially as Italy was a major power at that time and a permanent member of the ILO's governing body, led other governments to turn a blind eye to Italian practices. Throughout the interwar era, there was a similar form of collusion among governments when it came to Japanese worker delegates, also seen by the other worker representatives as not being independent (Grigorescu 2015, 206). In the end, the governmental interests in maintaining a broad membership in the ILO led government representatives to accept labor and employer representatives from virtually all authoritarian regimes, regardless of their actual independence. Even labor and employer representatives from Fascist Germany and Communist Soviet Union were accepted in the ILO proceedings when these countries joined the organization.

In 1926, the increasingly intergovernmental approach of the ILO became institutionalized through several changes to the Conference rules. That year, Italy introduced a motion to add two amendments to the standing orders. The first would not allow for future objections to the credentials of representatives that had already been recognized by a Labor Conference as valid. This would allow the Italians to curtail any future debates about their labor representative, who had been accepted by the credentials committee in the previous five years. The second motion was that if a nongovernmental representative was not nominated by his group to sit on any committee, he could appeal to a tripartite ILO body to place him on one or more committees. This amendment also referred to the Italian labor representative who, after being accepted by the credentials committee, was never voted by labor delegates to sit on any committee. Both amendments were adopted by the ILO Conference, despite labor protests (Alcock 1971, 75).

The intergovernmental perspective also dominated the ILO's approach in the late 1930s to the Soviet delegates. In 1937, when the Soviets sent a first delegation to the ILO conference, the credentials of both their labor and employer representatives were challenged. The challenge of the former delegate was based on the fact that trade unions in the USSR were subordinate to the government. In the latter case, the argument was that Soviet employers were simultaneously government officials. Both challenges were rejected due to the strong interests of government representatives in appeasing this powerful state (Galenson 1981, 35).

The degree of labor and employer ILO representatives' independence, of course, has had an important effect on the intergovernmental–nongovernmental nature of the organization. The reduced nongovernmental representatives' independence in the late 1920s and 1930s allowed governments to impose their will on the ILO. A good reflection of the intergovernmental–nongovernmental balance in the ILO is the percentage of votes in the international labor conferences in which at least one nongovernmental representative voted differently than its government. This measure has been used in previous research to express the aggregate level of independence of nongovernmental groups in the ILO (Haas 1962; Grigorescu 2015).

Figure 4.1 illustrates the evolution of this measure calculated for each year as an average of the percentages across all member states.[5] The figure shows that nongovernmental delegates tended to agree more with their governments throughout the interwar era and in second half of the Cold War. This should not be surprising considering the large number of authoritarian regimes throughout these periods. Conversely, in the immediate post–World War II era, before Communist Bloc countries joined the ILO, and in the immediate post–Cold War era, there was greater disagreement between governments and nongovernmental groups. Indeed, in these two periods, on average, about half of the time, at least one nongovernmental representative voted differently than their government. Another way to interpret these trends is that during the interwar era and most of the Cold War, the main differences in voting were *between states*, while in other periods there were also important differences between groups coming from *the same states*.

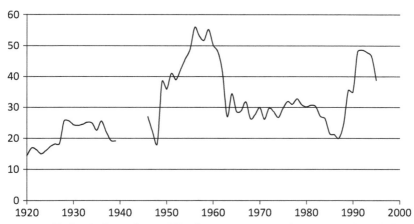

FIGURE 4.1. Voting independence (%) of nongovernmental representatives in International Labor Conferences.

[5] Based on records of proceedings of the International Labour Conference at www.ilo.org/public/libdoc/ilo/P/09616/, accessed February 23, 2018. See also Grigorescu (2015).

Not all battles surrounding the independence of labor groups unfolded in the ILO. The IFTU continued to promote important causes, such as the forty-hour work week, both pressuring the ILO directly and acting indirectly through the ILO national labor representatives from groups affiliated with the Union. IFTU not only supported independent labor representatives in the ILO, but also supported at the domestic level all truly independent labor groups in Italy, Germany, and other authoritarian states, never recognizing the government-sponsored workers' groups in these countries (Schevenels 1956, 182, 198–199). As Hitler and Mussolini eventually gained absolute political control, all independent labor groups in these countries were eventually crushed.

The question of nongovernmental representation in the ILO was not only problematic for authoritarian regimes. A very different type of problem of representation independence is reflected in developments immediately after the United States joined the ILO in 1934, soon after Franklin D. Roosevelt became president. His New Deal policies led to a strong role for government in multiple issue-areas. In the labor realm, he established the US Employment Service, a forum for workers and employers to exchange information. He also pushed for a number of new federal labor laws. The National Labor Relations Act defined unfair labor practices and established workers' rights to strike and collectively bargain. The Social Security Act created a safety net for the elderly, disabled, and unemployed. The Apprenticeship Act empowered the Labor Department to create regulations protecting the health, safety, and welfare of apprentices. The Fair Labor Standards Act established the forty-hour workweek, codified paid overtime and minimum wage, and introduced child labor legislation.

Not surprising, Roosevelt's activism in domestic labor issues spilled over to the international realm as he sought to have the United States join the ILO quickly. He had been a strong supporter of the organization as far back as the its first conference that took place in 1919 in Washington.[6] Even with such strong high-level support, US membership in the ILO was delayed for several reasons. First, there were still lingering tensions between the AFL and IFTU. At that time, the IFTU still dominated representation of labor in the ILO. Second, in 1935, the newly established Congress of Industrial Organizations (CIO) challenged the AFL's right to represent American labor interests in the organization. American government officials preferred that the decision of labor representation be made by labor itself. Although, in the end, the AFL was given the position on the US delegation, the infighting led to US labor playing a diminished role in the ILO in those last years before the war (Galenson 1981, 4–5). The expectations that the United States should play a very active part in the ILO were, however, reflected in the selection of American John Winant as ILO director-general in 1939 (Bellush 1968).

---

[6] At that time, as the Senate had refused to ratify the peace treaty and the United States was not a member of the League or ILO, there were very few American officials willing to help organize the conference. Roosevelt, who at the time was assistant-secretary of the Navy, offered conference organizers office space in the Navy building (Alcock 1971, 37).

GLOBAL GOVERNANCE IN THE LABOR REALM DURING
AND IMMEDIATELY AFTER WORLD WAR II

In 1940, soon after Germany occupied France, Winant decided it was too dangerous to maintain the ILO offices in Geneva and accepted an offer from the Canadian government to move the organization to Montreal. This decision allowed the ILO to continue some of its work during the war and was essential to its survival after 1945, even as its parent organization, the League of Nations, ceased to exist. In fact, the ILO is one of the few examples of a formally intergovernmental organization, albeit one that also had a strong nongovernmental character, surviving a major war. As seen in the previous chapter, the more intergovernmental health IOs in existence before World War I and World War II either ceased to exist after the wars or became far less relevant than before. Additionally, it should be pointed out that as authoritarian states such as Germany, Italy, and Japan left the ILO before the war, the organization shifted toward nongovernmentalism on the decision-making dimension.

However, to survive World War II, the ILO had to reduce its personnel to about one fifth of its original number (Bellush 1968). Most of the work of the small Montreal office involved collecting and disseminating information. The ILO also organized several meetings for Latin American countries that had not been affected by the war as much as those from other parts of the world (Stewart 1969, 52).

Most important, the ILO decided to organize a labor conference in New York in 1941. There were multiple reasons for having such a conference during the war. First, the organization's statutes required it for its day-to-day work, such as electing the governing body, adopting a budget, and approving its move to Canada. Perhaps more important, the conference was considered essential by ILO officials because it would show that the organization had an important role to play during the war and, hopefully, after it.

The conference indeed brought the ILO into the limelight. More than 200 delegates from thirty-four countries were present. Perhaps more important, it signaled that the United States supported the organization and was going to play an important role in its future. On the last day of the conference, US labor secretary Perkins surprised everyone by formally inviting delegates to hold a final sitting of the conference at the White House. As neither the ILO nor the United States had allotted funds for the travel of more than 200 people to Washington, Perkins explained to Phelan, then deputy director of the ILO (and, the following year, its director), that she was "going around with a hat" to raise money from some American employers. To answer Phelan's shock at such a "humiliating expedient," she added, "We often do that. It's in our tradition. When we can't get a thing done by Government, citizens get together and do something about it for themselves" (Phelan 2009, 304). At the White House, Roosevelt reaffirmed his support for the ILO and its tripartite structure:

In those days, the ILO was still a dream. To many it was a wild dream [...]. Wilder still was the idea that people themselves who were directly affected – the workers and employers of the various countries – should have a hand with Governments in establishing labour standards. [...] We must plan now for the better world we aim to build. In the planning of such international action, the International Labor Organization, with its representatives of labor and management, its technical knowledge and experience, will be an invaluable instrument for peace. Your Organization will have an essential part to play in building up a stable international system of social justice for all people everywhere. (ILO 1941, 156, 158)

To maintain its visibility and influence, in 1945, the ILO governing body traveled to London, where it hoped to gain support for its postwar role. There, the ILO officials met with Ernest Bevin, then British labor minister, who offered a very enthusiastic welcome. Bevin, a former trade union leader and Labour politician, assured the ILO representatives that he believed in the need for the organization, seeing it as an extension of the role that governments had to play in the reconstruction of the world economy. He argued that governments would need to plan their economies after the war because "laissez-faire will not do [...] The needs of the present age cannot be met with nineteenth century economics" (ILO 1943, 11).

Interestingly, this apparent pro-governmental (Keynesian) view held by Bevin and other British officials did not necessarily mean that they were prepared to give governments a greater say in the ILO. On the contrary, influenced by the same kind of strong labor pressures that were present during World War I, the British suggested that the ILO move to a more nongovernmental structure. Specifically, Bevin suggested that the ILO establish "industrial committees" where representatives of labor and employer groups focusing on specific industries could discuss topics before they reached the broader ILO forums. The British had created similar committees at the domestic level and now sought to export this bipartite model to the ILO, thus excluding government representatives. The British employer representative argued for this model: "Let them be bipartite, what has been done nationally in Britain can be done internationally" (cited in Stewart 1969, 55). Virtually all other officials, including British labor representatives, as well as the ILO leadership, opposed this idea and, in the end, the committees remained tripartite, like all other ILO bodies.

Toward the end of the war and in the first months of peace, the Soviet Union initiated a campaign to do away with (or at least radically transform) the ILO. The Soviets had always considered the organization as institutionalizing capitalist relations between workers and employers. They argued that this was not truly a workers' organization or truly democratic because labor representatives had only one vote while employers together with (capitalist) governments had three votes. Beyond the ideological aspects of this argument, in practical terms Moscow believed that it would stand to gain from moving the most important decision in the international labor realm from the ILO to international workers' organizations where it had greater influence (Alcock 1971, 182). It should be noted that while the Soviet plan appeared nongovernmental in nature, in fact it was not, due to the control its government had over its own trade unions as well as over those from a number of other countries.

In the meantime, ILO members decided to discuss the future of the organization in greater depth at the 1944 conference in Philadelphia. While the continued existence of the organization had been somewhat in doubt up to that point, the conference revealed a great deal of agreement among delegates that the ILO should continue its work after the war, perhaps also adopting some new rules to improve the way it functioned. The ILO's tripartite approach to labor thus won out over the purely labor union approach supported by the USSR.

The IFTU also continued to be very active during the war. As many leaders of free trade unions fled to the United Kingdom, IFTU moved its secretariat to London and kept in contact with most national groups (Schevenels 1956, 287). In February 1945, when the end of the war was in sight, IFTU leaders organized a World Trade Union Conference in London. The more than forty national delegations participating in the conference decided to replace IFTU with the World Federation of Trade Unions (WFTU). The founding conference of WFTU was held in Paris in October 1945. The most important difference between IFTU and WFTU was that the new organization also included representatives of the Soviet Union. The close relations between the United States, the United Kingdom, and the USSR from the wartime military alliance had spilled over into collaborations between labor representatives.

However, soon after WFTU's founding the emerging Cold War tensions led to a split in the new organization. As the USSR managed to wrangle control of WFTU from the United Kingdom, it began promoting this organization as a possible replacement for the ILO. It sought to keep any mention of the ILO out of the Dumbarton Oaks proposal. In 1949, the non-Communist unions seceded from WFTU, creating the International Confederation of Free Trade Unions (ICFTU).

When plans were being made for the San Francisco UN Conference on International Organization (UNCIO), the Soviets tried to keep ILO representatives out of meetings or at least not give them an official role. Instead, they requested that the WFTU be represented. This proposal was rejected by virtually all other states on the argument that the WFTU was a nongovernmental organization and should not be represented on equal footing with governments in an intergovernmental conference (UNCIO 1945, 152–154).

When it realized that the ILO was going to remain the principal global governor in the labor realm, the Soviet Union sought, once more, to alter the rules of the labor organization to fit more closely with its interests. It first tried to give the WFTU a stronger role in the ILO itself, well above the role given to other nongovernmental entities. When it did not succeed in altering the labor organization's rules, the Soviets requested the WFTU be allowed to participate in the work of the new Economic and Social Council (ECOSOC), the

UN organ that oversaw the work of the ILO. The increasingly tense relations between the Soviet Union and the United States led to heated debates that included strong ideological arguments involving that proposal. The American delegation argued that if the WFTU were allowed to take part in ECOSOC meetings, then so should other nongovernmental organizations, such as the AFL, even if they were only regional or national in character. The still very pro-United States UN General Assembly (GA) rejected a Soviet proposal to have only the WFTU as observer in ECOSOC and adopted an American one, giving both the WFTU and the AFL this status. More important for the future of the UN's relations with nongovernmental IOs, the GA instructed ECOSOC to adopt a framework for working with such nongovernmental entities in the future (UNGA 1946, 31–33). It is noteworthy, therefore, that Soviet efforts to give the WFTU a greater role in post–World War II global labor governance eventually led to an empowerment of nongovernmental IOs in the broader UN system, even though it didn't bring any real changes to the ILO.

Yet another proposal to alter the ILO's intergovernmental–nongovernmental balance originated in a Soviet initiative. The USSR sought to change the ILO's 2:1:1 voting system to one of 2:1:2, giving workers one additional vote. Interestingly, the formal proposal for this formula was made by a group of Latin American labor delegates, not by the Soviets. The formula was intended to reflect the increased presence of the state as employer in many countries. The plan was to have one of the two government delegates represent formal government structures, while the second would represent the nationalized industries. Similarly, the two labor delegates were intended to represent workers in the nationalized industries that, at that time, did not have trade unions and in the traditional private industries that were organized in trade unions. The Belgians proposed a 2:2:2 voting system, thus adding another delegate for the employers to also reflect the two types of industries. Interestingly, the debates surrounding this proposed change did not involve any arguments with ideological undertones. However, the initiative was supported by a number of nongovernmental labor groups, both from the USSR and from Western states.

Top ILO officials argued against any changes to the voting formula, suggesting that by giving a greater say to nongovernmental representatives and, implicitly, taking power away from governments, even if there were more conventions adopted by the ILO, fewer would be eventually accepted by parliaments. The ILO leadership had the support of the United States as well as of other Western powers that did not want to run the risk of having infighting between their two potential labor representatives. More important, they did not want Communist governments that controlled both their labor and employer delegates to receive six de facto votes (Alcock 1971, 182–183). In the end, the Soviets were not successful in changing any of the original ILO rules. The organization thus maintained an intergovernmental–nongovernmental balance similar to the one instituted at its founding, in 1919.

GLOBAL GOVERNANCE IN THE LABOR
REALM DURING THE COLD WAR

One important change the ILO was not able to resist in the immediate post–World War II era was its relationship with nongovernmental IOs. As mentioned, although the League Covenant referred to its work with "international bureaux" that was interpreted to include nongovernmental IOs, the ILO's official documents did not have similar stipulations. During the interwar era, it generally kept all such organizations – except for those representing national labor and employers – out of its activities.

In 1946, however, when the ILO altered its constitution to reflect its new status as the UN's first specialized agency, it amended Article 12 to stipulate that it should "make suitable arrangements for such consultation as it may think desirable with recognized non-governmental international organisations, including international organisations of employers, workers, agriculturists and co-operators" (ILO 1946).

Indeed, after World War II, virtually all new UN agencies introduced similar language. As mentioned, Roosevelt had relied on nongovernmental organizations to promote the UN to the American public, and his administration felt it now had to open the global organization to them in order to maintain their support. The United States was the main supporter of a greater role for nongovernmental IOs in the ILO. American representatives invoked ideological (pro-democracy) arguments when supporting this change.

The nongovernmental IOs the ILO began working with were few in number and generally affiliated with workers' and employers' groups already represented in the organization. This was primarily because these two groups were keen on keeping other nongovernmental actors outside the ILO so as to not dilute their own influence (Thomann 2008). In 1948, the arrangement between this small group of nongovernmental IOs was formalized by giving them "general consultative" status. Even today, only half a dozen nongovernmental IOs have this prestigious status that implies a standing invitation to participate in meetings of the ILO conference and governing body.[7] In these bodies, they have the right to observe, make oral statements, and circulate written ones.

By the mid-1950s, the intergovernmental–nongovernmental balance in the organization began shifting once more. While the Soviet Union refused to participate in the ILO from 1937 to 1954, after Stalin's death, it returned to the organization. It soon became apparent to Western states that some of the ideological battles they were fighting in other IOs were going to be even more difficult in the ILO, where labor groups from many member-states would often side with Moscow. As the smaller Soviet Bloc states were also joining the ILO during those

---

[7] See www.ilo.org/pardev/partnerships/civil-society/ngos/WCMS_201411/lang--en/index.htm, accessed February 23, 2018.

years, the United States and its allies moved quickly to allow more Western-based nongovernmental IOs to access the organization while they still had the necessary majority to shape the rules of the organization. Thus, in 1956, the ILO added a second group of "special list" nongovernmental IOs to the existing general consultative category (Ripinsky and Van den Bossche 2007, 72). The special list nongovernmental IOs do not represent employers or workers; rather, they focus on related issues considered relevant to the ILO. The organizations in this broader category only have observer status in the ILO conferences, but not in the governing body. They can also apply to observe lower-level ILO meetings. Early on, the special list nongovernmental IOs were ones that dealt with human rights and that promoted Western democratic values, such as Amnesty International.[8] The increase in the number of all these nongovernmental IOs accepted in the ILO led to a further shift of global labor governance toward nongovernmental-ism on the deliberative dimension of the continuum.

This shift is reflected in Figure 4.2, which gauges the number of nongovernmental IOs that were present at the annual international labor conference.[9] It should be noted that, in addition to the consultative status and special list organizations, others may apply for observer status in the ILO conference. However, for these other nongovernmental IOs, accreditation is more burdensome and uncertain. Therefore, the total number of nongovernmental IOs allowed to attend the annual Labor Conference reflects the push and pull

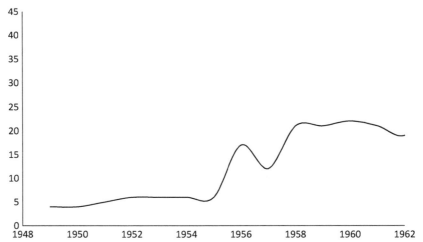

FIGURE 4.2. Number of nongovernmental IOs participating in International Labor Conferences.

[8] See www.ilo.org/pardev/partnerships/civil-society/ngos/ilo-special-list-of-ngos/lang--en/index.htm, accessed February 23, 2018.
[9] Based on data from records of proceedings of International Labour Conference at www.ilo.org/public/libdoc/ilo/P/09616/, accessed February 23, 2018.

of political disagreements between the two sides. The figure shows that this number indeed increased rapidly in the late 1950s. As Western influence in the ILO diminished, access of nongovernmental organizations appears to have advanced more slowly and, in some years, even experienced a decline.

In 1960, the "regional consultative" status was added as yet another category of nongovernmental IOs with access to the ILO. These have rights similar to those in the "general consultative" category, except that they can attend only meetings with a regional focus. The establishment of this category, however, did not simply reflect the West's willingness to accept more nongovernmental actors in the ILO. Rather, the United States and its allies pushed for the inclusion of this new category so that regional nongovernmental IOs from the developing world would be prevented from gaining general consultative status and, implicitly, a greater say in the ILO (Ripinsky and Van den Bossche 2007, 72). They appear to have been correct that developing countries would have sought greater influence for such organizations in the ILO. In 1980, despite the existence of the regional consultative status, the governing body granted the Organisation of African Trade Union Unity full consultative status (Osieke 1985, 70–71). Although this was seen as an exception, it reflected how, by that point, developing countries had gained a comfortable majority in the ILO and had a greater say in the functioning of the IO.

Cold War dynamics also influenced the broader debates in the ILO, beyond those focusing on nongovernmental IO access to deliberations. In the first few years after World War II, the United States increasingly used the organization as a venue to challenge global "creeping socialism" (Tipton 1959, 88). American officials were especially critical of some ILO conventions, such as the 1948 one on freedom of association and protection of the right to organize and the 1949 one on the right to collective bargaining. At that time, such conventions ran counter to trends in the United States, where McCarthyism saw the need for government to control labor conflicts in this new Cold War in a way that was similar to how they had been controlled during World War II. Indeed, in 1947, the US Republican Congress was able to override Truman's veto to pass the Taft-Hartley Act, restricting union activities and weakening the US labor movement.

In the ILO, American delegates, such as William McGrath, blamed the more left-leaning Western European countries for the creeping socialism in the organization. He argued:

Here is what has happened in the ILO, as I see it. For some years the "more power for government" boys had been itching to switch the ILO from an international labor organization to an international government organization. They pulled it off in 1944 at the ILO Convention in Philadelphia. (cited in Tipton 1959, 88)

This perception was based primarily on the domestic labor issues that the ILO took on and the conventions it adopted, rather than on the working rules of the organization.

The East-West tensions in the ILO became more visible after 1954, when the Soviet Union and its East Bloc allies joined the organization. During the Cold War, most of the heated disputes over labor issues took place among top-level officials who saw every development in this realm as very important for the broader relations between the two sides. The clashes between officials virtually always involved arguments with strong ideological undertones, as they were easily applicable to labor issues.

Many more Western states began using some of the same anti-Communist rhetoric the United States had used in the early 1950s. Such rhetoric was now primarily directed toward the encroachment of tripartism by Communist countries. Indeed, Soviet Bloc states did not have independent labor movements or truly nongovernmental employers. In fact, since the Soviet Union had lost its membership in the ILO in 1939, Stalin had reigned in even more than before the little independence labor unions may have had.

The first clash over ILO tripartism between the two sides of the Cold War began with the 1954 ILO conference. That year, the employers' group challenged the credentials of seven employer representatives from Communist countries. Some of the labor representatives also challenged the credentials of the Soviet and Czechoslovak labor delegates, arguing that they were not independent of the Communist government structures. As in the past, government delegates tipped the balance in the credentials committee and turned down all such challenges. Moreover, using the rules instituted at the proposal of Fascist Italy in the 1930s, the ILO seated a number of East Bloc employer delegates on governing body industrial committees, even though the employers' group had voted to keep them out of such forums. In this case, as in virtually all votes dealing with Soviet Bloc labor and employer representatives in the ILO, government delegates (sometimes with the exception of those from the United States and a few other states) and labor delegates took more conciliatory positions. Many Western governments wanted to maintain a more inclusive organization that would keep communication channels open between the two sides of the Cold War. Some believed that the League of Nations' inability to keep powerful countries such as Germany, Italy, and Japan involved in the IO had been partially to blame for the outbreak of World War II. In order to ensure that a similar breakup would not take place in the new UN system, most Western states often avoided confrontations with the Soviet Bloc in organizations such as the ILO. Western worker groups also sought a more moderate position in debates because they felt a degree of solidarity with workers from Eastern European countries.

Western employers were therefore virtually alone throughout the first half of the Cold War in seeking to strengthen tripartism in the ILO and, implicitly, in bringing the organization back to its original intergovernmental–nongovernmental balance. They requested the ILO constitution be amended to require that labor and employer delegates be independent from their governments, an item that, as mentioned, had not been addressed in 1919. The other two groups transformed this drastic initiative into a simple request that a committee draw up a report on the independence of such representatives. This "McNair report," released in 1956, embraced the more conciliatory approach of governments, rather than the feistier Western employers' position. It argued that when it came to employers, in many countries the distinction between governments and managers was becoming blurred. It also found that in the USSR, managers had "extensive powers and discretion and responsibilities and that a great deal is left to their independent judgement within the limits of the overall economic plan." Similarly, the report found that trade unions in the USSR "clearly possess a status in the life of the country of which all potentialities and powers within the country must necessarily take notice" (McNair 1956, 584).

Seeing that the McNair report would not bring about any real change, employers sought once more to alter the ILO constitution to stipulate that nongovernmental delegates need to be independent of their governments. A British employer representative declared that the ILO was not tripartite any more but rather a hybrid "government-tripartite" organization and argued, "Let us therefore have no more nonsense about retaining or maintaining the tripartite structure. We have already lost it" (ILO 1956, 134). Yet again, virtually all governments opposed altering the ILO constitution. The French, in particular, argued that the McNair report showed that it was difficult to discern between states where there was independence and others where there was not. American government representatives criticized the lack of nongovernmental representatives' independence and argued that there would come a time when Western states would have to choose between an organization with a more inclusive membership where the tripartite principle is neglected and a more exclusive, perhaps new, organization truly based on the tripartite principle. However, in the end, they, too, felt it was not possible at that time to change the ILO constitution (Galenson 1981, 39–40). Ironically, instead of taking any institutional measures to increase nongovernmental representatives' independence, the governing body changed its standing rules in 1960 to make it even easier for labor and employer delegates who were not selected by their groups to stand on industrial committees to be placed in such forums (ILO 1959, 31).

In time, even Western employers considered it useless to fight the tripartism battle. Many withdrew from committees where Eastern Bloc representatives had been placed using the new procedure. However, they were able to withstand pressures to have Communist Bloc employer delegates placed on the governing body. In contrast, the labor group began electing Soviet labor representatives to the governing body every year, starting in 1966. American labor delegates broke with their Western European counterparts over this issue. They also disapproved of the friendly relations between Western and Eastern European trade unions. The AFL-CIO's strong antipathy toward the unions from Communist states fueled its decision to leave ICFTU in 1969.

The issue of tripartism was not raised again in any major ILO forum until 1971. As Figure 4.1 shows, after Western governments had taken conciliatory positions toward employer and labor representatives in the late 1950s, voting cohesion between governments and nongovernmental representatives drastically increased. The decline in nongovernmental delegate independence was primarily due to the increase in the number of new states that had emerged from the decolonization process. Indeed, the ILO more than doubled its 1945 membership by the late 1960s. Most new members had not yet developed necessary domestic structures allowing labor and employers to be represented independently of their governments. Therefore, in the vast majority of these new national delegations, there was overly strong cohesion. All these developments contributed to the ILO moving toward increased intergovernmentalism throughout the 1960s and 1970s on the decision-making and deliberative dimensions.

Several developments unrelated to the question of tripartism slowly began affecting the power struggle in the ILO and, implicitly, the intergovernmental–nongovernmental balance. First, in 1970 American David Morse stepped down from the position of ILO director-general. While he had withstood Eastern Bloc pressures to appoint a Soviet assistant director-general, his British successor, Wilfred Jenks, succumbed to them. The United States was appalled by Jenks's decision because it had backed him with the understanding that keeping Soviet nationals from high-ranking ILO secretariat positions was essential for American interests. After the Soviet official was named to this second-highest position in the ILO, Congress sought to withhold funding for the organization. During the congressional hearings on this topic, George Meany, the head of the AFL-CIO and the US labor representative in the ILO, argued that the Soviet appointment

[...] is about the last straw because whatever assignment this man gets departmental-wise in the ILO, he will have hundreds of employees under his supervision [...] he will use that position to make each and every employee a Communist agent, whether he wants to or not. (cited in Galenson 1981, 115)[10]

The second important development that deepened tensions in the ILO was triggered by the Palestinian Liberation Organization's (PLO) application in 1974 for observer status. Israel opposed this status due to the inclusion in the Palestinian National Covenant of a commitment to the obliteration of Israel. The next day, developing countries, now holding a clear majority in the ILO, pushed for the adoption of a resolution condemning Israel for racial discrimination and violation of trade union freedoms. The United States strongly opposed it, arguing that the allegations in the resolution had not been taken up by any expert committee. Over the following year, the question of PLO observer status led to an extremely bitter rhetorical battle (ILO 1975).

---

[10] This position reminds us that although the ideological mechanism discussed in this book is primarily triggered by top government officials, there are instances when it can also involve representatives of nongovernmental groups.

In June 1975, when the PLO was formally admitted as an observer, the Israeli and American delegations walked out of the meeting. Two weeks later, Congress withheld US contributions to the ILO. In November 1975, Secretary of State Henry Kissinger gave formal notice of the United States' intention to withdraw from the ILO. The reasons for this decision were, in order: (1) erosion of tripartite representation, (2) selective concern for human rights, (3) accelerating trend to disregard due process, and (4) increasing and excessive politicization of the organization (United Nations 1975).

Despite efforts by ILO officials, Western governments, labor and employer representatives, and even the Pope to have the United States reconsider its position, the withdrawal took place on November 1, 1977. It thus took effect during the Carter presidency, even though the process had been initiated by the Ford administration. The final decision was in part due to Carter's broader commitment to international human rights and, in particular, to principles of due process and freedom of association (Beigbeder 1979, 235).

During the three years after the United States left the ILO, the organization struggled to deal with the departure of its largest financial contributor. Other states increased contributions but, even so, the ILO was left with a hole of about $30 million in its overall budget of $169 million (ILO 1978, 2). Western states' efforts to convince American government, employer, and labor officials to rejoin the organization and developing countries' willingness to drop some of their anti-Israeli rhetoric contributed to the US decision to return to the ILO in 1980. However, the most important concession made to American demands was the amendment in 1979 of Article 19 of the ILO's Conference Standing Orders, allowing voting by secret ballot. This made it easier for worker and employer delegates to vote independent of their governments, shifting the ILO toward greater nongovernmentalism on the decision-making continuum. In 1980, when the United States returned to the organization, it mentioned this change as a principal reason it believed there had been sufficient improvement in the organization to reconsider its decision (Shultz 1985). After the United States rejoined the ILO, the last decade of the Cold War era did not see much change in the intergovernmental–nongovernmental balance of the ILO or, more broadly, in the global labor realm.

GLOBAL GOVERNANCE IN THE LABOR REALM
IN THE POST–COLD WAR ERA

After the Cold War, labor and employer representatives continued to be the most significant nongovernmental actors in the ILO and, more broadly, in global labor governance. They also continued to guard their influence in the organization, keeping other nongovernmental entities outside of the decision-making and, whenever possible, even deliberative processes. Moreover, from around 1987 until the mid-1990s, the third wave of democracy appears to have translated into much more independent labor and employer groups, as reflected in Figure 4.1. It is this combination of increasingly independent labor and employer groups and their efforts to maintain their monopoly over nongovernmental influence in the ILO that led to an even smaller role for nongovernmental IOs in this organization starting in the mid-1980s. Indeed, the number of nongovernmental IOs allowed to participate at the annual international labor conferences declined from a maximum of 113 in 1988 to a minimum of 79 by 2001.[11]

The decline took place despite efforts from top-ranking ILO officials to reverse this trend (e.g., ILO 1997). A number of government and even nongovernmental representatives from the ILO also reacted to this decline by calling for a greater role for "civil society" in the ILO (usually interpreted as referring to nongovernmental IOs rather than to employer or labor groups). A study has shown that such democratic rhetoric increased in the ILO starting in the late 1990s, reached a high around 2003, and then declined again (Baccaro and Mele 2012). However, these pressures did not lead to an improvement in nongovernmental IO access to the organization.

The global governance of labor nevertheless did experience a shift toward nongovernmentalism in the 1990s and early 2000s. Yet, this shift took place due to developments outside the ILO rather than inside the organization.

With the rise in trade and the race to secure lower production costs in the competitive environment of the early 1990s, a great number of cases of child labor and other labor rights abuses came to the fore, especially in the apparel industry (Cavanagh 1997). At that time, it became apparent that despite the ILO's ability to adopt international agreements, it was "toothless" in monitoring them (Abbott and Snidal 2009; Baccaro 2015, 262). Labor rights advocates instead sought to find other forums to deal with such issues. Nongovernmental groups such as the ILRF and the Lawyers Committee for Human Rights took advantage of the negotiations in 1995 for the WTO and launched a "global New Deal" based on enforceable "social clauses" in trade agreements (Collingsworth et al. 1994). They expected that the enforcement of such clauses would work best if they were included as part of the new IO. However, the strong neoliberal ideology that virtually all powerful states had embraced, as well as the private material interests in developing countries where sweatshops had spread, led the majority of governments to reject this proposal, arguing that it would hinder free trade (Olsen et al. 2001, 161).

The eventual impetus for change came from a series of events that unfolded in the United States. In 1995, a group of indentured Thai immigrants were found in an apartment complex in El Monte, California, producing garments for major

---

[11] After 2001, the ILO altered its system of reporting participation in its annual conferences. Rather than including lists of all nongovernmental IOs that were *allowed* to participate, it listed organizations that *applied* to participate. Of course, not all applications were approved. Therefore, the information up to 2001 is not comparable to subsequent information. See www.ilo.org/pardev/partnerships/civil-society/ngos/ilo-special-list-of-ngos/lang--en/index.htm, accessed February 23, 2018.

American retailers. A few months later, it was discovered that the Kathy Lee clothing line was being manufactured in a Honduran factory employing children and in a New York sweatshop. These revelations led to more investigations and discoveries of sweatshops producing for big-name companies such as Gap, Nike, and Disney. The US government decided to strengthen the enforcement of existing labor laws through the Department of Labor and to adopt tougher legislation (Bartley 2007, 330). However, these actions primarily affected developments in the United States; those in the global realm were affected only slightly.

The demand for change in monitoring labor practices came primarily from the companies that had been shamed by these revelations. They moved swiftly to adopt voluntary codes of conduct for their producers. They also hired outsiders, virtually all nongovernmental, to monitor compliance with the codes. Activists, however, saw these efforts as nothing more than window dressing that allowed the companies to improve their damaged image but did nothing for the establishment of a broader set of labor standards. The American-based apparel industry sought to establish a common system of certification and labeling, but due to the same global competitive pressures, voluntary initiatives (such as the California Apparel Industry Certification Board and the Compliance Alliance) were short lived. As the more intergovernmental IOs did not step in to deal with such issues, and as NGOs had not developed a sufficiently global reach, the problems of child labor and sweatshops generally remained unresolved.

At that point, the Clinton administration decided to take on a more significant role. Yet, its "intervention," *encouraging* the creation of the private Apparel Industry Partnership (AIP), served solely to bolster private initiatives, not direct government action. It even supported the AIP and its successors financially. These measures were seen as compromises between doing nothing and building stronger domestic and intergovernmental regulations (Bartley 2007, 331). While some American officials, such as Labor Secretary Robert Reich, sought to have the ILO take the lead in monitoring the system, for example, by using a "social label," they were overruled by others in the Clinton administration (Zaracostas 1997).

In addition to pushing American businesses to come together in the AIP, US officials also encouraged nongovernmental organizations to take over the monitoring process. The administration was especially interested in having more nongovernmental IOs involved so that they could in turn pressure foreign companies and governments to establish a global monitoring system. The main organizations involved in developing international certification programs were the Lawyers' Committee for Human Rights and ILRF, which had both sought to have the WTO take on the monitoring of labor standards a few years earlier. In the end, as an observer noted, "the institutional entrepreneurship of these NGOs grew out of failures in intergovernmental arenas [...]" (Bartley 2007, 332).

By 1997, the ILO realized that it was being sidelined by a growing number of nongovernmental IOs and therefore tried to bring the new certification programs under its umbrella. Director-General Michel Hansenne felt that to make his organization more relevant, he needed to reach out to such nongovernmental groups (ILO 1997, 27–28). The nongovernmental IOs and corporations involved in the new international certification programs had little in common with the labor and employer groups represented in the ILO. Moreover, the global organization continued to be strongly influenced by the large number of developing member-states that saw the Global North–sponsored certification programs as mechanisms discriminating against their goods. The ILO leadership therefore presented its involvement in private initiatives as a way to influence the certification processes and to complement them with elements acceptable to the developing world. It emphasized the need to deal with potential job losses due to certification programs, pushed for the improvement of freedom of association in industries that were under the scrutiny of certification programs, and even raised questions about the legitimacy of private actors involved in certification programs (Baccaro and Mele 2012, 206).

Hansenne also proposed that the ILO take control of the programs. However, instead of bringing existing certification programs to the ILO, he first reached out to governments, proposing a convention through which states would establish their own "social label" programs and monitoring systems (ILO 1997, 30–31). Developing countries opposed this plan vehemently, calling it a form of trade protectionism. By 1999, other than the United States, a few other Western states, and most labor representatives, there was no support for the ILO becoming involved in certification programs, especially ones where nongovernmental IOs played a major role (Polaski 2006).

In 1999, when it became clear that governments would not accept a formal convention backing ILO certification programs, the new director-general, Juan Somavia, turned directly to the nongovernmental IOs involved in existing programs and sought to bring them into the ILO. Labor and employer representatives opposed this plan, as they saw the inclusion of new nongovernmental actors as encroaching on their own influence in the organization. Instead, they pushed for the adoption of an ILO resolution on "tripartism and social dialogue." Although the resolution acknowledged the need for the ILO to engage with a broader spectrum of "civil society" groups, it essentially reminded everyone that the ILO was run by governments, labor unions, and employers and stipulated that "the tripartite constituents will be consulted as appropriate in the selection of and relationships with other civil society organizations" (ILO 2002a, 26). This, of course, placed the traditional nongovernmental representatives in the ILO as gatekeepers to the organization for other nongovernmental actors. A few Western government representatives argued unsuccessfully that tripartism also implies broader civil society representation. Interestingly, when making their cases such speakers supporting a greater role for nongovernmental IOs also argued that governments had been "marginalized" compared to labor and employer representatives in the ILO (ILO 2002b, 4).

Faced with strong opposition from government and nongovernmental representatives, Somavia established a "high commission of eminent figures" to study how the ILO could move forward. The commission, made up of representatives of all three traditional ILO groups and from nongovernmental IOs, issued in 2004 the "Report of the World Commission on the Social Dimension of Globalization." The report emphasized how, due to changes brought about by globalization, governmental structures could no longer remain the sole channels of action for the ILO and advocated for a broader participatory approach that would bring more nongovernmental IOs into the organization. However, the ILO's members dug in, deciding to not alter the existing system.

In sum, at the beginning of the post–Cold War era, the ILO became less likely to work with nongovernmental IOs and include them in its deliberations in a trend that ran counter to the ones in other organizations from the UN system. Some have criticized this trend, arguing that currently, labor and employer groups in the ILO are not very representative of the global economy. These groups come only from formal economic sectors, not from the rapidly growing informal ones, which are especially present in developing states (Rodgers et al. 2009, 17).

Despite the failed efforts to have nongovernmental IOs play a stronger role *within* the ILO, their growing number and power (due primarily to the spread of democracy across states) led these organizations to launch international nongovernmental initiatives that became more influential *outside* the ILO. This led to an overall shift of global labor governance toward nongovernmentalism on all three dimensions.

Additionally, although the ILO has not been as accepting of nongovernmental IOs as other organizations in the UN system have, starting around 2000 it became more open to working with major corporations. That year it established its first public-private partnerships (PPPs). With support from the United States and other powerful Western states as well as from employer groups, often using arguments based on neoliberal ideologies, the 2006 ILO conference formalized this practice by adopting a set of principles for partnerships that were then included in the 2009 director-general's announcement regarding the implementation of PPPs. The document listed various forms that the partnerships could take, including development and implementation of projects, advocacy, and exchange of information. However, the first form of partnership on the list was "funding and donations in kind" (ILO 2009). Thus, the most relevant recent shift on the intergovernmental–nongovernmental continuum has not taken place on the ILO's deliberative dimension but, rather, on its financial one as it allowed for increased funding from corporations and foundations. By 2015, for the first time in ILO's history, corporations joined powerful states among the top donors to the organization.[12] However, it must be noted that the proportion of funding coming from corporations is still much smaller than in other major IOs over the same period, for example, the one in the WHO.

---

[12] See www.ilo.org/wcmsp5/groups/public/---dgreports/--exrel/documents/genericdocument/wcms206696.pdf, accessed February 23, 2018.

ANSWERING THE FIVE MAIN QUESTIONS:
SOME PRELIMINARY CONCLUSIONS

Figure 4.3 summarizes the evolution of the global labor realm with regard to its intergovernmental versus nongovernmental nature. It is analogous to Figures 1.1 and 3.4, reflecting changes in the global education and global health realms, respectively. Figure 4.3 notes in parentheses the main global governors for each time period. The dashed arrows represent failed attempts to bring about change, while the full arrows reflect successful ones.

To help visualize the shifts on this continuum better, I add Figure 4.4, which is analogous to Figure 3.5 representing the changes in the health realm. Figure 4.4 offers a better illustration of the intensity of changes than Figure 4.3 does. The level of intergovernmentalism on the vertical axis of Figure 4.4 begins at 0 in 1850, before the first global labor governance institutions emerged. For each time period, I add or subtract one unit on the vertical axis for each change toward intergovernmentalism or nongovernmentalism, respectively.

Both Figures 4.3 and 4.4 show that global labor governance has experienced numerous shifts across the intergovernmental–nongovernmental continuum over time. Moreover, when comparing Figure 4.3 to 3.4 and Figure 4.4 to 3.5, it appears that, overall, global labor governance was somewhat more nongovernmental than global health governance was. Indeed, in Figure 4.3, virtually all attempts to shift global labor governance toward the intergovernmental end of the continuum were unsuccessful. Also, most of the time, the line in Figure 4.4 is at or below the 0 axis.[13] However, as a reminder, these two types of figures should be interpreted with caution, as they represent the direction of the *changes* in global governance (and of their intensity in the case of Figure 4.4), not as much the levels of global governance.

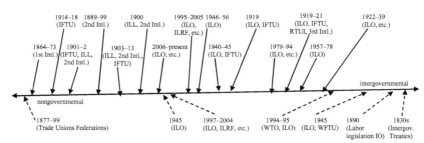

FIGURE 4.3. The nongovernmental–intergovernmental continuum in global labor governance.

---

[13] Even the exceptions (during the interwar era and the Cold War, when due to authoritarian states the ILO was very intergovernmental) never reach a level higher than +2 on the axis, while in the health realm they reach +4.

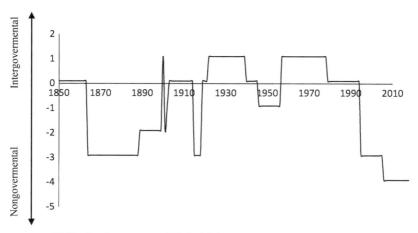

FIGURE 4.4. Shifts in the nature of global labor governance.

Table 4.1 complements the two figures. It offers additional information regarding not only the direction and intensity of the shifts across the
intergovernmental–nongovernmental continuum, but also the possible factors
that led to such shifts. The first column identifies the moments when there
were attempts to shift global labor governance across the intergovernmental–
nongovernmental continuum (with unsuccessful attempts noted with italic
letters). The second column lists the IOs where the changes were attempted.

The third column offers answers to the question *What types of changes
took place in the intergovernmental–nongovernmental nature of global governance?* The three subcolumns differentiate between changes on the decision-
making, financial, and deliberative dimensions. The last row indicates that
in the global governance of labor there were, in fact, more changes on the
decision-making dimension (fourteen) than on the financial (six) or deliberative dimensions (eight). This contrasts with the health realm, where there
were approximately equal numbers of changes on the three decision-making
dimensions. The difference may be due to the fact that the labor realm has had
more organizations where solely nongovernmental actors controlled the decision making (such as the First and Second Internationals, IFTU, and ILRF).
As their influence increased or declined, global labor governance experienced
shifts on the decision-making continuum. Moreover, the ILO institutionalized
voting rights for both governmental and nongovernmental representatives as
far back as 1919. Since then, the relative independence of the nongovernmental representatives (and implicitly, the nongovernmental nature of global governance decision making) has changed several times.

Column 4 summarizes the answers to the question *How strong was government activism in the most important countries promoting or opposing*

TABLE 4.1. *Summary of shifts on the intergovernmental–nongovernmental continuum in global labor realm (failed attempts in italic)*

Year(s)	IO(s) where change was attempted	(Q1) Type of change			(Q2) Major states supporting or opposing change and their ideology		(Q3) Evidence of ideology-based mechanism	(Q4) Evidence of institutional mechanism	(Q5) Evidence of system-level explanations
		(a) Decision-making	(b) Financial	(c) Deliberative	Support change	Oppose change			
1830s	*Intergovernmental treaties*	*+(NO)*	*+(NO)*	*+(NO)*		*All great powers*	*no*	*no*	*no*
1864	First International	–(NO)	–(NO)	–(NO)			no	yes	yes
1877–1899	*International trade union federations*	*–(NO)*	*–(NO)*	*–(NO)*			*no*	*yes*	*yes*
1889	Second International	+(NO)		+(NO)			no	yes	no
1890	*Labor legislation IO*	*+(NO)*	*+(NO)*	*+(NO)*	*Germany (+)*	*UK (–), France (–)*	*yes*	*no*	*no*
1900	ILL	+(NO)	+(NO)	+(NO)	Germany (+)	UK (–)	yes	no	no
1901	IFTU	–(NO)	–(NO)	–(NO)	UK (–)		no	yes	yes
1902	Second International, IFTU	+(AO)					no	yes	no
1903–1913	ILL	+(WO)			UK (+)		no	yes	no
1914–1918	IFTU, ILL	–(AO)	–(AO)	–(AO)			no	yes	yes
1919	ILO	+(NO)		+(NO)	UK (+), France (+)	US (–)	yes	yes	yes
1919–1921	Third International, RTUI	+(NO)			USSR (+)		yes	no	no

Year(s)	IO(s) where change was attempted	(Q1) Type of change			(Q2) Major states supporting or opposing change and their ideology		(Q3) Evidence of ideology-based mechanism	(Q4) Evidence of institutional mechanism	(Q5) Evidence of system-level explanations
		(a) Decision-making	(b) Financial	(c) Deliberative	Support change	Oppose change			
1922–1939	ILO	+ (WO)			Italy (+), Japan (+), Germany (+), USSR (+)	UK (−), France (−)	yes	yes	yes
1940	ILO	− (WO)					no	no	yes
1945	ILO, WFTU	+ (AO)		+ (AO)	USSR (+)		yes	no	no
1946–1956	ILO			− (WO)	US (−)	US (−), UK (−)	yes	no	no
1957–1978	ILO	+ (WO)		+ (WO)	USSR (+)	US (−)	yes	no	yes
1979	ILO	− (WO)			US (−)		yes	no	no
1994–1995	ILO; WTO	+ (NO)	+ (NO)	+ (NO)		All great powers	yes	no	yes
1995–2005	Nongovernmental IOs (e.g., ILRF)	− (NO)	− (NO)	− (NO)	US (−)		no	yes	yes
1997–2004	ILO			− (NO)	US (−)		no	yes	yes
2006–2015	ILO		− (WO)		US (−)		yes	no	yes
TOTAL		14	6	8	11		8	9	9

Key: NO: new organization; WO: change within existing organization; AO: change in relative importance among organizations; +: domestic activism or intergovernmentalism when referring to state or global governance, respectively; −: domestic passivism or nongovernmentalism when referring to state or global governance, respectively.

changes in the nature of global governance? Like Table 3.1, Table 4.1 shows that in the vast majority of cases, support or opposition to international changes went hand in hand with preferences for domestic activism (noted with + or − in both subcolumns of column 4). These findings offer support for H_1 and H_2. The bottom row indicates that there were overall eleven instances (of the sixteen successful attempts) where there is evidence of the domestic–international linkage.[14] Two exceptions involve, once again, developments during World War I and World War II. Three more involve the establishment of the First and Second Internationals and the empowerment of the Second International over IFTU. These last three changes resulted from actions of nongovernmental actors that were not supported by governments, yet were nevertheless successful.

Columns 5 and 6 respond to the following two main questions, respectively: *Did officials promoting intergovernmentalism or nongovernmentalism use arguments that invoked specific ideologies?* and *Which national institutions were represented in the international efforts to shift global governance toward greater intergovernmentalism or nongovernmentalism?* The bottom row shows that there are, yet again, almost as many cases supporting the ideology-based argument (eight) as the institution-based one (nine).

Column 7 responds to the question *Are there any system-level explanations for the shifts?* The last row suggests that there are nine instances where there are plausible system-level explanations for the shifts, slightly more than in the health realm. Moreover, in the labor realm there is only one instance (compared to four in the health realm) where system-level factors alone account for the changes in global governance. That case involves the nongovernmental shift that came during World War II, a development that is expected based on the system-level arguments presented in Chapter 2. However, even in that case, when one looks more closely, it becomes apparent that the aggregation of preferences and actions of powerful states were at least as responsible for this change as the system-level factors. Indeed, the shift took place primarily because powerful states like Germany, Italy, and Japan left the ILO when the war began and, therefore, the nongovernmental labor and employer groups in the IO became, on average, more independent.

The developments in the labor realm also show that system-level arguments can rarely account for the *direction* of changes toward intergovernmentalism or nongovernmentalism. For instance, throughout most of the nineteenth century, the increased economic interactions among states indeed led to a greater need for international collaboration in the labor realm. However, global factors cannot account for the fact that the first successful collaborative forums

---

[14] Moreover, it shows that even in cases where the attempts to alter global labor governance were *not* successful, the powerful countries opposing the changes had domestic preferences that ran counter to the direction of the proposed international shift.

were more nongovernmental (such as the First International and IFTU) and that later ones were more intergovernmental (such as Second International and ILL). One needs to also take into account the shifts away from the initial laissez-faire ideologies in powerful states, especially the United Kingdom, to understand why governments were slow to become involved in global labor issues.

The first major shift toward intergovernmentalism in this realm took place after World War I, with the establishment of the ILO. At that time, there were indeed several system-level factors that put pressure on governments to become involved in global labor governance. However, when one considers the very different positions held by the Americans and British at that time, it becomes clear that system-level factors need to be complemented with domestic factors to explain the hybrid nature of the resulting IO.

The rise of authoritarian governments in the interwar era, especially in some of the powerful states such as Italy and Japan, led to a decline in labor and employers' independence and, implicitly, to a more intergovernmental approach in the ILO. The increase in the number of authoritarian states during the Cold War had a similar effect. These developments offer support for the system-level arguments focusing on the impact of global democratic norms. However, the nature of the ILO was determined not only by the overall strength of democratic norms but also by the specific support for democracy in the most powerful states making up the organization. For example, while the USSR stayed out of the ILO in the first decade after World War II, the United States and its allies pushed the organization toward greater nongovernmentalism. Similarly, in order to explain the shift toward nongovernmentalism after 2000 that resulted from the systemwide rise in power of large corporations, one needs to take into account that the United States was the main supporter of this change. Indeed, the United States promoted the adoption of its own private-public partnership domestic model to the work of the ILO. In sum, as in the case of global health governance, even the most convincing system-level explanations of changes in the labor realm usually need to be complemented with arguments involving the preferences of the most powerful states. Almost all the shifts in global governance in this realm appear to have been shaped, at least to some degree, by domestic–international linkage mechanisms.

5

Global Governance in the Technical Standards Realm

This chapter discusses the evolution of global governance in the technical standards realm from the mid-nineteenth century to present. Like Chapters 3 and 4, it begins by noting how governments and nongovernmental actors initially became involved in this issue-area at the domestic level. It then follows the processes that led technical standardization to emerge as an issue involving international collaboration. As in the previous two chapters, the narrative follows the ebb and flow of global governance, keeping in mind the five main questions of the study. This allows me to assess in the concluding section of the chapter the changes that the main global governors underwent in terms of their intergovernmental versus nongovernmental nature and the possible explanations for such changes.

Given this chapter's focus is on *technical* standards (rather than all standards), it may appear even more difficult than in the previous two chapters to delineate between the global governors that should be included and those that should be left out of the analysis. However, also as in previous chapters, the existing literature offers a surprisingly coherent agreement on which standards are truly "technical."[1] This literature generally suggests that standards that are easily understood by all, as in the case of the early standards for weight and length, or labor standards specifying the maximum number of hours of work, are not technical in nature (Reuther 1956). Technical standards, by contrast, such as those in the electrotechnical, chemical, or medical realms, involve a high degree of expertise and are difficult for the general public to assess. The present chapter will focus only on such technical standards.

It should be pointed out that by excluding nontechnical standards, I do not bias the analysis of the intergovernmental or nongovernmental nature of

---

[1] See, e.g., the agreement among the several dozen authors in one of the first comprehensive studies of technical standards (Reck 1956).

global governance. Although at first sight, experts who deal with technical standards may appear to come from outside government structures, pushing the issue-area toward nongovernmentalism, in practice, governments have often established institutions to deal with questions of standardization and included such experts in their work. Even today in the United States, one of the countries with the greatest emphasis on nongovernmental standard-setting, a little more than half of all standards are in fact established by government institutions (Mattli 2003, 209). Thus, I consider that viewing technical standards as a very nongovernmental realm *by necessity* is flawed.

This chapter will show that, as in the cases of the health and labor realms, over time, the global governors of technical standards have experienced shifts across the intergovernmental–nongovernmental continuum. These shifts have, in turn, led to changes in the overall nature of global governance. I identify the main states supporting or opposing such changes and note their activist or passive domestic approaches to technical standards at that time. I also determine whether individuals involved in the promotion of changes represented top government institutions, lower-level specialized ones, or nongovernmental organizations. I point out instances when such individuals invoked ideological arguments. Lastly, as in Chapters 3 and 4, I offer possible system-level arguments for the shifts in global governance.

By following this format, the chapter answers the main questions of the study and identifies the causes for the shifts in global governance. The last section of the chapter summarizes the evolution of the technical standards realm in a way analogous to the two previous chapters. I conclude with several observations regarding the similarities and differences between the technical standards issue-area and the health and labor ones discussed earlier.

GLOBAL GOVERNANCE IN THE TECHNICAL STANDARDS REALM BEFORE WORLD WAR I

Standards have been adopted at the state level for thousands of years, starting with Egyptian rules for bricks and pots (Weidlein and Reck 1956, 5–6). While governments did not necessarily need to take on the task of standard-setting for such products, they did decide to become involved in the adoption of standards of the most common weights and measures because it was important for accurate taxation. Four millennia ago, Babylonian kings introduced uniform standards for weight, distance, area, and volume, and they established an official "testing house" where copies of the original standards were certified as accurate (Weidlein and Reck 1956, 8–9).

However, not all states became equally involved in the standardization of measures at all times. In fact, as such standardization could function at either the national or subnational level, it was often at the center of major disputes. For example, Chapter 35 of the Magna Carta refers specifically to the need for the state to develop common standards for weights and for measures of wine, ale, and corn. Similarly, one of the main demands of the French Revolution was the adoption of a national set of standards to replace the many different standards in each region through which local nobles were able to control trade in their territory.

Even after such revolutionary events, there were important differences between states in the types of standards that were seen as being a government's responsibility and those that were not. From one perspective, governments have had an interest in establishing some standards because "heterogeneity raises information and transaction costs, and thus may hinder the efficient conduct of trade" (Spruyt 2001, 372). But from a different perspective, it is very difficult for government institutions to take on all standards and to do so at a sufficiently fast pace to keep up with technological changes. Therefore, very often governments have allowed or even encouraged nongovernmental actors within specific industries to deal with national standards. Many of the nongovernmental networks that initially controlled such standards were based on guilds.

As industrialization brought about technologies that were increasingly complex and that the general public or government officials could not fully comprehend, standard-setting became technical, requiring expert input. Yet, even at that point, governments had a clear choice between becoming directly involved in the more sophisticated standards or stepping aside and letting only nongovernmental actors be the standard setters. The decision to adopt more governmental or nongovernmental standard-setting bodies has differed across time and states.

The most important distinction between domestic technical standard-setting systems mentioned in the literature is the American one, considered "fragmented, market driven and characterized by a high degree of internal competition," versus the European one, which is "hierarchical and highly coordinated" as well as "publicly regulated and subsidized" (Mattli and Büthe 2003, 23). The literature, however, acknowledges that such a simplifying classification misses the many differences between standardization systems, across both states and time (e.g., Tate 2001; Mattli and Büthe 2003, 23, fn 67). Indeed, virtually all national standardization systems have been considered to involve a mixture of multiple elements, some "cooperative," some "competitive," and some "coercive" (Greenstein 1992).

The differences between national technical standards systems has depended in great part on the historical moment at which they emerged. Thus, it has been argued that, as the United Kingdom and the United States were the first to adopt technical standards, they tended to favor market-based systems. The national standardization systems that developed somewhat later, such as French and German ones, were more likely to be coordinated because they could often accept standards that had been elaborated already in other countries. Standardization systems that emerged even later, such as the Asian ones, not only were in a position to determine which standards had worked better in other states but were able (and willing) to develop coercive mechanisms that gave governments a very important role in implementing standards. The literature has pointed out that the differences across the various approaches to standardization have also been based on other factors, such as the nature of the existing legal systems or the political views of the governments in power when national standardization systems emerged (Tate 2001, 444).

By the second half of the nineteenth century, after a number of technical standards institutions had been established within most major states, it became apparent that the process of standardization was necessary for efficient trade and communication not only within countries but also between them. However, the homogenization of standards across borders was often more complex than the process that unfolded within borders, as it needed to take into account long-engrained national practices.

The first international efforts involving technical standardization focused on telegraphy and were very intergovernmental in nature. The spread of telegraphy had substantially increased the speed of national and international telecommunications. In the 1840s and 1850s, the first two decades after the advent of the new form of communication, major states such as the United States, Prussia, the United Kingdom, and France already had tens of thousands of miles of telegraph wires within their borders (Rider 2007, 440). Almost immediately after telegraphy became an essential communications tool within states, it proved itself to be even more useful across borders. In the mid-nineteenth century, while it would take a letter about two months to travel from London to Singapore, the telegraph allowed for communications between the two cities in a matter of minutes (Roberts 2012). Throughout the 1850s and early 1860s, underwater cables were laid down first under the English Channel, then under other seas and even the Atlantic Ocean. By the early 1860s, the volume of international telegrams was increasing at an astounding rate. However, the process through which this form of communication worked across borders was still slowed considerably due to the differences in the technologies and languages used in each country. For example, in the 1850s, there were two employees from each state at a border telegraph station. One would receive the telegram on his domestic line, transcribe the text into a special form, and hand it across the table to his colleague, who would usually have to translate it (unless the two states used the same language) and send it out further on the other country's national telegraph system (ITU 2018).

The initial international efforts to streamline telegraph communications were initiated by Prussia, which as discussed in previous chapters, had a particularly activist government at the time. As the country became the dominant power among all German-speaking principalities, it took the lead in demanding a uniform technical telegraph system across these states, especially as they had the benefit of a common language. By the late 1840s, Prussia had signed more than a dozen bilateral telegraphy agreements with German-speaking states. These agreements were negotiated between government officials, including telegraphy experts who were part of government structures. In 1850, the Austro-German Telegraph Union (AGTU) became the first international telegraphy treaty that allowed other states besides the original two signatories to join the union, thus making it the first multilateral agreement in this realm (ITU 2018).

In 1865, twenty states adopted a more comprehensive agreement in Paris. In this case it was France – yet another country with strong government activist tendencies – rather than Prussia, that took the initiative. The telegraphic network was government-run in both countries, as it was in the vast majority of states at that time. French leadership in this realm was primarily due to Emperor Napoleon III's great personal interest in the new technology. Napoleon wanted France to be in a position to control as much as possible the decisions impacting this form of international communication (Roberts 2012; ITU 2018). The United Kingdom did not participate in the intergovernmental meetings because its telegraphy system was privately owned, rather than state-run. The government's lack of direct involvement in this realm did not allow it to join the IO until 1871, after the organization changed its rules to allow states to include in their delegations representatives of private telegraph companies. The United States, where all telegraph companies were also privately owned, joined the International Telegraph Union in 1908, after this change in rules.[2]

The strong intergovernmental nature of the Paris conference was further reflected in the high level of government representation. The conference was chaired by France's Foreign Minister Édouard Drouyn de Lhuys; all other states were represented by high-ranking ambassadors with plenipotentiary status. These officials were accompanied by experts drawn from their respective country's burgeoning government-run telegraphic institutions, and it was the latter who conducted most of the negotiations. However, the states' interests in controlling this important communications system was evidenced in the fact that only senior government representatives were allowed to vote on the final text of the agreement (ITU 2018).

In the end, the conference agreed on standardizing the signal's frequency as well as the strength and types of cables to be used. They also decided on a common system of tariffs that should be charged for telegrams. Furthermore, the participants chose the Morse code as the international telegraph alphabet. Although they agreed to protect the secrecy of correspondence and the right for everyone to use international telegraphy, they also reserved the right to stop any transmission they considered dangerous for state security, or in violation of national laws, public order, or morals (ITU 2018). The inclusion of

---

[2] See www.itu.int/online/mm/scripts/gensel8, accessed January 30, 2019. Although telegraphy had developed in the United States more than in other countries, this country did not participate in the 1865 conference because at that time it was still fighting its civil war. American telegraphy companies expressed more interest in international initiatives only after the war ended and after the first transatlantic cables became functional.

these reservations reflects the strong degree of governments' control over the convention.

The International Bureau of Telegraphic Administrations, the new organization that emerged from the Paris conference, was also very intergovernmental in nature. Only government representatives voted in the organization's decisions. Also, all funding for the organization came from governments. Last, but not least, all participants in the IO's meetings were formally considered to represent their governments, even if they were experts coming from domestic nongovernmental institutions (Lyall 2016, 8–11).

In 1868, states decided to alter the original 1865 convention by allowing for participation in the organization's meetings not just of experts from government agencies dealing with telegraphy but also those from private companies. The main impetus for this change came from countries where, in addition to government-owned telegraphy systems, substantial segments of the telegraphic system were in private hands. The Italians, the main proponents of this change, garnered sufficient support from other states to alter the rules.

Even in the 1868 meeting, representatives from ten private telegraph companies were allowed to participate in deliberations, alongside government representatives. The ten companies also took on financial obligations related to the IO (Lyall 2016, 31–32). With this change in the convention, the organization and, more broadly, global governance in the very young international issue-area of technical standards, shifted toward nongovernmentalism across both the deliberative and financial dimensions of the continuum. As the rules did not yet allow for representatives of private telegraphy to lead their national delegations or cast votes for their countries, I do not consider that any shift took place on the decision-making dimension of the continuum.

In the final decades of the nineteenth century, several other IOs emerged to take on issues of technical standard-setting. Virtually all such organizations were established with a very strong intergovernmental character, as was the case of the International Bureau of Weights and Measures (BIPM), established in 1875,[3] and the Central Office for International Carriage by Rail (OTIF), founded in 1893 (Murphy 1994, 47). The emergence of such organizations reflected the increased need for coordination in these realms due to the growth in trade and international transportation. Decision making in these IOs was in government hands, as had been the case in the telegraphy realm. This was to be expected, as their establishment was almost entirely the result of the consultations between government institutions from these issue-areas. Technical experts from outside government circles were rarely allowed to participate in meetings, making the organizations more intergovernmental than

---

[3] By this point, the more sophisticated systems of standardization had transformed the originally simple questions of weights and lengths into technical ones that necessitated a much stronger role for experts.

the International Telegraph Union on the deliberative dimension. Also, in the new IOs, only governments were responsible for financing. The shift brought about by the new IOs is therefore considered to have taken place only on the financial and deliberative dimensions.

France and Germany, two countries where government institutions were already dealing with such issues, were the main supporters of the new IOs. It should be noted that the United Kingdom was not an original member of either of these organizations, while the United States was a member of the former but, as expected, not the latter (Conference du Metre 1875).

Toward the end of the nineteenth century and at the beginning of the twentieth, as electrical engineering advanced quickly, virtually all powerful states developed professional nongovernmental associations made up of physicists and electrical engineers who were eventually tasked with developing technical standards. In 1871, the United Kingdom was the first to establish such an organization, originally named the Society of Telegraph Engineers. In 1880, it changed its name to the Society of Telegraph Engineers and Electricians and, in 1889, it changed yet again, this time to the Institution of Electrical Engineers (IEE). The shift in name indicates that standardization in electrical engineering was initially strongly connected to the emergence of the telegraph, a technology that, as mentioned, had led to the first efforts toward international standardization.

Throughout the 1880s and 1890s, the French, Austrians, Americans, Belgians, Canadians, Germans, and Italians (in that order) also established similar professional electrical engineering organizations. One of the main reasons such associations became involved in technical standards was that they allowed replication and advancements of each other's research (Büthe 2010, 297–298).

Despite the apparent similarities across the domestic electrotechnical standardization institutions, some states more than others tended to emphasize a more governmental approach to standard-setting in the electrotechnical realm. For example, in Germany, inventor and industrialist Ernst Werner von Siemens, who is credited with founding the electrical engineering discipline in his country, sought government support in 1886 to establish a national organization that would develop electrical standards, the Physikalisch-Technische Reichsanstalt. He felt that by being the first state to adopt such standards, Germany would be able to take the lead in this realm (Loya and Boli 1999, 71). In other states, however, the technical experts preferred to keep governments out of their work. In his study of international standard-setting in the electrotechnical realm, Büthe argues that the differences between the early Anglo-Saxon nongovernmental approach to electrical engineering standards and the governmental tradition in Continental Europe derived from the fact that for the former, "self-regulation was among the hallmarks of the traditional liberal professions (law and medicine) which they sought to emulate" (2010, 313).

Soon after their establishment, these national societies began sending representatives to international electrical congresses. Throughout the 1880s and 1890s, the congresses agreed upon a common set of electrical units that all states were to adopt, such as the ohm, ampere, and volt. The experts quickly realized, however, that standardization through international meetings that took place only every several years was much too slow to keep up with the rapid changes in their field. Indeed, the global need for coordination had increased in the scientific realm and in the rapidly growing electrotechnical industry. Therefore, in 1904, at the sixth Electrical Congress in St. Louis, they decided to establish an organization to deal with international standards on a continuous basis. Two years later, they met in London for a special session that formally created the new organization, the International Electrotechnical Commission (IEC).

The IEC's headquarters were placed in London, where they remained until after World War II. Its first director-general, Charles Le Maistre, was a British electrical engineer who simultaneously held positions in the IEE and in the British Engineering Standards Committee, even after being named director-general of IEC. In fact, in the first years of the IEC, in order to allow Le Maistre to continue working in both the domestic and international organizations, the IEE and IEC shared office space in the same building. Le Maistre led the IEC for almost fifty years, until his death in 1953 (Yates and Murphy 2008, 17–18). Due in great part to his leadership, the new international electrotechnical organization followed the model of the British IEE, the oldest and most influential national electrical engineering institution (Büthe 2010, 312–313).

Of the various elements that the IEC adopted from the IEE, the most relevant for this study is the strong nongovernmental nature of the organization. All member-countries in the IEC were initially represented by their national nongovernmental electrotechnical societies. Each state was allotted one vote that was cast by such representatives. IEC's funding also came from nongovernmental national institutions. Unlike the International Telegraph Union, where states paid different amounts depending on the degree to which they each were involved with the organization, in the IEC, all national delegations paid equal dues.

In the IEC's first years, government representatives rarely participated in the organization's meetings. The exception was in cases where a nongovernmental society had not been established in a state. Even in these instances, the rules of the organization provided for government officials to be replaced with representatives from nongovernmental electrotechnical societies as soon as they were established.

It should be noted, however, that the process leading to the *decision* of establishing the very nongovernmental IEC to deal with electrotechnical standards was fairly intergovernmental in nature. Although virtually all of the representatives at the 1904 St. Louis meeting that established the IEC came from nongovernmental electrotechnical societies, the congress documents referred to them as "official representatives appointed to the chamber of *government* delegates" (International Electrical Congress 1904). Moreover, the final report of the conference called for the Chamber of Delegates to consider the establishment of "an international commission representing the governments concerned" and requested "its members to bring this report before their respective governments" so that "the recommendation of the Chamber of Delegates [may] be adopted by the governments represented [and] the commission may eventually become a permanent one" (International Electrical Congress 1904). Therefore, when summarizing the evolution of global governance in the technical standards realm at the end of this chapter, I will consider that the shift toward nongovernmentalism in this realm came only in 1906, when the IEC adopted its official (very nongovernmental) rules, while the 1904 meeting was, at most, an unsuccessful attempt to shift global governance toward intergovernmentalism.

One possible explanation for the strong intergovernmental character of the 1904 meeting is that up to that point, all international initiatives dealing with technical standards, such as the International Telegraph Union, BIPM, and OTIF, had involved government officials. Many of the experts meeting in St. Louis had been involved in international telegraphy forums and, most likely, had come to consider that governments needed to give their consent for a new IO (even if it was to be nongovernmental) before such an organization became functional.

The initial intergovernmental approach of the 1904 meeting was quickly replaced with a much more nongovernmental one. By the opening of the 1906 IEC founding conference in London, the delegates were not referred to in any of the official documents as representatives of governments. The proceedings of the 1906 meeting list delegates by the "authorities by whom they were appointed" (IEC 1906). Such authorities were all nongovernmental electrotechnical societies, with the exception of those from Hungary and Spain, who came from government institutions.

However, even in the 1906 meeting, some speakers continued to oppose the decision to make the IO very nongovernmental or, at least, to give it too much power. For instance, a French representative suggested that the new IEC limit itself and not formulate too many standards, as it would not be able to implement them without the support of governments. The British quickly countered this objection by arguing that their own (extended) experience had shown the nongovernmental solution worked well and that governments need not become involved in their work. This argument emphasized the practical advantages of the nongovernmental choice rather than the ideological aspects. The United Kingdom and the United States, the two countries with the strongest nongovernmental traditions in the electrotechnical standards realm, were the most adamant supporters of a nongovernmental IEC. Together, they managed to fight back most efforts to make the new IO more intergovernmental (IEC 1906).

When the German delegate suggested that governments should be allowed to at least send representatives to IEC meetings, alongside the nongovernmental national representatives, virtually everyone present (but especially the British and Americans) opposed this provision vehemently. The German delegate had to quickly explain that what he had meant was that such government representation should take place only when the country did not have a nongovernmental institution dealing with electrotechnical standards. He went on to argue that when proposing this rule, "there had been no desire whatever to have *bureaucratic* influence imported into the Commission"[4] (IEC 1906, 6).

The strong shift toward nongovernmentalism that took place in the international technical standards realm by the 1906 London meeting was also reflected in the fact that a British proposal to allow industry representatives access to deliberations passed easily (IEC 1906). This, of course, implied that yet another type of nongovernmental actor would be present in IEC's deliberations. The apparent consensus on this point was due in great part to the fact that, as the official minutes of the meeting indicate, most national electrotechnical organizations already "included Manufacturers as they were more interested in the matter than anyone else" (IEC 1906, 18).

In fact, Germany included in its delegation to the London meeting Alexander Siemens, the head of the British division of the influential German company bearing his name. Siemens chaired the most important session at that meeting, the one deciding on the new organization's rules. Similarly, Ikisuke Fujioka, the founder of the Toshiba company in Japan, was very active in the 1906 IEC meeting and in later ones. The IEC continued throughout its history to include such industry representatives in its meetings, pushing the organization even further toward nongovernmentalism on the deliberative dimension.

Up until the outbreak of World War I, the IEC's work intensified as the electrotechnical field developed rapidly. During this time, the organization remained very nongovernmental. It should be pointed out, however, that there were also some intergovernmental elements visible in its work. For instance, in 1908, at the IEC's second meeting after its establishment, the conference was initially supposed to be opened by the British minister of war, who had expressed his great interest in questions of standardization. When the minister was called away elsewhere, he was replaced by Arthur Balfour, who had just stepped down as prime minister and was, at that time, leading the opposition in Parliament (IEC 1909). The presence of such high-ranking officials in IEC meetings suggests that governments were interested (if not yet influential) in the IO's work.

Additionally, as many new nongovernmental electrotechnical societies emerged in states that had not had such societies before, it was up to their

---

[4] The added emphasis is intended to show that IEC delegates saw their own work as not being bureaucratic, in addition to (or as a result of) it being nongovernmental in nature.

respective governments to "approve" their participation in the IO, replacing the previous government representatives. Although there is no indication that such governments used this power to control IEC representation, it suggests that the organization was not completely free of potential government interference.

There were several other IOs that took on issues of technical standardization before World War I, and all were very nongovernmental (Coonley 1954, 42). For example, in the International Aeronautics Federation (IAF), established in 1905, there were no governments represented in meetings.[5] Similarly, the International Commission on Illumination (ICI), established in 1913, was formed solely from national nongovernmental committees.[6] In both cases, the IOs brought together the representatives of domestic institutions dealing with these issues that, at that time, were nongovernmental. As in the case of IEC, virtually all such smaller technical standards organizations were initiated by powerful states, primarily by the United Kingdom and the United States. Although individually these organizations played only minor roles in the broader global governance of technical standards, as they focused only on very narrow issues, together they contributed to a shift toward nongovernmentalism across all three dimensions. Furthermore, they emerged with an even more nongovernmental character than the IEC, and they maintained that character in the years leading up to World War I.

In the years immediately prior to World War I, IEC experienced a shift from its original very nongovernmental character to a more intergovernmental one as the number of government representatives at its meetings increased steadily. As a reminder, at the 1906 IEC conference, only two states were represented by government officials. By the 1913 Berlin conference, five of the countries present were represented by government officials and, implicitly, gave decision-making power to governments. Moreover, many of the delegations that were led by nongovernmental representatives now included numerous government officials.

Even the United Kingdom, with its strong laissez-faire traditions, sent delegations with almost equal numbers of individuals coming from government and nongovernmental institutions (IEC 1914). This change to the United Kingdom's approach to IEC coincided with a shift in the country's domestic activism. In December 1905, a Conservative government replaced a Liberal one and took a much more hands-on approach, passing a series of acts of social legislation that are considered to have laid the foundations of the British welfare state (Cannon 2015, 565). During that period the United Kingdom as well as many other states began including in their expanded government institutions offices dealing with standardization. Individuals from these new offices joined the nongovernmental delegates in the IEC meetings in the years immediately before World War I.

[5] See www.icao.int/about-icao/History/Pages/civil-aviation-pre-icao.aspx, accessed April 13, 2019.
[6] See www.cie.co.at/about-cie, accessed April 13, 2019.

The shift toward intergovernmentalism in IEC also took place across the financial dimension, as all domestic institutions represented in the IO, whether governmental or nongovernmental, now contributed to the IO's budget. It is due to such changes in representation, financing, and participation starting around 1913 that I consider the IEC (and the entire international technical standards realm) to have experienced a shift toward intergovernmentalism across all three dimensions of the continuum.

GLOBAL GOVERNANCE IN THE TECHNICAL STANDARDS
REALM DURING AND IMMEDIATELY AFTER WORLD WAR I

Throughout World War I, virtually all international institutions, whether more intergovernmental like the International Telegraph Union or more nongovernmental like the IEC, ceased to function because it became virtually impossible for national representatives to meet. However, the tremendous significance of industry for the war efforts led IEC representatives to emphasize in their first postwar meeting that standardization was now an even more relevant issue. A reflection of the importance of international standardization efforts is the fact that Arthur Balfour, who had opened the very first IEC meeting in 1908, also spoke at the first IEC meeting after World War I, but now in his capacity as British foreign secretary (IEC 1919).

The influential American and British postwar idealist political thought emphasized the importance of international cooperation in all realms, including standardization. Idealists argued that if states worked together to achieve their many common goals across all issue-areas, future wars could be averted. An example of this argument is Le Maistre's 1919 speech before the new American Engineering Standards Committee (AESC), where he stated that "if we can bring together the engineers of the English-speaking races, it will shortly be one of the greatest helps toward peace of the world" (AESC 1919, 6).

In the immediate post–World War I years, global governance in virtually all issue-areas appeared to experience a shift toward intergovernmentalism reflected primarily by the emergence of the all-important League of Nations. As discussed, this shift is expected during periods that immediately follow wars (e.g., Shanks et al. 1996).

Article 24 of the League's Covenant sought to place many of the previously independent existing organizations (whether more intergovernmental or nongovernmental in nature) under the umbrella of the new IO if they "consented." Some organizations, such as the Universal Postal Union, agreed to this arrangement (Coonley 1954, 42). Others, such as the International Telegraph Union and IEC, the two most important organizations in the technical standards realm at that time, did not (Hills 2002, 183).

Overall, the initial 1919 attempt to shift global governance in the technical standards realm toward intergovernmentalism by giving the League a greater role was unsuccessful on the decision-making and financial dimensions. However, it was eventually successful on the deliberative dimension, as League officials were nevertheless allowed to attend meetings in the forums of the major technical standardization organizations. The initiative of including technical standards IOs under the League umbrella and of allowing League representatives in the deliberations of such IOs belonged to the League's staff, not to governments (although governments did not appear to oppose it).

The advancement of standardization in the electrotechnical realm quickly became a model for achieving better coordination for standardization in other technical realms, both domestically and internationally. After World War I, national standardization bodies, dealing simultaneously with multiple issues, began emerging across numerous states. With few exceptions, all such bodies were very nongovernmental in nature (Ping 2011, 17).

As in the case of the electrotechnical industry, the United Kingdom led the way. Charles Le Maistre became the most powerful advocate for establishing national standardization bodies around the world. Indeed, the British Engineering Standards Committee, established in 1901, was the first comprehensive national standard-setting body. In 1918, it changed its name to the British Engineering Standards Association (BESA). From the start, this organization did not allow for any government involvement in its work. Le Maistre was named its first secretary. As mentioned, he continued to work for BESA even after he was named the head of the IEC.

The German Institute for Standardization was established in December 1917. Although this organization emerged as a nongovernmental entity, it resulted from a process that was initiated by the German military even before the war (US Department of Commerce 1929, 76). Likewise, the French Permanent Commission for Standardization was established in 1918 (US Department of Commerce 1980, 2). The United States (1918), Belgium (1919), Austria (1920), Italy (1921), Sweden (1922), Norway (1923), Russia (1925), Japan (1929), China (1931), and many other states followed suit (Ping 2011). As one would expect in the immediate aftermath of World War I, many governments showed interest in standardization. Therefore, even though in the end the vast majority of standardization organizations were nongovernmental in their first few years, they at least considered an important role for governments. Moreover, there were important differences among countries with some, such as France, accepting a stronger government role in standardization while others, such as the United States, keeping the government "at arm's length" (Mattli 2003, 205–206).

It should be pointed out, however, that even the very nongovernmental American system was established after some debates in which a number of individuals proposed a government agency to deal with all technical standards. The meetings that led to the founding of the nongovernmental AESC in 1918 included not only representatives of nongovernmental organizations but also those from the Navy, War, and Commerce Departments. A significant number of those present argued that it was advisable for the government to take control of the new organization. This position was expressed both by government officials and by individuals who were not part of government structures. However, those in favor of a nongovernmental organization, led by new AESC chairman Comfort Adams (a professor of electrical engineering), carried the day (AESC 1918).

Adams's main arguments for the establishment of an American standardization organization derived from the powerful Taylorist ideology that emphasized improving economic efficiency, especially through increased labor productivity. At the founding meeting of the AESC, he argued: "the productive capacity of the individual, on the average, is not sufficient to create the wealth he wishes as a return for his labor. We must either face the possibility of a Bolshevik movement in this country or devise some means for increasing the average productivity of labor. This can be done by cooperation and standardization, which go hand in hand" (American Engineering Standards Committee 1919, 70). Indeed, Taylorism had been criticized by Lenin, who had argued that this ideology was nothing more than a "'scientific' system of sweating" more work from laborers (1975). However, it should be pointed out that even in this case, one of the very few in which an ideological argument was used in the standardization realm, the purpose was simply to support the establishment of a new organization, not to promote a more nongovernmental or governmental model.

The lingering tensions between those who supported a more governmental American standardization organization and those supporting a more nongovernmental one were considerably reduced after Le Maistre's visit to the AESC in summer 1919. He was invited to the United States by Adams, who had been a great admirer of the British standardization system. Le Maistre promoted the British nongovernmental standardization model in many other countries, especially those in Commonwealth such as Canada, Australia, New Zealand, and South Africa (McWilliam 2002, 252).

The nongovernmental model was indeed embraced by most countries establishing broad national standardization institutions in the immediate post–World War I era. The decisions in such institutions were adopted by representatives of the many narrower nongovernmental organizations that focused on very specific technical issues. These smaller nongovernmental organizations also funded the national standardization societies. In fact, when they faced financial difficulties, national standardization organizations tended to turn to private corporations rather than to their governments. Lastly, even though government officials were present in some of the founding meetings, once the organizations were established, deliberations were virtually always only among nongovernmental representatives.

GLOBAL GOVERNANCE IN THE TECHNICAL
STANDARDS REALM IN THE INTERWAR ERA

Soon after so many new domestic standardization institutions emerged, Le Maistre became the most active promoter of an international standardization body. In 1925, he organized a conference in Zurich to convince the new national standardization organizations to establish an International Federation of National Standardizing Associations (ISA). Throughout that year, several more international meetings took place to determine the scope and rules of the new organization. From the first negotiations, it became clear that the ISA would be very nongovernmental as it was a collaborative project among nongovernmental national technical standards organizations.

Le Maistre wrote the initial proposal and, as expected, presented an organization that was very similar to the nongovernmental structure of BESA and IEC, the two organizations that he oversaw. His plans for the ISA were as ambitious as those for the other two organizations. Most important, he saw it as a new standards-*setting* authority (Yates and Murphy 2008, 22). The American delegates were the most adamant opponents of this idea, requesting rather that the organization be one of information exchanges about national standards, not one to adopt mandatory standards. Most other countries sided with the United States. The compromise reached was that the ISA would not take on standard-setting in its first years and engage in such activities only "after the new organization had considerable experience" (AESC 1926). Despite this setback, virtually all other important elements from Le Maistre's proposal remained and, in 1926, the ISA become the first international organization to deal with standards from a multitude of technical realms. The ISA was headquartered in Switzerland, with Le Maistre named one of two secretary generals alongside the Swiss Huber-Ruf.

Decision making in the ISA was in the hands of national associations that, with very few exceptions, were nongovernmental. These associations were also responsible for financing the IO. Some government representatives would, however, be present in the ISA's official meetings, thus making the organization at least somewhat intergovernmental on the deliberative dimension. However, as the ISA was even more nongovernmental than the IEC at that time, and as it reflected an expansion of nongovernmentalism across a much broader set of technical standards than what had existed before, I consider the emergence of the ISA to represent a clear shift toward nongovernmentalism on all three dimensions.

Le Maistre's initial high hopes for the ISA were not met. The organization was never considered to have amassed the necessary "considerable experience" to develop its own standards. Its information-sharing system led, according to one official, to "printed bulletins that never became more than a sheet of paper" (Kuert 1997, 15). Perhaps even more important, the United Kingdom and the United States, the two main countries involved in the establishment of the ISA and the ones that were the most adamant supporters of a nongovernmental approach to technical standards both domestically and internationally, never truly participated in the organization because of important differences between their inch systems and the metric ones of virtually all other members. Moreover, the United States did not even join the organization until 1929 because of lingering problems the AESC inherited from divisions it experienced during its establishment (Yates and Murphy 2007, 19). Just a few weeks after the ISA received this important new member, the market crash and the subsequent decline in worldwide trade dampened the enthusiasm for the international cooperation principles at the basis of the ISA and of other interwar IOs.

The strong competition between major economies contributed to the watering down of the ISA's work even before the economic downturn of the 1930s. Tensions between the United Kingdom and the United States in the standardization realm were a reflection of the broader competition between these two powerful economies. While the United Kingdom promoted increasingly common standards across the Commonwealth, the United States sought closer cooperation in standardization with countries from the Western Hemisphere, such as Brazil. The main supporter of American standardization was Herbert Hoover, who served as the third US secretary of commerce from 1921 to 1928.[7] In 1928, when Hoover was running for president, Le Maistre wrote: "The policy of the American government is one of backing business, rather than doing business. The Department of Commerce has tremendous influence throughout the country, and is able to bear a persuasive propaganda, which undoubted plays no small part in Mr. Hoover's campaign" (cited in McWilliam 2002, 204). The more hands-on government approaches to promoting standardization based on national economic interests became stronger in many other powerful states throughout the 1930s.

Despite the problems that led to the ISA's reduced international role during its two decades of existence, it also had a number of successes, such as the adoption of a standard inch–millimeter conversion ratio, a standard for placing sound on motion picture films, and the standard sizing of paper (Coonley 1954). More important, the experiences of the ISA paved the way for the establishment of the International Organization for Standardization (ISO),[8] the principal global governor in this realm after World War II, which has served as the prototype for international standardization work since then (Kuert 1997, 15).

The ISA was not the only important actor in international standardization during the interwar era. Other technical standards IOs that had been in existence for some time, such as the IEC and the International Telegraph

---

[7] It may be worth noting that Hoover was the only US president to have practiced engineering.
[8] The acronym ISO was derived from the Greek "isos," meaning equal. See www.iso.org/about-us.html, accessed April 13, 2019.

Union, continued to flourish. In fact, in 1932, the latter merged with the very intergovernmental International Radiotelegraph Union, thus establishing the International Telecommunication Union (ITU), also a very intergovernmental IO.[9]

Interestingly, as the ITU became more powerful in the second half of the interwar era, it also began shifting toward nongovernmentalism on the decision-making and financial dimensions. The shift was in great part due to the United States taking on a more important role in the IO starting in the 1930s. Before that, even though it had been a member of the organization since 1908, it rarely sent delegations to meetings. In the second half of the interwar era, as the United States began participating in the ITU on a regular basis, it included in its delegation representatives of private corporation alongside its government representatives.[10] As mentioned, starting in 1868, the rules allowed for this practice. However, in time, the United States pushed the ITU even further toward nongovernmentalism by sending delegations that did not include *any* government officials. The most important nongovernmental representatives in US delegations at that time were those from the all-powerful American Telephone and Telegraph Company (AT&T). Indeed, after the government settled its 1913 antitrust challenge of AT&T's growing monopoly in the phone and telegraph industries, the telecommunications giant became more interested in international standards (CCIR 1929, 27). Other countries followed the nongovernmental American model and in the years just prior to World War II, the ITU began giving industry representatives a greater say. Such nongovernmental representatives would sit and often vote in the ITU's technical committees (CCIF 1945). Moreover, the ITU rules were again altered to allow private entities to be the sole representatives of national delegations if governments chose to not be present in meetings (CCIF 1945). By 1938, the US delegation to the ITU was made up only of AT&T representatives. That year, several other delegations were comprised solely of representatives of private companies (CCIF 1938). In contrast, in the 1929 meetings, all ITU delegations had been headed by representatives of national "administrations" (CCIR 1929). The new privileges that private companies had gained in terms of voting were contingent, however, on their contributing financially to the IO (CCIF 1945, 43). In sum, the increased influence of the United States led the ITU to shift in the 1930s toward nongovernmentalism across two dimensions of the continuum, the decision-making and financial ones (while participation in meetings continued to be open both to governmental and nongovernmental representatives). However, overall, the organization remained more intergovernmental than other IOs in the technical standards realm.

---

[9] See www.itu.int/en/history/Pages/RadioConferences.aspx?conf=4.41

[10] The United States continued to be a leader in terms of nongovernmental representation in the ITU. Throughout time, it has included more representatives of private companies in its ITU delegations than any other state (see, e.g., International Telecommunication Union 1964, 6).

Thus, throughout the interwar era, the still fairly intergovernmental ITU co-existed with the more nongovernmental IEC (that remained virtually unchanged throughout that period) and the new, very nongovernmental, ISA. There were no real efforts to bring existing international organizations dealing with technical standards, such as the ITU and IEC, into the ISA or into any other umbrella organization (e.g., IEC 1927). In part, this was due to the fact that all international technical standards organizations became less active and eventually sank into "hibernation" as the global economic depression deepened (IEC 1934).

GLOBAL GOVERNANCE IN THE TECHNICAL STANDARDS REALM DURING AND IMMEDIATELY AFTER WORLD WAR II

The ISA unsuccessfully attempted to continue its activities after World War II began. But by 1941, virtually all of the organization's work had ceased. The IEC, ITU, and other international technical standards organizations similarly stopped functioning around the same time.

Despite the fact that technical standards IOs were inactive during World War II, the conflict appeared to spark even greater interest in standardization at the domestic level. In the late 1930s and early 1940s, many of the national standardization organizations turned to their governments to seek guidance for the war effort. As mentioned, even in countries that had embraced more nongovernmental approaches to standardization, such as the United Kingdom and the United States, there had always been some support for governments playing a role in this realm. For example, in 1919, even though Adams had managed to convince all other members of the emerging AESC to keep the process nongovernmental, there was not sufficient support to include in this new organization a commission to deal with aircraft standards. Instead, AESC members requested that the government take on this issue or, at a minimum, that Congress specify that a nongovernmental standards body should be responsible for such standards (Yates and Murphy 2007, 18).

Of course, the shifts toward government involvement were not just the result of nongovernmental actors' preferences to sometimes limit their own prerogatives. They were also due to government officials often feeling that their intervention would be beneficial. The aforementioned case of Herbert Hoover taking a more hands-on approach to standardization when he was US secretary of commerce in the 1920s is one such example. Another is the attempt of Samuel Stratton, director of the governmental National Bureau of Standards, who tried unsuccessfully to bring the AESC under the control of his agency.[11]

---

[11] The agency was established as part of the US Department of Commerce. See www.nist.gov/node/774226, accessed April 17, 2019.

Not surprising, US governmental efforts to become involved in technical standard-setting became more visible during World War II. Indeed, throughout the war, the National Bureau of Standards became the main actor in national standardization efforts, both in issues that were directly relevant for the war efforts (such as weapons production) and in ones that were indirectly relevant (such as the production of consumer goods) (Cochrane 1966). This shift was at least in part due to the Roosevelt administration taking a more activist approach in all realms, not just in standardization.

Perhaps the most important development in the technical standards realm during World War II did not unfold in the domestic realm but rather internationally. Even though IOs with broad membership, such as ISA and IEC, ceased to function, international standardization collaboration among a handful of allies increased substantially during the war.

An oft-cited example of the need for standards coordination between allies is that the differences between American and British screw threads added about £25 million to the war effort (*The Economist* 1945). By late 1941, American, British, and Canadian officials from both government and nongovernmental standardization bodies began meeting to discuss the formation of a coordination standards committee between their countries. The emergence of the committee reflected the shift toward intergovernmentalism in this realm not only during the war but also in the first few years after it ended. The committee gave governments the main decision-making role. Additionally, it was funded solely by governments. However, experts from outside government circles were part of the deliberations, thus implying that the shift took place across only two of the three dimensions.

Throughout the discussions that led to the establishment of the wartime international forum, it quickly became clear that the leaders of the nongovernmental standardization bodies did not want to permanently hand over control of their work to governments. Even if there was, understandingly, some government involvement in nongovernmental standardization institutions during the war, they felt it should only be temporary. Additionally, the ASA (the successor of the AESC) emphasized that the new international forum, the UN Standards Committee, should not have the authority to set standards; rather, it should simply allow for coordination among national committees. The general international agreement on this point led to the eventual addition of the word "Coordinating" to the title of the organization: the UN Standards Coordinating Committee (UNSCC) (Yates and Murphy 2007, 22).

During the war, government officials accepted all of the nongovernmental actors' conditions. While this may not be surprising in the case of the United States and the United Kingdom, who were the two main drivers of the wartime coordination process in the standards realm, it should be pointed out that other countries involved in the UNSCC, such as Australia, Canada, New Zealand, and even the Soviet Union (which had observer status), also went along with the strong demands of the nongovernmental groups.

The UNSCC set up an office in London and another in New York. During its fairly short history, it did not have time to take on many standards and, overall, did not have a serious impact on the war effort. In fact, it was only in May 1945 that the organization actually decided on which standardization projects to take on.

The main role of the UNSCC in the global standardization movement came, however, from the fact that it sparked even more intense international cooperation in technical standard-setting. As the organization had been set up with only a temporary (two-year) status, its members quickly decided to find ways to continue the work of the UNSCC in times of peace, though they did realize that if they built a new organization on the UNSCC's structure, they would leave out (at least in the short term) the countries that had fought on the other side of the war. However, if they built the new organization around the ISA, they would embrace an organization where nonmetric countries such as the United Kingdom and the United States had played (and were expected to play) a small role (*The Economist* 1945). In the end, they decided to create a completely new organization, the International Organization for Standardization. There was a general agreement that the new ISO would continue the very nongovernmental practices of the ISA.

In sum, it is important to point out that during the war, global governance in technical standards experienced a more intergovernmental approach, contrary to expectations based on the existing literature (e.g., Shanks et al. 1996). Similarly, the quick reversal to nongovernmentalism immediately after the war was unexpected, at least if one considers only existing system-level arguments. Moreover, unlike the immediate post–World War I era, where the League sought to absorb some technical standards IOs, there were no similar attempts to have the new UN control the work of organizations such as the ISO or IEC.

Representatives from eleven victorious Allied states met in New York in October 1945 to create the ISO. A second meeting (often referred to as "unofficial") followed in Paris in July 1946 (UNSCC 1946a). The agenda for the New York conference was prepared by representatives from domestic standardization organizations from the United States, the United Kingdom, and Canada. Throughout the entire ISO founding process, many other states (such as the Nordic countries, France, the Netherlands, Switzerland, and the Soviet Union) offered proposals and counterproposals for the new organization. At one point, in fact, there were three draft-proposals for the IO's constitution, one backed by the United States, the United Kingdom, and Canada; one by France; and one by the Switzerland and the Nordic countries (UNSCC 1946b).

The "executive committee" (made up of American, British, and Canadian representatives) started by laying down three "foundation values" for the new organization. The first called for the organization to be composed solely of "national standardization bodies" (UNSCC 1945). Interestingly, most of the debates surrounding this point did not refer to the nongovernmental versus governmental nature of such national bodies, as all representatives in the New York meeting came from nongovernmental structures and appeared to assume that the new organization would reflect their domestic institutions. In fact, the first draft of the new IO's constitution called the organization The International Standards Coordinating *Association* (emphasis added). The word "Association," which had also been used in the name of the ISA, was considered at that time, as today, to generally refer to nongovernmental entities.

The main debates on this first point focused on the question of whether states that did not yet have *national* standardization bodies nevertheless could be represented in the *international* organization in some form (most often by their governments). Although the American delegation pushed for the adoption of such a practice (similar to the one already in place in the IEC), the British and French representatives opposed it. Yates and Murphy suggest that one possible reason for this opposition was that these two great powers sought to maintain control over the domestic and international affairs of their colonies (2007, 26, fn 80). Those supporting a more exclusive IO won out.

The second "value" proposed was that the new organization should deal with only the coordination of standards rather than their establishment. On this issue, the most adamant supporters of the less intrusive organization were the American and British representatives. Although not present in New York, the Soviet and Chinese delegations were later the most supportive of an organization that would develop mandatory standards for members. The division on this particular issue was especially relevant considering that the Soviet and even the Chinese representatives came from governmental or at least quasi-governmental domestic structures rather than from truly nongovernmental ones (UNSCC 1946a).

Despite British and American opposition to an international organization that would *adopt* standards, the majority of states present at the ISO's founding conferences were eventually able to stipulate that the standards would indeed become mandatory if all members of the organization agreed. Later, this rule was altered to allow for such mandatory standards when no member *specifically vetoed* a proposal. This subtle shift from coordination of domestic standards in the ISA and the UNSCC to the adoption of international standards in the new ISO was reflected in the eventual decision to drop the word "Coordination" from the title of the new IO.

The third proposed "value" called for the formation of technical committees. This proposal appeared to be the least controversial and was swiftly accepted by all representatives present at the ISO's establishment. This decision opened the door for some of the narrower and older technical standards organizations to become part of the new ISO, and implicitly to develop a similar set of rules for their work. The IEC, the most active and significant international body to deal with technical standards before World War II, decided at its first postwar meeting (in 1946) to "affiliate" itself with the ISO but simultaneously emphasized that it was to maintain its independence (IEC 1946). Such quasi-independence became common for most technical committees and organizations affiliated with the ISO when it came to decisions on standards. However, in terms of their budgets and even decision-making rules, they all virtually came under the ISO's wing and thus accepted the broader IO's initially very nongovernmental character (Coonley 1954, 40). Their affiliation with the ISO led them to be affected by that organization's subsequent back-and-forth shifts along the intergovernmental–nongovernmental continuum.

The apparent overall general agreement among those present in New York was short-lived. Differences surfaced at the 1946 Paris meeting, which had been intended primarily to help deal with the question of the ISA. While the United States and the United Kingdom, two countries that had stayed out of the ISA, wanted to simply dismantle the old organization and allow the new ISO to take on its work, a number of fairly vociferous representatives from smaller states, all very active members of the ISA, felt that the process was rushed and did not give the necessary attention to the work the interwar organization had completed (UNSCC 1946a).

Those from the Nordic countries and the Swiss, who had not been represented in New York, declared that the first draft of the ISO constitution was simply unacceptable. While primarily opposed to the unceremonious way in which the ISA was being dismantled as well as to the lack of recognition for the work of Secretary-General Huber-Ruff, they also voiced other concerns. Perhaps most important, these countries argued against the decision to give the permanent members of the UN Security Council permanent seats on the ISO council. This proposal was based on the fact that the five most powerful members had been given permanent seats or other advantages in many other IOs that emerged immediately after the war (UNSCC 1946a, 2–3; 1946c, 14). The debates in Paris led to a compromise through which such permanent seats would be held for only the first five years of the ISO and then be eliminated.

It should not be very surprising that the new organization involved permanent seats for the great powers. At that time, most IOs that were being established were shaped by the same type of power politics that had been behind the founding of the UN. After all, even the UNSCC that the ISO was replacing had been very intergovernmental and driven by great power interests. Moreover, its very name (that included the term "United Nations") gave rise to the false impression that it was yet another IO affiliated with the UN.

The smaller countries also requested greater equality when it came to the funding of the organization. Previous IOs either had made all member-states equally responsible for funding the budget or had found schemes requiring wealthier states or ones that were expected to use the organization more often to pay larger shares. The New York proposal sought to give great powers a disproportionate advantage in controlling the budget. This decision was intended to be used later by the same great powers to request a "veto" in ISO decisions. In the end, this issue also led to a compromise. It was decided that half of the IO's budget would come from contributions based on a country's international trade, one quarter from contributions based on population, and one quarter from equal contributions (UNSCC 1946d).

The Paris meeting led to some additional changes. The official name of the organization was altered yet again to the International Standards Association. Additionally, for the first time, the Paris draft of the IO's constitution stipulated that the organization may provide "international standards" when "no national standardizing body dissents" (UNSCC 1946c).

It is also noteworthy that the Paris conference specifically discussed whether only "recognized states" could be part of the IO. As the process of recognition was an intergovernmental one, this implied that membership in the new organization was based not only on nongovernmental decisions and processes (1946a).

At a third and final meeting in London in October 1946, the pendulum swung back toward intergovernmentalism as representatives from Czechoslovakia, seconded by France and the Soviet Union, proposed to go back to the term "Organization" rather than "Association." Interestingly, even in such debates, the arguments used to support one title or another for the IO were not ideological in nature. Instead, they argued that the term "Organization" was preferable because by that point the word "was being increasingly used in the titles of International Bodies such as UNESCO" (UNSCC 1946d, 11). Despite efforts by the Americans, Norwegians, and Danes to revert to the word "Association," those favoring a more intergovernmental approach to standardization garnered the necessary majority to adopt the International Organization for Standardization title. In sum, although the rules and procedures of the new organization were very similar to the ones of the ISA, thus making it almost as nongovernmental as its interwar predecessor, there was nevertheless a small shift toward intergovernmentalism, at least in name. What is important for the present study, however, is that in terms of the actual change experienced by the global governance of technical standards, the shift that took place in the immediate post–World War II era was clearly toward nongovernmentalism, as the ISO took away the important decision-making and financial roles governments had held in the wartime UNSCC. There was no shift on the deliberative dimension, as representatives of nongovernmental groups as well as government officials participated in the IO's meetings.

The immediate post–World War II era also saw a push toward intergovernmentalism initiated by some of the new intergovernmental IOs. For example, as early as June 1946, even before the ISO was formally established, UNESCO contacted Le Maistre, seeking formal ties with the new organization and offering its "recognition" in exchange for an annual report it would receive from the ISO. UNESCO even suggested at that time that it could support some future ISO work financially (UNESCO 1946).

This initiative did not have any real effects for some time. However, starting in the 1960s, the initial apparently innocuous agreement between the two organizations eventually opened the door to having ISO programs funded by UNESCO and allowing the latter organization's representatives to take part in the former's meetings. In time, other very intergovernmental organizations such as the UN Industrial Development Organization (UNIDO) and the ILO also participated in ISO deliberations and in some cases even in financing the standardization organization's work.

GLOBAL GOVERNANCE IN THE TECHNICAL
STANDARDS REALM DURING THE COLD WAR

Despite the relative agreement behind the establishment of the very nongovernmental ISO as the principal global technical standards governor immediately after World War II, the Cold War saw a number of clashes regarding the preferred way of dealing with international standardization. One primary disagreement, as should be expected, was between the Western and Eastern Cold War blocs and unfolded primarily from the end of World War II to the early 1970s. A second disagreement unfolded between the United States and Western European states and appeared to have two "rounds," the first in the 1960s and a second in the late 1980s.

The East–West tensions of the Cold War quickly became apparent even in the international technical standards realm. The United Kingdom and the United States, which had been behind the establishment of the IEC and ISA, were also the motors of the process leading to the establishment of the ISO as a very nongovernmental IO. The Soviet Union, which embraced a very governmental approach to technical standards domestically, also became interested and involved in the establishment of the IO. Although the Soviet Union did not take part in the initial UNSCC meeting in New York, it joined the other states at the Paris and London meetings.

Its interest in the work of the new organization was reflected in its strong demands that Russian become an official language of the ISO. The Soviet delegation was also the most outspoken proponent of giving powerful countries permanent seats on the ISO Council (UNSCC 1946a; IEC 1947). Most important for the present study, the Soviet Union and some of its Eastern European allies began demanding a much "stronger" ISO as early as their first participation in debates, at the July 1946 meeting in Paris. By "stronger," they specifically meant that ISO decisions should become mandatory for states (UNSCC 1946a, 7–8), arguing that some standards are too important to simply remain voluntary and therefore require government action.

In response to Soviet demands, an American delegate pointed out that the nongovernmental nature of the organization precluded it from adopting mandatory standards. He offered the example of some standards related to questions of illumination that, although relevant for airplane safety, the nongovernmental illumination IO could not impose on states. Such standards became mandatory only once they were taken on by the intergovernmental International Commission for Air Navigation (UNSCC 1946a, 9).

Lastly, during the Paris meetings, the Soviets also requested that only national standards organizations "recognized by official law" should be allowed to take part in the ISO's work (UNSCC 1946a, 8). Such a proposed legal process of recognition implied that government institutions would be responsible for selecting the organizations involved in international standardization. The British delegation opposed this proposal, arguing that in the United Kingdom and most other states there was no legislation identifying "official" national standards-setting bodies. These exchanges were only the first of the Cold War where the more governmental Soviet approach to standardization clashed with the more nongovernmental Western one. During the Paris and London meetings that set up the ISO, the Soviets had very few allies and therefore lost most battles for a more intergovernmental organization.

As relations between the two future sides of the Cold War were still relatively amiable when the ISO was founded in 1946, the American delegation eventually supported the Soviet demand to introduce Russian as an official language for the new organization's work as long as the USSR would cover the costs for translation to and from the language. This apparent token of good will, as well as the recognition that the Soviet Union did not have much support for its other more important proposals for changing the ISO, led to its delegation eventually accepting the very nongovernmental approach to the organization.

Throughout the Cold War, the Soviet Union and its allies continued to seek ways of pushing the ISO closer to their own models of governmental standard-setting. The open disagreements on this question were primarily between national delegations, not between the government officials and representatives of nongovernmental groups within states (as was the case in the ILO, discussed in the previous chapter). It should also be pointed out that such initial disagreements were not laden with ideological undertones as similar East–West debates were in some other IOs. Instead, both sides preferred using pragmatic arguments, suggesting that their solution was simply more effective (e.g., ISO 1952).

By the 1960s, the divisions between the East and West also began focusing on the funding of the organization. As the ISO budget was creeping up, Eastern European states suggested that governments (not just the national standardization organizations) be allowed to contribute financially to the organization. The proposal was also supported by the few developing countries that participated in the ISO's work at that time, explaining that their nongovernmental national standardization bodies did not have the necessary resources to contribute to the increasing work of the organization. The American delegation was able to gather sufficient support to defeat the proposal for (partial) government funding of the ISO (ISO 1967).

In time, much of the ISO's budget, as well as that of the national nongovernmental standardization organizations, began being funded from private sources. While most of the organization's funding continues to come from national member organizations (both from the more governmental ones and from the more nongovernmental ones), almost half of the budget is currently based on sales of its documents. Moreover, many of the participants in the work of the technical committees are paid by the private companies that appoint them.

By the late 1960s, more developing countries with very governmental standardization systems joined the ISO. This led to the organization becoming increasingly intergovernmental in nature on the decision-making and financial dimensions. Taking into account the greater role of governments in its work, ISO leadership began recommending in 1970 that member-countries "strengthen cooperation *between governments* in the field of standardization policy and, on a national basis, to offer better coordination of their standards with international standards and stronger support to national standardization bodies" (ISO 1970; emphasis added). In 1973, the Bulgarian delegate to the ISO General Assembly openly requested that the organization be transformed into a formal intergovernmental organization (ISO 1973). Such official changes (whether to financing, proposed in 1967, or to decision making, proposed in 1973) never took place, suggesting that the Soviet Bloc's attempts to shift global governance toward intergovernmentalism were not successful.

Despite continued Western opposition to making the ISO a formal intergovernmental organization, by the late 1970s, the IO nevertheless appeared to accept the new reality. The 1979 ISO annual report pointed out that governments were increasingly becoming interested in standards and that a shift away from purely nongovernmental national standardization bodies to "mixed" nongovernmental-governmental national committees had occurred (ISO 1979, 16). In 1980, the ISO secretary-general declared that more than half of the national standardization organizations represented in the ISO were in fact governmental ones, thus implying that the organization de facto had become more intergovernmental than nongovernmental (Sturen 1980). Although this change to the ISO's character was not a formal one, it was nevertheless significant, both on the decision-making dimension and the financial one, as the majority of national delegations contributing to the ISO's budget were governmental in nature. There was no change on the deliberative dimension, as both government and nongovernmental representatives continued to take part in ISO meetings.

The second important clash relevant to the intergovernmental versus nongovernmental nature of the ISO took place between the developed Western European countries and the United States. As mentioned, even during the interwar era, powerful countries had competed with each other in the international standardization realm, seeking individual economic advantages. As European integration began to advance throughout the 1960s, the European Commission sought to develop its own technical standards, especially in the automobile industry, where these countries were falling behind Japanese auto-makers (Bousquet et al. 2008). The Commission pushed for more common technical standards among European Community (EC) members. The tensions between the various national economic interests led to a cumbersome intergovernmental standard-setting process in the EC that was eventually deemed a failure, even by the European Commission (Micklitz 1998, 574). As this change took place only at the European level and not at the global level, I do not consider it a shift in *global* governance. It is nevertheless important because it triggered a change at the global level. Indeed, even though the EC efforts failed to produce the kind of standards that would have helped the European markets, the United States decided to counter any possible future European initiatives by moving the discussions on international standards to the General Agreement on Tariffs and Trade (GATT), where it was more likely to influence outcomes than in the EC (Murphy and Yates 2010, 93).

Throughout the 1970s, the GATT Tokyo Round negotiations led to the adoption of the Agreement on Technical Barriers to Trade. This agreement promoted the use of common standards as a way to avoid the usual technical barriers to trade and, by doing so, spurred the need to develop even further technical standards through global organizations such as the ISO and IEC (not in GATT) (Middleton 1980). By the 1980s, GATT acknowledged the central role of the ISO in the technical standards realm (ISO 1988, 61). This change led to a shift toward nongovernmentalism in decision making, as it is a case of a very intergovernmental institution (GATT) deciding to give the decision-making role in the technical standards realm to the much more nongovern-mental organizations (ISO and IEC). This decision, however, did not alter the nature of financing and deliberations in global technical standards governance.

The decision to have GATT accept standards adopted by the more nongov-ernmental ISO and IEC (as well as the decision to shift standard-setting deci-sions from European to global organizations) was supported by the United States. In fact, it would have been very difficult for the United States to allow an intergovernmental body to develop standards for GATT because its own domestic standard-setting institutions were primarily nongovernmental. It would have had to deal with the complex problem of integrating representa-tives of such nongovernmental structures in global intergovernmental ones.

Another relevant development that altered the nature of global governance in the technical standards realm throughout the Cold War was that a number of international organizations with strong intergovernmental character that did not deal with standardization issues began working more closely with the ISO. As mentioned, the pressure for the ISO to work with organizations from the UN system had been present almost since its inception (ISO 1997b, 28). By 1967, the UN began paying greater attention to the ISO and recognized it as a "specialized organization for standardization" (ISO 1967, 36).

In 1969, UNESCO, which had reached out to the ISO even as the orga-nization was being established in 1946, eventually granted the organization consultative and associate status in its category A, the closest form of liaison for UNESCO with a nongovernmental organization. That same year, UNIDO also granted ISO consultative status. UNIDO used this relationship to call on the opinions and expertise of the ISO in their technical assistance program on standardization. In 1970, the two organizations set up regional workshops in Addis Ababa and Cairo for training personnel involved in standardization. The relationship between the ISO and the many very intergovernmental organizations implied that officials from such IOs could take part in ISO meetings, thus shifting the nature of the organization toward intergovernmentalism on the deliberative dimension.

Perhaps more important for the changes in global governance of technical standards during the Cold War era were the decisions by a number of very intergovernmental organizations to take on work in the area of technical standardization. Such changes took place while some of the more intergovernmental organizations that had dealt with technical standards even before World War II continued their work. The ITU, for example, remained fairly intergovernmental in nature throughout the first half of the Cold War. For private actors such as firms or technical standards experts to take part in ITU work, they now needed to be part of a national delegation appointed by a government. Moreover, none of the new important telecommunications multinational corporations could be represented, as they did not formally belong to any one single state (Mattli 2003, 222). In the 1980s, although Western states sought to open the ITU to more nongovernmental actors, developing countries opposed such changes, feeling that any increase in the power of private firms and standardization experts would lead to a decline in their own influence in the organization (Mattli 2003).

One significant IO that began its standardization work during the Cold War is the UN Economic Commission for Europe (UNECE). Although the UNECE has conducted standardization work in multiple technical realms, its main contribution has been in automobile safety. As one of five regional commissions of the UN established in 1947 to promote economic cooperation in Europe, UNECE struggled during the Cold War to find collaborative projects that would be acceptable to both the Western and Eastern parts of this divided continent. Its main goals were in fact extensions of the immediate postwar priorities of the UN Relief and Rehabilitation Administration (UNRRA), such as rebuilding the European infrastructure, especially in the realm of transport and energy. Most important for the issue of standardization was the founding at that time of the European Central Inland Transport Organization (ECITO), later transformed into the Inland Transport Committee (ITC) of UNECE. The ECITO and later ITC were primarily intended to deal with the problems of bottlenecks in the national and international traffic flows, taking on issues related to traffic safety and customs arrangements. For that reason, when the UN held its 1949 Conference on Road and Motor Transport, it turned to the UNECE (and ECITO) to draw up a global Convention on Road

Traffic and a Protocol on Road Signs and Signals (Berthelot and Raymont 2007, 34). Over the past seven decades, the UNECE has managed to maintain its monopoly over the important issue-area of transportation safety standards among all international organizations and to continue adding to its broad set of standard-setting tasks in this realm.

Another important organization that became involved in technical standards during the Cold War was the World Health Organization. Starting in 1953, the WHO began adopting pharmacology standards (WHO 1956). It is interesting to note, however, that the organization hesitated for a while to deal with other types of standards. For example, when the question of "biological standardization" came up in the mid-1950s, the WHO preferred to have the highly nongovernmental International Association of Biological Standardization (currently the International Alliance for Biological Standardization), take on this issue. The WHO established relations with this organization in the late 1950s[12] but did not become directly involved in biological standardization work until the late 1980s (WHO 1988). Even then, most of this work as well as the work in the pharmacology standards realm, was done by nongovernmental organizations working with the WHO and by individual experts from outside of the IO's structures.

Perhaps the most important role played by the WHO in the technical standards realm developed through its work with the Food and Agricultural Organization (FAO) as part of the Codex Alimentarius, a very intergovernmental standards body established in 1962. While both the WHO and FAO had dealt with some food standards even in the 1950s (WHO 1994), by joining forces they felt that their work would advance substantially (FAO 1963, 6).

The intergovernmental nature of the Codex Alimentarius was taken as a given from the start. This was the case even though it was recognized that many members of the FAO and WHO did not yet have domestic government institutions to implement Codex standards. In fact even today, Codex officials consider that one of the greatest problems faced by their organization is the difficulty that states often have implementing the international standards they adopt.[13]

WHO and FAO officials accepted early on that some standards in the food safety realm could be *initiated* by nongovernmental entities, including the ISO (FAO 1962). Moreover, in the Codex Alimentarius, much of the work has been conducted by experts coming from outside government circles (Codex Alimentarius 1986, 4). However, despite the presence of such nongovernmental actors in the organization, the institution has remained very intergovernmental. Its funding has come solely from governments.[14] All of its decisions are sent to member-states for ratification and implementation.

---

[12] See www.iabs.org/index.php/who, accessed April 17, 2019.

[13] Personal interview with WHO official involved in Codex Alimentarius, June 6, 2016.

[14] In fact, in its first few decades, such funding was provided solely by developed countries. See, e.g., WHO (1966, 1).

Even its relations with more nongovernmental international standards organizations are tepid. For instance, it was only in 1985 that the ISO and Codex developed official relations and the former organization began publishing standards adopted by the latter (FAO 1985).

In sum, although throughout the Cold War the fairly nongovernmental ISO has dealt with the vast majority of technical standards, a handful of much more intergovernmental IOs such as the FAO, UNECE, and WHO carved out their own niches in such work, especially in the 1960s and to some degree in the 1970s. This process has contributed to the overall shift toward intergovernmentalism in this realm across all three dimensions. Moreover, the emergence of these new very intergovernmental actors in the technical standards realm led to the more nongovernmental ISO and IEC having to work more closely together with the new organizations and, at a minimum, allow their representatives to attend many of their meetings. By 1979, twenty-five organizations that were formally intergovernmental in nature attended the ISO's General Assembly (ISO 1979). This compares to 1967, when only one such organization attended the ISO General Assembly (ISO 1967).

The spread of intergovernmental global governors in the 1960s in the international technical standards realm seems to run counter to expectations that as organizational density increases (as was the case in the first two decades of the Cold War) more nongovernmental rather than intergovernmental organizations flourish due to their more flexible nature (Abbott et al. 2016). However, it should be noted that the types of standards that were pursued by very intergovernmental organizations, such as those in the realm of health, traffic, or food safety, were the kinds that had already required government input at the state level in many countries. One can therefore consider that this intergovernmental shift was triggered by the emergence of many new domestic government institutions in such narrow issue-areas pushing for more international coordination, as H_2 suggests.

The initiatives to have all these very intergovernmental organizations take on technical standards belonged primarily to IO officials seeking to expand their work in this increasingly crowded realm. Additionally, the decision to not deal with all technical standards within one IO but rather have multiple such institutions working on different types of standards was primarily promoted by the United States (ISO 1958, 14). Its support for a competition-driven approach was most visible in the telecommunications realm (Krasner 1991). The Soviets, as mentioned earlier, were the ones who promoted the idea of having a stronger ISO that would take on the narrower work of other standardization organizations. The proposal to shift the global governance system toward greater nongovernmentalism (by bringing some of the intergovernmental technical standards work under the umbrella of the ISO) may appear to be unexpected coming from a statist Soviet Union. However, in fact it is not surprising considering that throughout the Cold War in the USSR, and in many other states, standardization was in the hands of government entities, and implicitly such countries had their interests represented by government officials in the ISO. Therefore, bringing all international standardization processes in one increasingly intergovernmental IO was in line with Soviet activist preferences for centralization of tasks.

As expected, the Soviet view of having all standards dealt with in the ISO was supported by the organization's secretariat. In his speech to the 1955 ISO General Assembly, Hilding Törnebohm, then president of the ISO, argued:

Since international standardization is pursued outside the regular ISO activities, we might ask: was it necessary to organize ISO and, prior, to that, ISA, when standardization work was being carried on anyway? I can easily answer that question. Naturally, it was desirable to establish an international organization for each individual matter. Theoretically, each of the ISO's Technical Committees could work quite independently of the others. However, I am sure that no explanations are required for you to understand that it would be quite inadvisable to have an organization of this type. Very often the commissions of the Technical Committees are intimately related. A closely allied organization appears to be the most suitable, not to say imperative. (ISO 1955, 14)

A last important attempt to change the global governance of technical standards during the Cold War involved the emergence and eventual inclusion of consumer groups in both the deliberations and decision making of IOs. This development is relevant because it reflects the participation of representatives of a much broader nongovernmental category of actors in international standardization decisions than simply those of experts and producers.

Although most significant changes with regard to nongovernmental consumer groups took place in the post–Cold War era and therefore will be discussed in greater detail below, it should be mentioned that the ISO sought as early as the 1960s to include in its work some representatives of such groups. At that time, a special panel was set up to discuss how the ISO could best deal with consumer safety standards, consumer information, and participation of consumers in the standard-setting process. In 1970, the panel reported its recommendation to the ISO General Assembly. Interestingly, within that panel it was the technical director of the Consumers Union of the United States who called for international government intervention to secure safety standards. He explained that in the United States, real safety standards had been put in place only through government intervention and that, unfortunately, mandatory legislation had been adopted only "after some tragedy had occurred" (ISO 1970, 25). However, other members of the panel disagreed with the American view, and argued that mandatory legislation was not necessary to protect consumers and that private organizations could resolve questions of consumer safety without having governments intervene in the process (ISO 1970, 26–27).

The ISO standardization experts did not look kindly on the addition of a new type of actor in the standard-setting process within their organization. Some objected that it would be difficult to find consumer representatives with enough technical knowledge to participate in such a process and that technical experts had so far done a good job developing standards that took into account consumer needs. Others pointed to the high costs involved in implementing safety standards in developing countries. Yet others cautioned against certification systems involved in consumer safety standards that could "become barriers to trade, thus reducing the consumer's choice" (ISO 1970, 28). More important, the American representative to the ISO disagreed with his conational, arguing that the latter's perspective "was unnecessarily and improperly designed to downgrade the good faith and ability of the private standards bodies in [the] USA" and that "those bodies were fully capable of dealing effectively with standardization problems, and in particular of evolving standards for product safety and if necessary making them compulsory" (ISO 1970, 28).

The organization's reticence to include a new type of nongovernmental actor in its work led to a delay of eight more years before it established a formal body that would give consumers a say in its work. Eventually, in 1978, the ISO Committee on Consumer Policy (COPOLCO) was established (ISO 1979). Its self-proclaimed goals have been to help consumers benefit from standardization, provide information to consumer groups, advise the ISO on consumers' needs, and (lastly) make recommendations on standardization work.[15] Despite the formal establishment of the body, in the first decade of COPOLCO's existence, the ISO hardly engaged with consumer groups. Technical experts' opposition to consumer participation in ISO meetings was reflected in the 1979 General Assembly debates where the only comments made after the first COPOLCO report were negative. One representative pointed out that there had been some difficulty with the definition of "consumer" and implicitly with the representation of such consumers. Another requested that when consumer representatives attend meetings "they should be given thorough briefing on the technical realities behind standardization and the procedures of standards bodies, so as to enable them to make a realistic, informed and appropriate contribution to the discussions" (ISO 1979, 21).

The debate over COPOLCO unfolded across national lines. The effort to shift the ISO toward greater nongovernmentalism by empowering consumer groups was primarily promoted by the United States, a country that had a history of domestic institutions allowing consumers to have a say in standardization matters. The opposition from developing countries and even from some developed ones, such as France (ISO 1970, 25), initially led to a weak COPOLCO and, implicitly, no real shift toward nongovernmentalism in the ISO.

Consumer issues appeared to remain relatively dormant in the ISO throughout the rest of the Cold War. This fact was emphasized in the 1985 General Assembly, when the American representative complained that the ISO did not take on consumer-friendly programs and offered as examples a number of such programs that had been developed in the United States, especially through the

---

[15] See https://isotc.iso.org/livelink/livelink/fetch/-8925727/8925750/16474221/A_%2D_ISO_COMMITTEE_ON_CONSUMER_POLICY_at_a_glance.pdf?nodeid=19812790& vernum=-2, accessed April 17, 2019.

private sector (ISO 1985, 75). It is worth noting that, other than this intervention and the fairly brief formal yearly reports from COPOLCO, the ISO did not take up the question of consumers in a more substantial way until after the Cold War. For these reasons, I do not consider the formal establishment of COPOLCO in 1978 as a successful change. As I note below, the actual shift toward nongovernmentalism came around 2000, when COPOLCO became truly active and representative of nongovernmental consumer groups.

GLOBAL GOVERNANCE IN THE TECHNICAL STANDARDS
REALM IN THE POST–COLD WAR ERA

Some of the most important post–Cold War changes in the global governance of technical standards were triggered by events of the Cold War. Perhaps the most significant such change was initiated in European institutions in the late 1980s after the European Commission acknowledged in 1985 that its very intergovernmental standard-setting process was deeply flawed and called for a "new approach" to such tasks (Commission of the European Communities 1985). This new approach meant that while the Commission was to continue dealing with standards that were relevant for the environment, safety, consumer protection, and health, the other standards (a vast majority) would be adopted in the more nongovernmental European Committee for Standardization (CEN), established in 1961. The European Community member-states took on the obligation to accept the standards of the CEN and of other nongovernmental European standardization bodies. While this shift toward nongovernmentalism appears to have affected only European standardization, I will show that, just as in the case of the aforementioned intergovernmental shift at the European level in the 1960s, the nongovernmental changes in the 1980s eventually impacted the *global* governance of technical standards.

The arguments used to support the decision to have the EC accept CEN standards were presented in terms of the practical advantages that they brought to standardization, not in ideological terms. Indeed, the EC standardization process had proven to be very slow, especially at a time when important technologies were advancing quickly and European states appeared to be falling behind their competitors. EC members felt that the nongovernmental approach would be more efficient.

The understanding that international nongovernmental standardization bodies were more efficient was significantly based on the example of the ISO, which had been moving quickly in developing technical standards in the early 1980s. Figure 5.1 shows that by 1985, the global standardization organization was adopting about 600 new standards each year, twice as many as in 1979.[16]

---

[16] Based on data provided by the ISO central secretariat in personal correspondence on February 7, 2019.

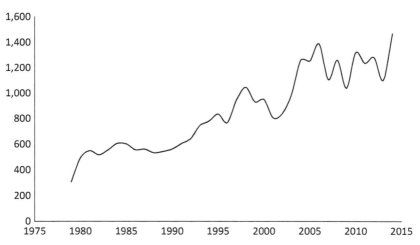

FIGURE 5.1. Number of standards adopted annually by the ISO.

The 1985 shift toward the "privatization of standards governance" in Europe (Mattli 2003, 211) had the desired effect, increasing the speed of standardization. While in 1986 European standards organizations[17] established fewer than 50 new standards, by 1991 they were developing more than 400 new standards annually and by 1996, ten years after the shift toward nongovernmentalism, they reached almost 2,000 new standards a year (Mattli and Buthe 2003, 3). By that point, European technical standardization was outpacing that of the ISO. Indeed, as Figure 5.1 shows, during that same 1986–1996 period, the number of new ISO standards had only increased from about 600 to 800.[18] Because of this, by the mid-1990s Europeans were considered to have taken on the role of "first movers" as the ISO began accepting many ready-made CEN standards (Mattli 2003, 213). At that point, the United States felt it was losing its ability to influence global technical standard-setting. It therefore tried to level the playing field in the increasingly competitive, technology-driven global economy by having the ISO once more become the main global governor.

One important way the United States felt it could accomplish this was by pushing the ISO toward even greater nongovernmentalism. After all, compared to the CEN, the ISO had many more member-states that were represented by government officials rather than by private actors. In a competitive environment and at times of high levels of organizational density, as in 1980s and 1990s, one indeed expects nongovernmental actors to be more

---

[17] The numbers refer to the total output of standards of both CEN and CENELEC, CEN's sister electrotechnical standardization organization.
[18] If we also include IEC standards, the total number of new global standards increased at about the same pace, from approximately 800 to 1,200. See Buthe and Mattli (2003, 3).

flexible and efficient than intergovernmental ones, such as the EC (Abbott et al. 2016). Moreover, by the mid-1990s as many countries had moved away from the more statist Soviet domestic model of standardization, the ISO could now shift toward greater nongovernmentalism. Indeed, as countries that transitioned to democracy after the end of the Cold War embraced more nongovernmental domestic systems of standardization, the ISO shifted toward greater nongovernmentalism on all three dimensions of the intergovernmental–nongovernmental continuum.

Another factor contributing to the speed with which global standards were being adopted in the post–Cold War era was the increasingly interconnected global economy. The emergence of the World Trade Organization (WTO) in 1995 reflected, in part, the need to deal with a number of nontariff barriers to trade after its predecessor, the GATT, had reduced tariffs worldwide to an all-time low. Among the nontariff barriers that were at the center of the 1986–1994 Uruguay round of negotiations were the technical ones. By some calculations, about 80 percent of all global trade is affected by some form of technical standardization (OECD 1999). The WTO emerged with a clear mandate to deal with such barriers. Rather than becoming directly involved in drafting technical standards, the WTO decided to adopt the standards established by global organizations such as the ISO and IEC, just as GATT had (e.g., WHO 1994, 23; Smythe 2009, 95). This initiative was primarily promoted by the United States as yet another way to increase the importance of global standards-setting IOs where it could influence outcomes, rather than in European ones where it could not.

The WTO's decision to cede an important part of its decisions to nongovernmental entities can be understood as a shift on the decision-making dimension, similar to the one that unfolded in the 1980s when GATT also accepted ISO and IEC standards.[19] Moreover, the collaboration between these organizations implies that representatives of the more nongovernmental ISO and IEC had access to the deliberations of the more intergovernmental WTO. It also implies that WTO officials could now be present for some ISO and IEC deliberations (Smythe 2009, 96). Overall, therefore, I do not consider that the WTO's involvement in technical standards led to any real shift on the deliberative dimension of the continuum. Also, the financing of international standard-setting did not change at that time.

In Europe, the new nongovernmental approach to standardization proved to be so promising that by 1995, the European Commission announced it would even extend this model of standard-setting to realms that had traditionally been seen as the monopoly (or near-monopoly) of governments: biotechnology, environmental policy, and telecommunications. By 2000, some food safety

---

[19] While there are some very intergovernmental IOs (such as the Codex Alimentarius) among those from which the WTO accepts standards, the majority of them, and the most significant ones such as the ISO and the IES, are very nongovernmental.

standards and even standards from the defense realm were dealt with through the new European nongovernmental approach (CEN 2000).

The ISO – which had been increasingly attentive to developments in its quasi-rival, CEN – also started taking on social issues that previously had been dealt with only through government and intergovernmental institutions. The first demands for the organization to deal with such issues had emerged as early as the 1970s. At that time, a number of governmental and nongovernmental organizations, especially from the developing world, sought to establish a set of codes of conduct for companies that functioned internationally. The codes would deal with issue of marketing, labor standards, and relations with host governments (Murphy and Yates 2010, 82–83). While those early efforts did not produce any results, by the late 1980s and early 1990s, the ISO began considering a number of standards with important social implications. In 1987, it adopted the first standard in the ISO 9000 family, for "quality management systems." This initiative was primarily promoted by the United Kingdom and the United States to develop common government procurement standards (Seddon 2000). In 1992, the British Standards Institution was the first national standardization organization to adopt environmental management standards. In 1993, the ISO 14000 standards series also took on environmental management issues following the British model (Clements 1996).

Also in the 1990s, a number of nongovernmental entities, such as Clean Clothes Campaign and Rugmark, established a set of narrow corporate responsibility standards (Nadvi and Frank 2004). In 2000, the UN decided to promote a Global Compact through which companies could sign on to accept a series of human rights and environmental standards. That same year, major companies pushed for the adoption of the Social Accountability (SA) 8000 standards that focus primarily on employees' working conditions.[20] By 2004, an ISO report called for the establishment of the ISO 26000 standards to deal with companies' social responsibility (Tamm Hallström 2008). In 2008, the ISO took on standards for health care, the traditional "turf" of the very intergovernmental WHO.[21]

Of course, the simple inclusion of social issues (that are difficult to consider truly "technical" in nature) in the purview of the ISO is not directly relevant to the focus of this study. However, it is important to mention this process because it led to consumer groups pushing even harder for a role in international standard-setting now that the ISO and CEN had taken on standards with greater societal effects. In the ISO, as discussed earlier, COPOLCO had been established in the second half of the Cold War era to allow for some consumer input in the standard-setting process. Standards experts, however, did not look kindly on introducing yet another nongovernmental group in the IO's work.

---

[20] See www.iisd.org/business/tools/systems_sa.aspx, accessed April 17, 2019.
[21] See www.iso.org/caring-about-health-and-safety.html, accessed April 17, 2019; also, e.g., see entire issue of *Focus*, the ISO's magazine, for March–April 2016.

Therefore, COPOLCO never became the strong voice of consumers initially envisioned. Consumer International (CI), which represents more than 200 consumer organizations from around the world, has been the only global consumer organization allowed to participate in the ISO's work. Yet, even in the case of the CI, their representatives have been able to take part only in lower-level technical ISO committees. They have not had access to the upper-level ones where important decisions are adopted. Moreover, lack of funding often hampered CI representatives from even attending important technical meetings where they were allowed to participate (ISO 1997a). Last, but not least, this lack of funding has led to competition among consumer groups to gain support from their governments, especially in developing countries. Governments often funded such organizations to allow them to travel to ISO meetings and to train their staff (ISO 1997a). In sum, the efforts to open up the ISO to more nongovernmental actors were not truly successful, even in the 1990s.

The European Association for Consumer Representation in Standardization (ANEC), the main representative of consumer interests in the CEN, is also financed from governmental and intergovernmental sources (especially from the European Commission) (Mattli 2003, 220). Despite this financial dependence of consumer groups on intergovernmental sources (similar to the one in the ISO), the CEN has been more accepting of nongovernmental consumer groups than the ISO has. In fact, in the 1990s, the CEN established a completely new category of "associate members" that allowed social partners such as the ANEC to take part in its work (EU 2000). Mattli has argued that the main reason for this difference between the CEN and the ISO when it comes to acceptance of additional actors is the demand for greater EU transparency and accountability following the 1992 Maastricht Treaty (2003, 219).

Nongovernmental consumer groups appear to have had an even harder time carving out a role for themselves in the more intergovernmental technical standards IOs such as the ITU or Codex Alimentarius (ISO 1997a, 78). In the 1980s, although Western states sought to open the ITU to more independent nongovernmental expert participation, developing countries opposed such changes, feeling that any increase in the power of private firms and standardization experts would lead to a decline in their own influence (Mattli 2003, 222).

Additionally, although in the mid-1990s the ITU considered emulating other UN organizations by being more open to nongovernmental IOs (O'Siochrú 1995), it eventually did not change its relations with such nongovernmental actors. In fact, for a long time, the ITU remained the only organization in the UN system where nongovernmental IO participation in debates required paying a substantial fee that, of course, discouraged such groups from taking part in the organization's work (CONGO 2006, 10).

Proponents of a greater role for consumer representatives in the ISO and in other IOs in the post–Cold War era, as well as of greater access for other nongovernmental actors in the ITU and other organizations, used democratic normative arguments. In most cases, such arguments went unchallenged but did not lead to change (e.g., CONGO 2006).

Due to their lack of representation in the ITU, nongovernmental actors turned to other organizations, especially the European Telecommunications Standards Institute (ETSI), which was established in 1988. The ETSI has allowed for a broad array of members, including network operators, equipment manufacturers, users, and, of course, government agencies. It also granted votes to such entities based on a weighted system (ETSI 2018). As the ETSI and other new organizations became increasingly involved in telecommunications standardization work, the traditional turf of the ITU, developing countries reconsidered their positions. By the late 1990s, they began opening participation in the ITU's standards committees to nongovernmental actors, hoping to reassert the relevance of the ITU where they had a voice (Hawkins 1999, 163).

The Codex Alimentarius also made it very difficult for nongovernmental groups (such as those representing consumer interests) to be involved in its work. However, in 1999 the organization finally adopted a set of principles that formally allowed such nongovernmental organizations to receive observer status, thus giving them access to documents and the ability to speak in meetings (Smythe 2009, 97). It has been pointed out that the vast majority of such nongovernmental organizations represent industries rather than consumers. That is in great part because the former are more prepared to fund the participation of their representatives at Codex meetings (Smythe 2009, 98). The funding problem is especially acute for environmental and consumer groups from developing countries.

The above suggests that despite efforts to minimize the role of nongovernmental groups in individual technical standardization IOs in the post–Cold War era, overall, there have been important shifts in this realm toward nongovernmentalism on the deliberative dimension. The change came in the 1990s in European IOs and (in part because of the changes in Europe) in the 2000s in global IOs.

ANSWERING THE FIVE MAIN QUESTIONS: SOME PRELIMINARY CONCLUSIONS

Figure 5.2 illustrates the evolution of the intergovernmental versus nongovernmental nature of global governance in the technical standards realm from the mid-nineteenth century to present. It is analogous to Figures 1.1, 3.4, and 4.3. I note in parentheses the main global governors for each time period. The dashed arrows represent failed attempts to bring about change, while the full arrows reflect successful attempts.

Figure 5.3 is analogous to Figures 3.5 and 4.4. Although it does not indicate who the main global governors in the technical standards realm are, it offers a better illustration of the intensity of changes in this realm than Figure 5.2 does. The level of intergovernmentalism on the vertical axis of Figure 5.3 begins at 0 in 1850, before the first global technical standards IOs emerged. Then, for each time period, I add or subtract one unit on the vertical axis for

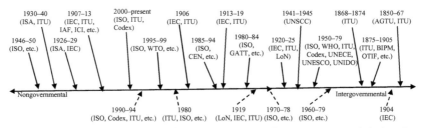

FIGURE 5.2. The intergovernmental–nongovernmental continuum in global technical standards governance.

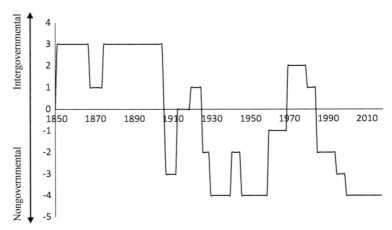

FIGURE 5.3. Shifts in the nature of global governance in the technical standards realm.

every change on one dimension of the intergovernmental–nongovernmental continuum. Figures 5.2 and 5.3 both show that, over time, global governance in this realm has experienced more than a dozen shifts across the intergovernmental–nongovernmental continuum.

Table 5.1 complements the two figures. It not only includes information regarding the type, direction, and intensity of the shifts across the continuum but also considers the factors that led to such shifts. By doing so, it offers answers to the five main questions I pose for the global governance of technical standards. The first column identifies the moments there were attempts to shift the global governance of technical standards across the intergovernmental–nongovernmental continuum (with unsuccessful attempts in italic). The second column lists the IOs where the changes were attempted.

The third column answers the first main question: *What types of changes took place in the intergovernmental–nongovernmental nature of global governance?* I differentiate in the three subcolumns between changes on the

TABLE 5.1. *Summary of shifts on the intergovernmental–nongovernmental continuum in global technical standards realm (failed attempts in italic)*

Year(s)	IO(s) where change was attempted	(Q1) Type of change			(Q2) Major states supporting or opposing change and their ideology		(Q3) Evidence of ideology-based mechanism	(Q4) Evidence of institutional mechanism	(Q5) Evidence of system-level explanations
		(a) Decision-making	(b) Financial	(c) Deliberative	Support change	Oppose change			
1850–1865	AGTU, ITU	+ (NO)	+ (NO)	+ (NO)	Prussia (+), France (+)		no	yes	no
1868	ITU		– (WO)	– (WO)	Italy (–)		no	yes	no
1875–1893	BIPM, OTIF	+ (NO)	+ (NO)	+ (NO)	Germany (+), France (+)		no	yes	no
1904	*IEC Congress*	+ (NO)			All states		*no*	*no*	*no*
1906	IEC	– (NO)	– (NO)	– (NO)	UK (–), US (–)	France (+)	no	yes	yes
1907–1913	IAF, ICI	– (NO)	– (NO)	– (NO)	UK (–), US (–)		no	yes	yes
1913	IEC	+ (WO)	+ (WO)	+ (WO)	UK (+) and other great powers		no	yes	no
1919	*League, ITU, IEC*	+ (AO)	+ (AO)				*no*	*no*	*yes*
1920	League, ITU, IEC			+ (AO)			no	no	yes

(continued)

TABLE 5.1 (*continued*)

Year(s)	IO(s) where change was attempted	(Q1) Type of change			(Q2) Major states supporting or opposing change and their ideology		(Q3) Evidence of ideology-based mechanism	(Q4) Evidence of institutional mechanism	(Q5) Evidence of system-level explanations
		(a) Decision-making	(b) Financial	(c) Deliberative	Support change	Oppose change			
1926	ISA	– (NO)	– (NO)	– (NO)	UK (–) and other great powers		no	yes	no
1930	ITU	– (WO)	– (WO)		US (–)		no	yes	no
1941	UNSCC	+ (NO)	+ (NO)		UK (+), US (+)		no	yes	no
1946	ISO	– (NO)	– (NO)		US (–), UK (–)	USSR (+)	no	yes	no
1950–1979	WHO, FAO, UNECE	+ (AO)	+ (AO)	+ (AO)	US (–)	USSR (+)	no	no	no
1960–1979	*ISO*	+ (WO)	+ (WO)		*USSR (+)*	*US (–)*	no	yes	yes
1970	ISO, UNESCO, UNIDO			+ (AO)			no	no	no
1970–1979	ISO	+ (WO)	+ (WO)		USSR (+)	US (–)	no	yes	yes

Year(s)	IO(s) where change was attempted	(Q1) Type of change			(Q2) Major states supporting or opposing change and their ideology		(Q3) Evidence of ideology-based mechanism	(Q4) Evidence of institutional mechanism	(Q5) Evidence of system-level explanations
		(a) Decision-making	(b) Financial	(c) Deliberative	Support change	Oppose change			
1970–1978	ISO			– (WO)	US (–)		no	yes	no
1980–1984	GATT, ISO, IEC	– (AO)			US (–)		no	yes	yes
1980s	ITU			– (WO)	US (–)	Developing countries (+)	no	yes	no
1985–1994	CEN, ISO	– (AO)	– (AO)	– (AO)	US (–)		no	yes	yes
1990–1994	ISO, Codex, ITU			– (WO)	US (–)		yes	yes	yes
1995	WTO, ISO, IEC	– (AO)			US (–)		no	yes	yes
2000s	ISO, ITU, Codex			– (WO)	US (–)		yes	no	yes
TOTAL		13	13	12	12		1	14	8

Key: NO: new organization; WO: change within existing organization; AO: change in relative importance among organizations; +: domestic activism or intergovernmentalism when referring to state or global governance, respectively; –: domestic passivism or nongovernmentalism when referring to state or global governance, respectively.

decision-making, financial, and deliberative dimensions. As in the analogous tables from Chapters 3 and 4, I also distinguish between changes brought about by the establishment of new organizations (NO), those due to developments within existing IOs (WO), and changes among organizations (AO) due to shifts in the relevance of some IOs compared to others. Additionally, I note when the shifts were toward greater intergovernmentalism (+) or nongovernmentalism (–). The last row indicates that in the global governance of technical standards, there were about the same number of changes on the decision-making (thirteen), financial (thirteen), and deliberative dimensions (twelve).

Column 4 summarizes the answers to the question *How strong was government activism in the most important countries promoting or opposing changes in the nature of global governance?* This column suggests that in the international technical standards realm, as in the case of the health and labor realms, great powers' support for or opposition to intergovernmentalism (+) or nongovernmentalism (–) almost always coincided with government preferences for domestic activism or passivism (noted with + or –, respectively). The only case in which we do not see a direct connection between great powers' domestic preferences and the type of global governance they are promoting unfolded during the first half of the Cold War, when American and Soviet interests in gaining greater control over international standardization led them to support forms of global governance that were unlike their domestic institutions.

Column 5 responds to the third question of this study: *Which national institutions were represented in the international efforts to shift global governance toward greater intergovernmentalism or nongovernmentalism?* Column 6 summarizes the answers to the fourth question: *Did officials promoting intergovernmentalism or nongovernmentalism use arguments that invoked specific ideologies?* The two questions are intended to help distinguish between the institutional and ideological mechanisms linking domestic and international preferences.

The bottom row shows that there is considerably more evidence supporting the institutional mechanism (fourteen) than the ideological one (one). This is expected, as the technical standards realm is less conducive to the use of ideological arguments and more prone to pragmatic ones such as those that emphasize the speed with which decisions are reached.

Column 7 responds to the fifth question: *Are there any system-level explanations for the shifts?* The last row indicates that there are eight instances where there are plausible system-level explanations for the successful attempts to alter global governance, about the same number as in the two other issue-areas discussed in the previous chapters. Only one of these eight cases, the one involving the shift toward intergovernmentalism immediately after World War I, cannot simultaneously be explained using domestic–international linkage arguments. Yet, even in that instance, the relevance of system-level arguments is questionable. Indeed, the end of the war led to the establishment and empowerment of the very intergovernmental League of Nations as a way to deal with the problems perceived to have sparked the war. This is, of course, expected based on the system-based arguments discussed in Chapter 2. However, the decision to allow League officials to participate in the meetings of nongovernmental technical standards IOs such as IEC (the only real change that pushed global governance toward intergovernmentalism) can primarily be explained by focusing on the interests of the IO officials, rather than on the global pressures to have governments collaborate more after a major war.

Moreover, in most of these cases where system-level factors appear to have contributed to global governance shifts, they cannot account for the direction of those shifts. Indeed, the first IOs to emerge in this realm appeared at times of increased economic and especially informational interactions between states, as system-level arguments discussed in Chapter 2 would suggest. However, these factors cannot explain why the global governors that were established during such times were sometimes more intergovernmental (e.g., the ITU) and other times more nongovernmental (e.g., the IEC). More important, the establishment of the very intergovernmental UNSCC during World War II and of the very nongovernmental ISO after the war run counter to system-level expectations based on the literature emphasizing the impact of conflict on the emergence of IOs (e.g., Wallace and Singer 1970, 257; Shanks et al. 1996).

System-level arguments do account, at least in part, for the nongovernmental shifts that took place in the 1980s in Europe and in the 1990s at the global level, when states shifted to the more nongovernmental CEN and ISO, respectively, rather than allow the more intergovernmental EC or WTO to be directly involved in standard-setting. Moreover, the CEN appears to have pushed the ISO toward even greater nongovernmentalism in a competition to be more efficient and garner increased control over international technical standardization. These are all instances that appear to be the result of increased organizational density, an important system-level factor explaining nongovernmental trends in global governance.

Finally, the shift toward intergovernmentalism in the ISO in the 1970s can be explained by system-level arguments related to the move toward authoritarian and statist approaches to governance experienced at that time. Conversely, the slow acceptance of nongovernmental consumer groups in the ISO and ITU in the post–Cold War era is partially due to the global spread of democracy. However, even in these last two cases, the system-level explanations go hand in hand with the domestic–international linkage explanations based on institutional factors. As powerful states became more authoritarian or democratic, domestic technical standards institutions in powerful states tended to be more governmental or nongovernmental, respectively, leading to similar intergovernmental or nongovernmental shifts in global governance. In sum, in the realm of technical standards, as in the health and labor realms, system-level explanations can only rarely (if ever) be used alone to explain changes in global governance. The domestic–international linkage arguments are essential for understanding developments in global governance.

6

Conclusions

THE PRINCIPAL FINDINGS OF THE EMPIRICAL CHAPTERS

The empirical chapters had two primary purposes. First, they offered support for this book's main argument: that individual global governors, as well as the aggregate global governance in specific issue-areas, are better understood as falling along an intergovernmental–nongovernmental continuum rather than simply into one of two dichotomous categories. By focusing on this continuum, we can observe the many subtle changes that take place in the intergovernmental or nongovernmental character of global governance. Second, the chapters assessed the plausibility of the two main explanations for global governance shifts across the intergovernmental–nongovernmental continuum.

The narratives in each of the three chapters, the summaries of developments (captured in Tables 3.1, 4.1, and 5.1), and the visual representations of the changes that global governance has undergone (in Figures 3.4, 3.5, 4.3, 4.4, 5.2, and 5.3) all offer strong support for my main argument. Each issue-area has experienced many shifts across the intergovernmental–nongovernmental continuum in the last century and a half. Altogether, I identified fifty moments when global governance was altered in each of the three issue-areas. Many of these moments involved multiple simultaneous shifts across the decision-making, financial, or deliberative dimensions. Overall, the fifty moments of change led to ninety-four shifts across individual dimensions of the continuums. For the entire period from 1850 to 2015, this represents an average of approximately one shift every five years in one specific issue-area.[1] Figure 6.1 and Table 6.1, which offer an aggregate view of all developments from the three chapters,

---

[1] The relatively high number of shifts in the technical standards realm (thirty-eight) compared to the health and labor realms (both twenty-eight) may be due to the decision to not consolidate all IOs into larger ones in this issue-area. Implicitly, there are more IOs dealing with technical standards and therefore more opportunities for shifts across continuums.

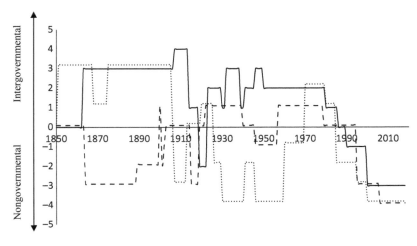

Key: —— health realm;   – – – labor realm;   ·········· technical standards realm

FIGURE 6.1. Evolution of global governance in the health, labor, and technical standards realms.

indeed show that over the past century and a half there have been many shifts, both towards greater intergovernmentalism and nongovernmentalism, in a continuous ebb and flow of global governance.

Table 6.2 considers all moments when there were shifts on the intergovernmental–nongovernmental continuum from Table 6.1 but, rather than focusing on the characteristics of the shifts, it includes information from Chapters 3–5 regarding the degree to which I found support for the two main hypotheses connecting domestic and international developments as well as for additional system-level arguments. Table 6.2 indicates that in thirty-eight of the fifty moments when there were shifts in global governance, their direction matched the domestic preferences for more hands-on or hands-off approaches to domestic governance in the most powerful states. Altogether, the three chapters uncovered evidence of the ideology-based mechanism in about one third of all moments when shifts occurred and of the institution-based mechanism in about two thirds of all such moments. In 12 percent of all moments, both mechanisms appeared to function simultaneously.

The findings thus support the main explanations for shifts across the intergovernmental–nongovernmental continuum, captured by H_1 and H_2. Specifically, ideology-based and institution-based linkages between the domestic and international preferences of the most powerful states have often led to changes in the nature of global governance.[2]

---

[2] Moreover, I found that in many instances when attempts to alter global governance were not successful, this was primarily due to powerful states opposing shifts that ran counter to their domestic (and international) preferences.

TABLE 6.1. *Summary of all shifts on continuums in health, labor, and technical standards realms*

	Number of moments when shifts took place	Number of all shifts across continuum	Shifts toward intergovernmentalism	Shifts toward nongovernmentalism	Shifts on decision-making dimension	Shifts on financial dimension	Shifts on deliberative dimension	Shifts due to emergence of new organizations (NO)	Shifts due to changes within existing organizations (WO)	Shifts due to changes in relevance among organizations (AO)
Global governance of health	16	28	13	15	9	9	10	14	12	2
Global governance of labor	16	28	12	16	14	6	8	16	8	4
Global governance of technical standards	18	38	17	21	13	13	12	18	10	10
TOTAL	50	94	42	52	36	28	30	48	30	16
Proportion from all shifts	–	–	45%	55%	38%	30%	32%	51%	32%	17%

TABLE 6.2. *Summary of all instances supporting main explanations of the shifts*

	Number of moments when shifts took place	Instances when changes matched preferences of powerful states	Instances with evidence for ideology-based mechanism	Instances with evidence for institution-based mechanism argument	Instances with evidence supporting both ideology-based and institution-based mechanisms	Instances supporting system-level arguments	Instances supporting system-level arguments but not domestic–international linkage arguments
Global governance of health	16	12	7	9	4	7	4
Global governance of labor	16	11	8	9	2	9	1
Global governance of technical standards	18	15	1	15	0	8	2
TOTAL	50	38	16	33	6	24	6
Proportion from all shifts	–	76%	32%	66%	12%	48%	12%

The following sections of this chapter will go into greater depth in explaining the shifts toward intergovernmentalism and nongovernmentalism. They will do so by summarizing the answers to the five questions that were asked in each empirical chapter. The first question refers to the types of shifts that took place. The second question assesses the plausibility of the hypothesized linkages between domestic developments and global ones. The third and fourth questions are intended to disentangle the two main causal mechanisms behind such linkages captured in hypotheses H_1 and H_2. The fifth question considers the existence of system-level explanations for the shifts.

After considering the degree to which the empirical chapters support the arguments laid out in the introductory and theory chapters of the book, I also discuss the instances in which these were not supported. Specifically, I consider all cases where despite the *lack* of such domestic–international linkages, global shifts nevertheless took place, as well as those where domestic preferences for a more activist or passive approach to domestic governance *did not* translate into global shifts on the intergovernmental–nongovernmental continuum. These "deviant cases" (George and Bennett 2005, 21) help me identify additional factors that allow us to understand the causes of shifts and suggest directions for future research in seeking more complete answers to the questions driving this book. The last sections of the chapter draw a series of conclusions regarding the theoretical and practical implications of the book's findings.

THE TYPES OF SHIFTS ACROSS THE INTERGOVERNMENTAL–NONGOVERNMENTAL CONTINUUM

The first main question asked in each of the three empirical chapters was *What types of changes took place in the intergovernmental–nongovernmental nature of global governance?* The discussions of all such changes in Chapters 3–5 signaled when the shifts were toward intergovernmentalism or nongovernmentalism. I also distinguished between shifts across the three dimensions of the continuum (decision-making, financial, and deliberative) as well as between shifts that took place due to the emergence of new organizations, due to changes within an existing organization, and as a result of changes in the relative importance of existing organizations.

Table 6.1 includes the breakdown of all of these different types of shifts. It shows that the proportion of shifts toward intergovernmentalism (45 percent of all shifts) is comparable to the one toward nongovernmentalism (55 percent). In other words, the history of these three issue-areas involved a true ebb and flow across the intergovernmental–nongovernmental continuum, rather than a continuous movement in only one direction. All three issue-areas exhibited a somewhat higher number of shifts toward nongovernmentalism than toward intergovernmentalism: fifteen-to-thirteen in the health realm, sixteen-to-twelve in the labor realm, and twenty-one-to-seventeen in the technical standards realm. The slight discrepancy can be viewed as a result of the unusual developments of the post–Cold War era, when all nine shifts led to increased nongovernmentalism. Before this period, there had been an almost equal number of shifts in either direction.

Table 6.1 also shows that there were similar numbers of shifts across the decision-making (thirty-six), financial (twenty-eight), and deliberative (thirty) dimensions. This supports the argument from the introductory chapter that all three dimensions are relevant for understanding changes in the intergovernmental–nongovernmental nature of global governance and that actors have sought to increase their control over various IOs by altering the ways in which such organizations made their decisions, were financed, and deliberated.

Although there is a fairly equal distribution of types of shifts in terms of their direction and dimension, Table 6.1 shows that there are some important differences in terms of the number of shifts that resulted due to the emergence of new IOs (51 percent of all cases), those that took place due to later changes within existing IOs (32 percent), and those that resulted from changes to the relative importance of one IO compared to others (17 percent). The differences in these numbers are expected, especially if one takes into account the time periods during which they unfolded. Indeed, a close look at Tables 3.1, 4.1, and 5.1 reveals that until around World War I, the vast majority of changes took place through the emergence of new IOs. However, once organizations were created to deal with the three issue-areas, their rules could be changed to alter the nature of global governance. Later, when even more IOs emerged, various international actors could choose from among the many existing organizations the ones that best fit their preferences. In fact, over the past few decades it appears that changes within IOs and those among IOs were just as common, if not more so, than those resulting from the establishment of new organizations.

However, for the narrower purposes of this first study of shifts across the intergovernmental–nongovernmental continuum, it is important to simply point out that all three strategies of change were used at one time or another by great powers. Indeed, in about one third of all cases, global shifts resulted from changes within existing organizations through slow processes akin to those discussed as "layering" in the historical institutionalist literature (e.g., Thelen 1999). One such example is that of the ILL in the years before World War I. Although the organization was established with a nongovernmental character in 1900, by 1913 most members had slowly altered the makeup of their delegations by including more government representatives. They did not, however, choose to establish a new and more intergovernmental labor IO. Similarly, during the Cold War, the Soviet Union and its allies did not move to establish a new, more intergovernmental, IO to replace the very nongovernmental ISO and they did not choose to transfer the standardization work to another existing IO that was closer to their intergovernmental preferences. Instead, they sought to alter de facto representation in the organization, thus pushing it toward greater intergovernmentalism.[3]

Also, there were sixteen shifts on the intergovernmental–nongovernmental continuum that took place because powerful states turned to existing IOs other than the main global governor (the "select" category of institutional choices discussed by Jupille et al. 2013). In such cases, they usually chose organizations that were closer to their intergovernmental or nongovernmental preferences, rather than establishing new IOs or changing existing ones to match their preferences. In turn, this led to shifts on the intergovernmental–nongovernmental continuum in global governance. Such a process unfolded, for instance, in the 1980s in the health realm when the United States began working more through the World Bank, which had already moved toward greater nongovernmentalism rather than continue promoting programs through the WHO that it felt had remained too intergovernmental. Similarly, in the 1990s, powerful Western states pushed much of the standardization work in the telecommunications realm to the more nongovernmental ETSI, as the ITU was reluctant to shift from its very intergovernmental character. In any case, although there are some differences in the frequency with which various types of shifts took place on the intergovernmental–nongovernmental continuum (in terms of their direction, dimension on which they unfolded, or strategy used), the above summary suggests that none of them can be considered rare occurrences.

Figure 6.2 brings together all changes across the three issue-areas, distinguishing between the dimensions of the intergovernmental–nongovernmental

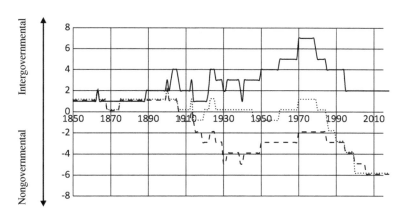

Key: ——— : decision-making dimension; – – : financial dimension; ····· : deliberative dimension

FIGURE 6.2. Overall evolution of global governance for all issue-areas across the three dimensions.

---

[3] It should be pointed out that at the time these shifts were taking place, there were no formal changes to ILL or ISO participation rules. Rather, these are both examples of how informal processes can affect the functioning of IOs.

continuum. The figure illustrates that there were periods when all three dimensions exhibited similar trends. Specifically, there were simultaneous shifts toward nongovernmentalism in the first decade of the twentieth century and then toward intergovernmentalism just before World War I. Most visibly, in the 1960s and 1970s, global governance on all three dimensions experienced shifts toward intergovernmentalism and, starting in the 1980s, shifts toward nongovernmentalism, yet another reflection of the unusual nongovernmental character of the end of the Cold War and the post–Cold War era. Overall, in about half of all moments experiencing changes, the shifts took place simultaneously on at least two dimensions.

Just as important, Figure 6.2 shows that there were many moments when the three dimensions of the intergovernmental–nongovernmental continuums *did not* experience similar trends. There were instances when the changes took place on only one or two dimensions. There were periods in which all three dimensions experienced similar shifts, but the changes did not take place at exactly the same time. Perhaps most telling is the fact that although the past two decades have indeed seen multiple shifts toward nongovernmentalism (as the existing literature has often pointed out), such shifts more often took place on the financial and deliberative dimensions and rarely on the decision-making dimension. This may be interpreted as meaning that over the past few decades, even though governments may have been willing to allow nongovernmental actors to contribute financially to the functioning of major IOs and to take part in deliberations, they have generally sought to maintain control over decision-making processes.

These observations offer further support for the initial decision to distinguish between changes in decision making, financial arrangements, and deliberations. By following shifts across the three separate dimensions, we gain a more nuanced understanding of developments in global governance. Additionally, the distinction between dimensions allows us to understand that for most periods throughout history, there were different types of shifts across the intergovernmental–nongovernmental continuum. As mentioned in Chapter 1, we should not assume that changes across all three dimensions go hand in hand simply because the most recent few decades have exhibited fairly concerted shifts.

In fact, it is important to emphasize that had the present research focused solely on the past few decades, as many existing studies have done, the conclusions would have been markedly different. One need only visualize how the graphs in Figures 6.1 and 6.2 would appear with time frames starting only in 1990, rather than in 1850.

The post–Cold War era (at least the 1990s and early 2000s), when the most powerful countries either had embraced democratic and free market values for some time (as in the case of the United States, Japan, and Western European powers), or had recently embraced one or both such values (as in the case of Russia and China), appears to be unique (e.g., Fukuyama 1992). In virtually all other time periods, at least one great power has opposed the ideological preferences of other powerful states. This text suggests that in the future (or even now), as ideological clashes between great powers once more become pronounced, it is entirely plausible that global governance may shift yet again toward intergovernmentalism and that such shifts may take place in different ways on each of the three dimensions.

THE MAIN EXPLANATIONS FOR SHIFTS ACROSS THE INTERGOVERNMENTAL–NONGOVERNMENTAL CONTINUUM

This section focuses on the questions that allow me to assess the plausibility of H_1 and H_2. As a reminder, question 2 refers to the plausibility of both hypotheses, without distinguishing between them: *How strong was government activism in the most important countries promoting or opposing changes in the nature of global governance?* Questions 3 and 4 seek to disentangle the two separate mechanisms behind H_1 and H_2: (3) *Which national institutions were represented in the international efforts to shift global governance toward greater intergovernmentalism or nongovernmentalism?* (4) *Did officials promoting intergovernmentalism or nongovernmentalism use arguments that invoked specific ideologies?*

The third column of Table 6.2 shows that in slightly more than three quarters of all instances of changes across the intergovernmental–nongovernmental continuums, the domestic activist or passive approach of governments matched the international intergovernmental or nongovernmental approach that they promoted, respectively. In the twelve instances when the changes that took place were not in the same direction as the preferences of the most powerful states, this was due to one of three possible reasons. First, as will be discussed in greater depth, there were six moments when system-level factors, rather than state-level ones, were responsible for changes in the intergovernmental or nongovernmental nature of global governance. In two other cases, also discussed in greater depth below, neither state-level nor system-level factors appeared to play a role. In three other instances (all in the labor realm), the changes were due to the emergence of nongovernmental institutions in the most powerful states, a development that is in accord with the one underlying H_2. However, contrary to the hypothesized institution-based mechanism, such changes were not supported by the *governments* of the most powerful states (as question 2 specifically asks), but rather solely by the nongovernmental actors from such states.[4]

Lastly, there is one instance when powerful states successfully promoted global changes that appear to be in the direction opposite of their domestic preferences. This happened in the first half of the Cold War in the technical

---

[4] This is yet another useful reminder that not only government actors, but also nongovernmental actors, shape domestic and international preferences.

standards realm, when the United States was promoting the use of the more intergovernmental WHO, FAO, and UNECE alongside the more nongovernmental ISO while the USSR sought to have all international standardization work in the ISO. This case is a reminder that states can have multiple *domestic* preferences that do not go hand in hand with each other and that can translate into multiple analogous *international* preferences that also do not always go hand in hand with each other. Indeed, at that time, while the United States supported more nongovernmental solutions both domestically and internationally, it also sought to spread the standardization work across multiple IOs (both intergovernmental and nongovernmental) and thus allow for competition among organizations, a decision based on principles that are also in tune with traditional American domestic preferences. The Soviet Union, on the other hand, preferred intergovernmental approaches over nongovernmental ones but also supported the centralization of tasks in IOs, just as it preferred centralization in its domestic institutions.

As mentioned, Table 6.2 shows that of the two arguments connecting domestic and international preferences, the institutional one appears to be supported more often (in 66 percent of all instances when changes occurred) than the ideological one (in 32 percent of all such instances).[5] While this finding is, of course, an important one, it needs to be interpreted with caution, as many cases in which the institution-based mechanism unfolded came from the technical standards realm, where the ideology-based mechanism appears to have functioned only once. By contrast, the ideology-based mechanism was only slightly less prevalent than the institution-based one in the health realm (seven versus nine instances) and labor realm (eight versus nine instances).

To some degree, this is to be expected, as the technical standards realm is more likely to involve pragmatic arguments regarding the most efficient way of adopting standards. It is less conducive to debates involving ideological arguments, while the labor and even health realms appear to be more conducive to such arguments. Had the case studies here included issue-areas that were even more open to ideological interpretations (such as human rights or,

---

[5] A possible explanation for this imbalance is simply that it may be more difficult to find evidence for the ideology-based mechanism. As a reminder, I identified such instances when finding state representatives using ideological arguments to support their positions. However, even though in many cases I did not find such a "trail of communication" (mentioned by Finnemore and Sikkink 1998, when discussing similar methodological problems in identifying norms), that does not necessarily mean that *unspoken* ideological preferences did not play a role in shaping developments. For instance, when the United States, the United Kingdom, and the USSR decided to establish an intergovernmental health IO after World War II, their agreement in terms of government activism in the health realm can explain the lack of ideological arguments (despite the existence of ideologies influencing all three countries' positions) used to promote the creation of the intergovernmental WHO. It is likely that there were more instances where ideologies contributed to the shifts and, therefore, that the discrepancy in the incidence of the two mechanisms may not be as great as numbers in Table 6.2 suggest.

perhaps, trade), there may have been more overall support for the ideology-based mechanism.

Additionally, this discrepancy may be because the technical standards realm has been generally more nongovernmental in nature than the other two issue-areas and therefore top government officials (who, as discussed, are the ones responsible for the domestic–international ideological connections) were less active in the processes of change. In sum, it is useful to conclude simply that this research has found support for *both* mechanisms and acknowledges that the specific type of linkage between domestic and international preferences may depend on issue-area.

Moreover, the role of ideological factors affecting global changes should not be neglected, even in issue-areas where one does not find strong evidence of their presence. As a reminder, I have argued that many of the domestic institutional changes leading to greater intergovernmentalism or nongovernmentalism can themselves be the result of ideological shifts in powerful states. Indeed, the decisions to have more nongovernmental domestic institutions in the technical standards realm in the United Kingdom and the United States were in great part based on ideological factors. Representatives of these nongovernmental institutions then became the main promoters of nongovernmentalism in global technical standards, thus contributing to the large overall number of cases that I counted as being institution-based for this realm.

It should also be noted that Table 6.2 indicates that in six instances there is evidence of both the ideology-based mechanism and the institution-based one. This does not mean that the study could not discern between the two mechanisms but rather that they functioned simultaneously. In the relatively few instances in which both mechanisms functioned simultaneously, one of two processes unfolded: In some cases, although the main representatives in international meetings were from lower-level specialized institutions (rather than top-level government officials) they nevertheless invoked ideological arguments. The case studies revealed a number of such instances for representatives from Italy when the IRU was being established and from Soviet Union when seeking to alter the ILO after World War II. Both are examples of ideologies being imposed by authoritarian systems on other domestic actors, including on lower-level officials from domestic organizations.

In other cases, the two mechanisms were simultaneously detected when top-level officials who did not actually take part in the international meetings nevertheless expressed their preferences for one form of global governance or another by invoking ideological arguments. For example, there were multiple such instances around the time the United States decided to leave the ILO during the Cold War.

The empirical chapters identify not only the *instances* when one particular causal mechanism or another is in place, they also help differentiate between the specific *effects* of the ideology-based and institution-based mechanisms leading to shifts in global governance.

Table 6.3 offers a breakdown by each mechanism and allows us to identify similarities and differences between their respective effects. The table shows that the two mechanisms led to approximately equal numbers of shifts toward intergovernmentalism (44 percent of all shifts resulting from the institutions based-mechanism and 50 percent from the ideology-based one) and nongovernmentalism (56 and 50 percent, respectively). Similarly, the institution-based mechanism does not appear to lead to a substantially greater number of shifts across any of the three dimensions: decision-making, financial, and deliberative. However, the ideology-based mechanism appears to favor shifts on the deliberative dimension and leads to fewer shifts on the financial dimension. This finding is not surprising. Allowing more types of actors to participate in IO deliberations is easily connected to democratic pluralist ideologies. The arguments for financial contributions, on the other hand, appear to be presented more easily in pragmatic terms.

Table 6.3 also shows that there are important differences between the instances when such shifts led to new IOs, led to changes within IOs, or led to changes in the relative importance of IOs. Almost half of the institution-based mechanisms led to the establishment of new IOs. Ideological mechanisms have only rarely led to changes due to choices of one IO over others.

The former finding is in tune with the argument made in Chapter 2 that officials from domestic institutions often act at the international level to secure resources and prestige for the organizations they represent. The establishment of new IOs with formal rules is more likely to lock in such benefits than is a simple change of rules in existing organizations or the use of one IO rather than another.

The latter finding suggests that choices for empowering one IO rather than another is presented primarily using pragmatic rather than ideological arguments. One instance[6] when this may not have been the case was when the United States decided toward the end of the Cold War to shift global health governance work from the WHO to the World Bank. It used ideological arguments similar to the ones it made when leaving UNESCO, around the same time, to show that it was adamant about its preferences and thus to induce other states to alter the very intergovernmental nature of the WHO. However, this decision was also due to the fact that the United States had much greater control over the World Bank (with a weighted voting system based on states' wealth) than over the WHO (with a one-country-one-vote system).

---

[6] Ideological arguments were also used unsuccessfully when the USSR called for having the WFTU rather than the ILO as the principal global governor in the labor realm in the first few years after World War II.

TABLE 6.3. *Outcomes of institution-based and ideology-based mechanisms*

Mechanisms leading to shifts	Types of shifts							
	Inter-governmental	Nongovernmental	On decision-making dimension	On financial dimension	On deliberative dimension	Due to emergence of new organizations (NO)	Due to changes within organizations (WO)	Due to changes in relevance among organizations (AO)
Ideology-based mechanism	12/24 50%	12/24 50%	9/24 37%	5/24 21%	10/24 42%	10/24 42%	11/24 46%	1/24 4%
Institution-based mechanism	30/68 44%	38/68 56%	27/68 40%	22/68 32%	19/68 28%	30/68 44%	15/68 22%	9/68 14%

Although not addressed in Table 6.3, it is worth mentioning that the establishment of new IOs led to almost as many shifts toward intergovernmentalism (twenty-one) as to nongovernmentalism (twenty-three). However, there were differences between the effects of shifts that took place because of changes in the importance of some IOs relative to others (five led to greater intergovernmentalism, while ten led to nongovernmentalism) and those due to changes within existing IOs (ten led to greater intergovernmentalism and nineteen toward nongovernmentalism).

The few instances of shifts toward intergovernmentalism as a result of interactions between IOs appears to offer support for the argument in the existing literature that when there are multiple organizational options (i.e., there is a high level of organizational density), actors tend to prefer nongovernmental solutions over intergovernmental ones (Abbott et al. 2016). Additionally, the more likely shift toward nongovernmentalism as a result of changes within organizations and among organizations may be due to recent developments. Indeed, while IOs emerged to deal with a myriad of global governance issues through the Cold War, recent decades have seen a relative decline in the establishment of new IOs compared to previous eras (Shanks et al. 1996, 598). This trend has coincided with (but is not causally related to) the trend toward greater nongovernmentalism over the past few decades. Therefore, when seeking to shift global governance toward nongovernmentalism in the post–Cold War era, actors' choices were more likely to be between changing rules within existing IOs and embracing ones that already had rules that they preferred rather than establishing new IOs.

SYSTEM-LEVEL EXPLANATIONS FOR CHANGE

The fifth main question addressed in all three empirical chapters was *Are there any system-level explanations for the shifts?* Table 6.2 indicates that in almost half the moments when there were changes across the intergovernmental–nongovernmental continuum, there was evidence for some of the system-level explanations discussed in Chapter 2. Moreover, in six such moments, the system-level arguments were supported even while the domestic-level ones were not. It is also important to note here that there were two additional moments when changes occurred but neither the arguments emphasizing domestic–international connections nor any of the system-level ones noted in the literature could explain them. All such cases will be discussed in greater detail in this section.

As will be recalled, based on extensions of arguments from the existing literature, I expected shifts toward intergovernmentalism soon after major wars. I also expected shifts toward nongovernmentalism during major wars, global economic decline, increased economic and informational flows, waves of democracy, and high organizational density. The three previous chapters have offered examples of all such factors affecting the intergovernmental or nongovernmental nature of global governance. However, I have found an almost equal number of instances when the system-level factors led to shifts in directions *opposite* from the ones expected based on existing arguments from the literature.[7]

For example, in the health realm, cooperation in more intergovernmental organizations, such as the OIHP and LNHO, indeed broke down during World War I and World War II, while nongovernmental IOs such as the ICRC and IFRC played more important roles. However, in the labor realm, while only the more nongovernmental IFTU continued to function during World War I, during World War II, it was the more intergovernmental ILO that remained the principal global governor, even if it had to reduce the volume and scope of its work. Additionally, in the technical standards realm, World War II led to a dramatic shift from the more nongovernmental ISA to the very intergovernmental UNSCC, contrary to expectations based on system-level factors that were discussed in Chapter 2.

The global economic downturn in the 1930s led to a shift toward nongovernmentalism in the health realm when governments could not afford to spend much on the LNHO but the nongovernmental RF stepped in to contribute almost half of the IO's budget. However, during the same period the international labor realm shifted toward intergovernmentalism, despite experiencing the same global economic downturn.

There was also evidence of shifts toward both intergovernmentalism and nongovernmentalism immediately after major wars. After World War I, there was a shift toward nongovernmentalism in the health realm. However, during that same period, the labor realm experienced a shift toward greater intergovernmentalism with the emergence of the ILO.

There were some instances in which the increased global economic and informational flows led to shifts toward nongovernmentalism, as the literature predicts (Boli and Thomas 1997, 1999). Some of the best examples can be found in the first decade of the twentieth century when the very nongovernmental IEC, IAF, and ICI were established in the technical standards realm. However, during that same period, the increased economic and information flows led to intergovernmentalism in the health and labor realms when the ILL and OIHP were created.

---

[7] As a reminder, the discussions of system-level arguments explaining shifts toward intergovernmentalism or nongovernmentalism from Chapter 2 often led to different expectations depending on the body of literature being used. Some arguments were derived from literature focusing solely on developments involving IGOs and others from literature solely on INGOs. Unfortunately, as the literature review of Chapter 2 revealed, few existing studies discuss the *relative* impact of system-level factors on the intergovernmental versus nongovernmental character of global governance. This suggests yet another problem generated by the traditional dichotomous intergovernmental–nongovernmental approach to the study of global governance.

The democratization processes of the second half of the nineteenth century did indeed bring about a greater role for civil society organizations at both the state level and the international level, as the literature predicts. These changes eventually led to the establishment of a number of nongovernmental initiatives such as the founding of the ICRC (in Dunant's very nongovernmental original vision) or of the First International. Post–Cold War democratization also led to an increase in the number of nongovernmental actors in many states and to international nongovernmental actors playing greater roles in global governance, as the literature predicts (Tallberg et al. 2013). However, it should be pointed out that, especially in the post–Cold War period, the push for nongovernmentalism appears to have been due just as much, if not more, to only a handful of powerful states that had been democratic and supportive of greater roles for nongovernmental actors for a long time. It is difficult, therefore, to determine whether it was indeed the system-level wave of democracy or the specific support of powerful states promoting their own domestic nongovernmental principles that led to the global shift toward nongovernmentalism.

And finally, the argument based on organizational density is supported by some of the shifts toward nongovernmentalism. For example, when there was an increase in the number of overlapping IOs in the global health realm after World War I, the initial plans for a very intergovernmental IRU were altered because the new organization was viewed as competing with the more nongovernmental ICRC and IFRC. In the end, the IRU had to shift toward greater nongovernmentalism by including the ICRC and IFRC in its work. Similarly, in the second half of the Cold War, the many international institutions states could choose from when seeking to deal with technical standards led them to adopt more nongovernmental approaches by embracing IOs such as CEN and the ISO rather than working through more intergovernmental ones such as the EC and GATT, respectively. Also, the global governance of labor shifted toward greater nongovernmentalism in the post–Cold War era when states appeared to prefer having the many new nongovernmental organizations take on the question of labor conditions in the garment industry, rather than have the intergovernmental ILO or WTO become involved.

However, as in the case of the other system-level factors discussed above, the three issue-areas also revealed instances when the increase in organizational density led to shifts toward intergovernmentalism. One such example unfolded during the Cold War when virtually all of the new IOs that took on technical standards (such as FAO, UNECE, and WHO) were very intergovernmental compared to the more nongovernmental ISO. It was also the case in the 1920s when many new health IOs emerged and yet the very nongovernmental LRCS (backed by the United States) was brushed aside in favor of the much more intergovernmental LNHO (supported by the French and British).

This last example illustrates a broader point. As in most cases in international relations, it is rare that systemic factors can single-handedly explain developments.[8] They establish conditions that make it more likely for agents to take action. However, they cannot account for when and why such agents actually take advantage of the opportunities afforded to them by the system and when they do not. Indeed, as this section has emphasized so far, the vast majority of system-level explanations refer to cases where arguments based on domestic–international linkages are *also* supported. The preferences and actions of the most powerful states are the immediate causes of change.

For example, throughout the second half of the nineteenth century, increased global economic interactions had created incentives for states to coordinate with each other when establishing labor legislation. However, the initiatives to establish a more intergovernmental IO to deal with this issue were not successful until the beginning of the twentieth century when domestic developments in Germany brought about a change in that powerful country's preferences in the labor realm. Only after this major power joined existing efforts to create a more intergovernmental labor IO (one that had been initiated by smaller states such as Switzerland) was the shift in global governance possible. Even then, other great powers did not allow for the creation of a truly intergovernmental IO. It took another decade for powerful states such as France and especially the United Kingdom to alter their positions and to transform the fairly nongovernmental ILL into a more intergovernmental one.

Similarly, as early as 1919, states felt the pressure to deal with the spread of diseases across borders that had been brought about by the terrible systemwide conditions following World War I. However, the nongovernmental approach represented by the LRCS was not replaced with the more intergovernmental one of the LNHO until the mid-1920s when the United States, with its very nongovernmental preferences, retreated from its leadership role in international affairs and when the United Kingdom applied its more government-activist approach to global health governance.

To summarize, it appears that while system-level factors can sometimes explain *when* it is likely to expect a change in the nature of global governance, they can rarely, if ever, account for the direction of shifts. Indeed, as mentioned, the number of instances when system-level factors led to shifts in the expected intergovernmental or nongovernmental direction was approximately equal to the instances of such changes in the direction opposite to the one expected. Moreover, when system-level factors did have an impact, it was more likely that they acted at the same time with one or both of the domestic–international linkage mechanisms (H_1 and H_2) and it was such mechanisms that determined the

---

[8] One of the best known acknowledgments of this fact was mentioned by Kenneth Waltz, perhaps the strongest proponent of the "third image" (i.e., of system-level analyses). He argued that systemic theories cannot be expected to predict individual events just as the law of gravitation cannot predict the "wayward path of a falling leaf" (1979, 121).

actual direction of change.[9] On the other hand, domestic-level mechanisms did not always require the presence of system-level factors in order to bring about change. In more than half of all cases when ideology-based or institution-based mechanisms operated, the relevant system-level factors were not even present.

It should be pointed out, however, that the importance of combining system-level and state-level processes derives from the two main hypotheses. As a reminder, I posit that the domestic shifts that matter are the ones that unfold in the most powerful states. This implies that global shifts can take place either (1) when there are changes in domestic preferences of states that continue to be the most powerful in the system or (2) when the relative power among states (a system-level characteristic) changes and new actors with different preferences than the previous ones have a greater say in global governance.

Despite the above argument that most system-level factors were relevant only when domestic level factors accompanied them, the three empirical chapters do reveal six instances when this was not true. How can one explain these exceptions of system-level factors single-handedly leading to changes in the intergovernmental versus nongovernmental nature of global governance?

A closer look at these exceptions shows that three such moments were somewhat expected, in that they unfolded during major wars. Global governance in the health realm shifted toward nongovernmentalism during both World War I and World War II as the more intergovernmental organizations ceased to function but the more nongovernmental Red Cross organizations played important roles. Similarly, in the labor realm, during World War II, as many states left the ILO altogether and the governments of most of the remaining states were too caught up in war efforts to become very involved in labor issues, global governance shifted toward nongovernmentalism. Thus, there are instances (albeit very few in number) when system-level factors were so powerful that they did shape global governance, while governments and nongovernmental actors played hardly any role in the changes.

However, the three other moments when shifts took place apparently solely due to system-level factors reveal that IO officials (rather than government officials or representatives of nongovernmental groups) played decisive roles in the shifts across the intergovernmental–nongovernmental continuum. In the health realm, top officials from the LNHO (especially its director, Ludwik Rajchman) were behind the shift toward nongovernmentalism that came with the RF gaining a greater role in the IO's work. During the first half of the Cold War, there was a similar attempt by WHO officials to seek financial contributions from nongovernmental entities and thus make the organization more nongovernmental. Although the original initiative was unsuccessful, it later led to increased collaborations between the WHO and many small nongovernmental

---

[9] See Grigorescu and Baser (2019) for some initial evidence (based on statistical analyses) that domestic factors are more likely than system-level factors to account for shifts toward intergovernmentalism.

organizations and to an eventual shift on the deliberative dimension of global governance. Also, after the League of Nations was established, top officials from the new IO sought to bring many of the existing technical standards organizations, both more intergovernmental and more nongovernmental, under the League's wing. Although initially they were not very successful, organizations such as the ITU and IEC eventually accepted the participation of League officials at their meetings, thus shifting the IOs and global governance toward greater intergovernmentalism on the deliberative dimension.

Top IO officials were also behind the two instances when neither system-level factors nor the hypothesized domestic–international linkages appear to have played a role, but there were nevertheless changes across the intergovernmental–nongovernmental continuums. Both such cases unfolded during the Cold War in the technical standards realm. Starting in the 1950s, the leadership of a number of very intergovernmental IOs such as FAO, UNECE, and WHO sought to expand their organizations' work into standardization, despite opposition from the more nongovernmental ISO and IEC, which wanted to maintain their near-monopoly in this realm. Also, in the 1970s, top officials from very intergovernmental organizations such as UNESCO and UNIDO were finally able to have the more nongovernmental ISO open up to them and allow their representatives to take part in ISO meetings.

All of the above cases remind us that IO bureaucracies often have the interests and resources to play important roles in shaping the nature of global governance, whether alone or together with governmental and nongovernmental domestic and international actors. In some cases, such IO officials were the ones who used opportunities presented by the system-level factors and acted to push global governance toward greater intergovernmentalism or nongovernmentalism. However, the case studies also suggested that when such IO officials pushed global governance in a direction that major states truly opposed, the shifts were relatively short lived. For example, when the United Kingdom and other great powers felt that Rajchman, the powerful director of the LNHO, had created a much too activist IO, they simply maneuvered to have him replaced from his influential position.

CASES THAT THE TWO MAIN ARGUMENTS CANNOT EXPLAIN: POSSIBLE DIRECTIONS FOR FUTURE RESEARCH

As this is the first study of the intergovernmental–nongovernmental continuum, it has purposely focused only on the most powerful explanations of shifts, the ones connecting domestic preferences to international ones. It has also considered some instances when, although the two principal explanatory mechanisms were not present, changes nevertheless took place. Such cases were explained primarily based on system-level factors, especially global conflict, democracy waves, and increases in organizational density. The above discussion also suggested that we need to look more closely at the potential role of IO officials to understand the shifts across the intergovernmental–nongovernmental continuum.

This section considers several more explanatory factors and suggests some possible directions for future research that would help account more completely for the intergovernmental or nongovernmental nature of global governance. One way to identify such additional factors is to turn to the cases discussed in Chapters 3–5 when the hypothesized mechanisms seemed to function but the attempts to shift global governance were not successful. Such cases can be found among the ones that were presented in italic letters in Tables 3.1, 4.1, and 5.1. While in the narrative of the empirical chapters the small number of such exceptions in each issue-area makes them appear simply as anomalies, taken together they may suggest some important additional explanations for the shifts on the intergovernmental–nongovernmental continuum. Overall, in seven instances in which the institution-based mechanism was in place and five instances in which the ideology-based mechanism was in place, the attempts to shift global governance were not successful.

Most unsuccessful attempts to alter global governance when one of the two mechanisms appeared to be functioning were due to the insufficient power of those actors promoting the changes, something that is expected based on H_1 and H_2. Examples of such instances are those in which labor groups sought a more nongovernmental ILO when the organization was being established, or the one of Italy initially promoting a very intergovernmental IRU in the 1920s, or of the USSR trying to make the ISO more intergovernmental in the organization's first years.

Another set of interesting cases includes those in which even though at least one of the two mechanisms was in place, proposed shifts toward nongovernmentalism did not occur because they involved multiple nongovernmental actors vying for greater influence in IOs. Indeed, as Chapter 4 has shown, labor and employer representatives in the ILO have been the principal opponents of including more nongovernmental organization in the IO's work, even when governments of powerful states sought such changes. Similarly, the nongovernmental experts in the ISO have sought to weaken COPOLCO, the body that is intended to give consumer groups a greater say in the standardization realm. Also, in recent decades, representatives of nongovernmental organizations having official status with the WHO joined forces with developing states to reduce the role of large foundations and corporations in the global health IO (Richter 2012). What all these cases suggest is that the more types of nongovernmental actors there are that have the potential to play important roles in an IO and in global governance, the more likely it is that they will challenge each other for greater influence and thus slow down or stop altogether the process, leading to greater nongovernmentalism.[10]

---

[10] It should be pointed out that this argument appears to run counter to the one suggesting that increased organizational density will lead to a choice for nongovernmentalism.

Additionally, these examples are a reminder that nongovernmental actors' interests and actions, not just those of governments that have been emphasized in this book, are important for understanding possible shifts across the intergovernmental–nongovernmental continuum. This suggests that further research could seek ways to bring together the more government-centric approaches characteristic of political science (which also characterize the present research) with the more nongovernmental ones which are generally emphasized by studies of global governance in sociology (e.g., Boli and Thomas 1997, 1999).

A last case worth discussing is the one of the United States promoting the establishment of the WHO and then joining the organization. At first glance, this process supports the argument that a powerful state's preferences for government activism (as was the case of the United States during the Roosevelt and Truman presidencies) translate into shifts toward intergovernmentalism. Indeed, this is the interpretation captured in Table 3.1 and in all subsequent relevant tables and figures. However, a closer look at those events reveals that after the United States originally was a main promoter of establishing the WHO, it then wavered and it seemed like it would not join the organization, but it eventually became a member, albeit somewhat later than other states. It is these two intermediary moments that appear as anomalies and deserve further attention (even though they are not visible in any of the tables and graphs). These moments are important because had the United States never ratified membership in the WHO, it could have pushed for a more nongovernmental approach to the global governance of health, as it did after World War I, when it did not play any role in the very intergovernmental LNHO and instead supported the very nongovernmental LRCS.

The main reason the United States hesitated to embrace the WHO was that the 1946 elections brought about a change in Congress and an ideological shift from the very pro-governmental approach of the Roosevelt and Truman administrations. This event offers an example of how domestic government structures are relevant for understanding a state's potential shifts in embracing a more intergovernmental or nongovernmental approach, as discussed in Chapter 2. In authoritarian systems, such as the USSR, or even in a parliamentary system, such as the United Kingdom, division between the executive branch of government (that commits to joining an IO) and the legislative branch (that ratifies that decision) is not very strong. In a presidential system, such as the American one, shifts toward greater intergovernmentalism or nongovernmentalism can take place because of changes in either the executive branch or the legislative branch.[11]

---

[11] Of course, the best known example of how a split between the two branches of government in the American system affected the country's support for an IO unfolded after World War I when Woodrow Wilson was the main architect of the League of Nations but was not able to garner sufficient support from the Senate to have the United States actually join the organization.

More broadly, the issue of ratification of treaties is a reminder of the broader argument that there are domestic actors besides the executive branch of government, and representatives of domestic institutions may vie for representation in an IO that may affect the intergovernmental or nongovernmental nature of global governance. For example, it should also be mentioned that when the Senate opposed the United States joining WHO, professional groups from the medical establishment fought for membership in the organization. Similarly, in the 1990s, the American press raised the visibility of the appalling labor conditions in the garment industry and praised the nongovernmental groups that were seeking solutions to such problems. However, it is just as important to note that in both cases, it was the executive branch of government that eventually chose the more intergovernmental solution in the case of the WHO (by eventually joining the organization) and the more nongovernmental one in the labor realm (by keeping the question of how to deal with poor labor conditions in the garment industry out of the more intergovernmental ILO). Thus, while the additional domestic actors indeed sometimes appear to influence international outcomes, Chapters 3–5 found very few such instances. In fact, the best example of the legislative branch affecting international developments is the aforementioned one when the United States hesitated to join the WHO, a case that is not even captured in the tables summarizing the changes on the intergovernmental–nongovernmental continuum. This suggests that overall, such additional actors played only minor roles in shaping the nature of global governance.

The second surprising US decision in the first years of the WHO's existence was that the Senate changed its mind and eventually accepted the country's membership in the IO. The main reason for that reversal what that the US Senate realized the importance of the organization for future Cold War dynamics, specifically for the security of US partners, such as Egypt. This case, of course, offers another illustration that the likelihood of having states embrace a more intergovernmental approach may also be related to the specific issue-area. Some recent research has shown that when "sovereignty costs" are high, as in the case of the security realm, governments often selfishly seek to keep the issue-area to themselves rather than allow nongovernmental actors to play a meaningful role (e.g., Tallberg et al. 2013; Grigorescu and Baser 2019). Other examples of this argument can be found in cases when governments became involved in technical standards of telecommunication as early as the mid-nineteenth century or in all technical standards during World War II, at times when these issues were seen as essential for their respective countries' security concerns. They chose an intergovernmental solution rather than allowing or encouraging nongovernmental actors (such as IEC or ISA) to control the technical standards work. More broadly, this example of how issue-areas can exhibit certain characteristics that make them more prone to adopting intergovernmental rather than nongovernmental solutions reminds us that it is important to study in greater depth the differences between issues. While the institutionalist literature has emphasized such differences in the ability of states to develop collaborative arrangements (e.g., Snidal 1985; Martin 1992), it has yet to tackle the question of this book, regarding the choice between intergovernmentalism and nongovernmentalism.[12]

In sum, the present sections of this chapter as well as the previous chapters suggest that to fully understand the forces behind shifts across the intergovernmental–nongovernmental continuum, there is a need to expand the research of this book to focus more closely on additional actors such as domestic legislatures, the multiple and often conflictual nongovernmental groups in the international realm, and IO officials. Additionally, future research should focus on other issue-areas to assess whether the findings of this study can be generalized even further, and to identify the factors that can generate differences across issues.

RELEVANCE OF THE FINDINGS FOR THEORIES OF INTERNATIONAL RELATIONS

The most obvious theoretical contribution of this book derives from the conceptualization of the intergovernmental–nongovernmental continuum and its three dimensions. By refining our understanding of "intergovernmentalism" and "nongovernmentalism," we can improve our theoretical arguments and the way we test them. The potential relevance of this more fine-tuned approach is comparable to those of other multidimensional continuums such as those focusing on democracy (Marshall et al. 2010) and globalization (Dreher 2006).

A second important contribution of this study to theory-building is that by emphasizing three different dimensions of the intergovernmental–nongovernmental continuum, it shows that apparently disparate bodies of literature discussing how IO decision making (e.g., Shanks et al. 1996; Boli and Thomas 1997, 1999), finances (e.g., McCoy et al. 2009; Graham 2015), or deliberations (Steffek et al. 2008; Tallberg et al. 2013) are controlled either by governmental or nongovernmental entities are in fact related and come together to explain a larger puzzle. In this sense, the present study can be seen as subsuming a great deal of previous work and offering generalizable conclusions that cut across the three dimensions and various bodies of literature.

A third important theoretical conclusion is that systemic factors alone can rarely explain important changes in the international realm. They usually need to be complemented with additional factors, most often derived from the domestic level, to further specify the interests of the actors who shape global developments. Of course, as mentioned in the introductory and theory chapters of this book, this important argument has been made previously many times. It came as a reaction to the dominant system-level arguments

---

[12] An important exception is the recent work of Abbott et al. (2016).

of neorealism that, as Ruggie suggested, needed to fuse traditional power considerations with social purpose (1982, 382). It also came as a reaction to later neorealist-neoliberal debates that sought to show that either relative gains or absolute gains shape international outcomes. However, neither of these system-level theoretical approaches offered an explanation as to why actors were sometimes guided by one type of gain and at other times guided by another. Some authors, such as Milner (1992, 481), pointed out that what both system-level approaches were missing was a state-level explanation for international preferences. This text shows how even the character of global governance that, at first sight, might appear to be the least likely aspect in international relations to require an explanation based on domestic politics, is indeed greatly shaped by the ideologies and domestic institutions of the most powerful states. In this sense, the present research contributes to one of the most important debates in international relations.

Additionally, it is worth reiterating that this study builds on the existing new liberalism literature (e.g., Moravcsik 1997). It illustrates how two different forms of this approach (ideational liberalism and republican liberalism) can be used to explain, both separately and together, important global developments. I have shown that both of the hypothesized mechanisms can account for shifts in global governance. This last chapter has also emphasized that one of the two mechanisms may be more common in certain issue-areas and during certain time periods than in others. This offers a reminder that the broader question of when different types of domestic–international linkages are more likely to be relevant has not been explored sufficiently by the new liberalism literature and merits more attention.

Finally, by emphasizing the domestic sources of changes in global governance, this book can account for the many and relatively rapid shifts that have taken place in global governance. Indeed, while systemic factors such as increases in global informational and economic flows, waves of democracy, or changes in global power structures take place over long periods of time, domestic changes are more likely to unfold rapidly. The ideological and institutional shifts that took place after each group of domestic political elites in powerful states was replaced by another (often through regular electoral cycles) appear to match much better with the rhythm of the ebb and flow of global governance than system-level shifts. In sum, this book has shown that the connection between domestic changes and global ones is not haphazard; rather, it is a long-standing phenomenon that can account for important international developments.

PRACTICAL RELEVANCE OF FINDINGS

There are several reasons the findings of this book have practical relevance. First, and most important, the understanding that individual IOs and the global governance of issue-areas is never truly either intergovernmental or nongovernmental, but rather a mix between these two extremes, is important because it allows us to recognize that there are multiple possible types of practical solutions (rather than just two) when dealing with the most important global problems we face.

The understanding of global governance as a continuum also pushes us to look beyond the more obvious actors who appear to be in control. The argument that powerful IOs are themselves influenced by other actors (governmental or nongovernmental), leads to more complete answers to the all-important question of "Who governs the globe?" (Avant et al. 2010) One of the most important conclusions of the present book is that the answer to this question may be even more complex than the literature has so far suggested and deserves even more detailed research.

By discussing the three dimensions of the intergovernmental–nongovernmental continuum, this book suggests that a complete analysis of such influence needs to assess not only who is involved in the actual decision making but also who contributes to the funding of organizations or to shaping their agendas and actions through deliberations. As both more intergovernmental and more nongovernmental IOs have been increasingly pushed to make their budgets transparent in response to demands for greater accountability (e.g. Blagescu and Lloyd 2006; Grigorescu 2007), it is now possible to assess more accurately the degree to which governments, as well as foundations, corporations, and other nongovernmental actors, control finances and work in each realm. Past research on IO budgets has led to a better understanding of how governments have used their financial contributions to gain greater influence in the international realm (e.g., Graham 2015). Similar research can now assess whether and how other actors beyond governments control the finances of such organizations and, implicitly, the degree to which they affect global governance.

Similarly, IOs are increasingly under pressure to make public the names of organizations and individuals with whom they consult.[13] By revealing such information, IOs now make it possible to determine in a more precise way how much influence governmental and nongovernmental actors actually have in deliberations and, implicitly, how they shape the global ideational environment. In other words, they allow us to answer the question of who is behind what happens in global governance. More specific studies of such influence will allow us to avoid impressionistic accounts and gain a more accurate image of real-world events.

Also, with the introduction of the intergovernmental–nongovernmental continuum, this text shows that there is much greater change in global governance than the usual dichotomous approaches would suggest. Moreover, it shows that such changes have led to almost equal shifts toward both

---

[13] See, e.g., EU website with information about such consultations at https://ec.europa.eu/info/about-european-commission/service-standards-and-principles/transparency_en

intergovernmentalism and nongovernmentalism. One of the most important secondary findings related to this primary finding is that the changes in the post–Cold War era appear to differ from those in most other periods. Indeed, as Figures 6.1 and 6.2 suggest, this period experienced considerable shifts toward nongovernmentalism across all three dimensions and all three issue-areas considered in this book. As mentioned in the introduction, this finding is in tune with the growing body of literature discussing the increased role of nongovernmental actors in international relations (e.g., Matthews 1997; Tallberg et al. 2013).

However, the study also suggests that this is one of the very few instances where we have seen such concerted shifts in one particular direction. This observation, coupled with an expected heightened interest in this most recent era, may lead to erroneous conclusions regarding the future of global governance. Just as democracy has been seen as advancing and then retreating in waves and counterwaves, the empirical chapters of this book suggest that we have also experienced back-and-forth changes in the intergovernmental and nongovernmental nature of global governance. In other words, after several decades of shifts toward nongovernmentalism, we should expect, sooner or later, the reverse shifts toward intergovernmentalism.

Such reversals are expected not only because of system-level factors such as the recent global authoritarian tendencies (Zakaria 1997) and the erosion of the economic liberal model (e.g., Haass 2018). Based on the findings of this book, they are expected primarily because of two additional potential factors. First, the shifts in power that are giving China an increasing role in global governance (e.g., Lynch and Groll 2017), coupled with this country's more government interventionist approach to domestic politics, suggest that we should see a movement toward greater intergovernmentalism worldwide and a decline in the influence of nongovernmental actors. There is already some evidence of this trend. Incipient research on two new and very intergovernmental IOs that China recently established, the New Development Bank (NDB) and the Asian Infrastructure Investment Bank (AIIB), indicates that this rising power has instituted a similarly strong governmental grip on international collaborative arrangements to that in the domestic realm, leaving no real role for nongovernmental actors (e.g. Dove 2016).

Second, the ideologies and institutions embraced by Western leaders appear to also be shifting. In the United States, the Trump administration appears to have increased the role of government in trade, immigration, and several other issue-areas (even as it has sought to reduce such a role in other issue-areas). Perhaps more important, the "America First" approach has highlighted another important choice in global governance, the one between engagement and disengagement from world affairs. Indeed, the United States has left the Paris Agreement on climate change, the Trans-Pacific Partnership, and UNESCO. It also threatened to leave NAFTA and other international agreements and organizations. When the United States has previously retreated from a leadership role in global governance in the interwar era, other great powers have stepped in and shaped global institutions in ways that were closer to their own preferences. This observation leads us back to the previous conclusion, that China and other rising powers that have a more activist approach to domestic governance and are becoming more present than the United States in global governance may push the system toward greater intergovernmentalism.

Of course, because the ebb and flow of global governance is continuous, this text also suggests that even those shifts that appear to be looming in the near future (or that have already begun unfolding) may soon be followed, yet again, by domestic changes in powerful states such as the United States and China and by reverse shifts. Therefore, policymakers should not expect the current trends toward nongovernmentalism to continue for long and should prepare both for shifts toward intergovernmentalism and toward nongovernmentalism.

Last, but not least, this text has shown that the sources of preferences that very often shape global governance stem from domestic ideological factors and from parochial interests of domestic institutions rather than from pragmatic reasons. This, of course, leads to another essential question: Is either intergovernmentalism or nongovernmentalism a "better" form of global governance in a given issue-area and time period? Of course, this question is complex and requires much additional research. However, by acknowledging that there is such a choice and that we have many possible options on a continuum, this text has taken a first step toward answering it.

References

Abbott, Kenneth W. 2012. "The Transnational Regime Complex for Climate Change." *Environment and Planning C: Government and Policy*, 30(4): 571–590.

Abbott, Kenneth W., and Duncan Snidal. 1998. "Why States Act through Formal International Organizations." *Journal of Conflict Resolution: A Quarterly for Research Related to War and Peace*, 42(1): 3–32.

2009. "Strengthening International Regulation through Transnational New Governance: Overcoming the Orchestration Deficit." *Vanderbilt Journal of Transnational Law*, 42(2): 501–578.

Abbott, Kenneth W., Philipp Genschel, Duncan Snidal, and Bernhard Zangl. 2015. *International Organizations as Orchestrators*. Cambridge, UK: Cambridge University Press.

Abbott, Kenneth W., Jessica F. Green, and Robert O. Keohane. 2016. "Organizational Ecology and Institutional Change in Global Governance." *International Organization*, 70(2): 247–277.

Abel-Smith, Brian. 1992. "The Beveridge Report: Its Origins and Outcomes." *International Social Security Review*, 45(1–2): 5–16.

Alcock, Antony Evelyn. 1971. *History of the International Labor Organization*. New York: Octagon Books.

Allison, Graham T. 1969. "Conceptual Models and the Cuban Missile Crisis." *American Political Science Review*, 63(3): 689–718.

1971. *Essence of Decision: Explaining the Cuban Missile Crisis*. Boston, MA: Little and Brown.

Alter, Karen J., and Sophie Meunier. 2009. "The Politics of International Regime Complexity." *Perspectives on Politics*, 7(1): 13–24.

American Engineering Standards Committee (AESC). 1918. "Minutes 1918."

1919. "Minutes 1919."

1926. "Minutes 1926."

Andonova, Liliana B. 2010. "Public-Private Partnerships for the Earth: Politics and Patterns of Hybrid Authority in the Multilateral System." *Global Environmental Politics*, 10(2): 25–53.

Andonova, Liliana B., Thomas N. Hale, and Charles B. Roger. 2017. "National Policy and Transnational Governance of Climate Change: Substitutes or Complements?" *International Studies Quarterly*, 61(2): 253–268.

Archer, Clive. 1983. *International Organizations*. London: Allen & Unwin.

Avant, Deborah D. 2005. *The Market for Force: The Consequences of Privatizing Security*. Cambridge, UK: Cambridge University Press.

Avant, Deborah D., Martha Finnemore, and Susan K. Sell, eds. 2010. *Who Governs the Globe?* Cambridge, UK: Cambridge University Press.

Axelrod, Robert, and Robert O. Keohane. 1985. "Achieving Cooperation under Anarchy: Strategies and Institutions." *World Politics*, 38(1): 226–254.

Ayusawa, Iwao. 1920. *International Labor Legislation*. Columbia University dissertation.

Baccaro, Lucio. 2015. "Orchestration for the 'Social Partners' Only: Internal Constraints on the ILO." In *International Organizations as Orchestrators*, edited by Kenneth W. Abbott, Philipp Genschel, and Duncan Snidal. Cambridge, UK: Cambridge University Press, 262–285.

Baccaro, Lucio, and Valentina Mele. 2012. "Pathology of Path Dependency? The ILO and the Challenge of New Governance." *Industrial and Labour Relations Review*, 65(2): 195–224.

Balinska, Marta A. 1995. "Assistances and Not Mere Relief: The Epidemic Commission of the League of Nations, 1920–1923." In *International Health Organisations and Movements: 1918–1939*, edited by Paul Weindling. Cambridge, UK: Cambridge University Press, 81–108.

   1998. *A Life for Humanity: Ludwik Rajchman, 1881–1965*. Budapest: CEU Press.

Banks, Arthur S., and Kenneth A. Wilson. 2015. *Cross-National Time-Series Data Archive*. Jerusalem: Databanks International.

Barros, James. 1969. *Betrayal from Within: Joseph Avenol, Secretary-General of the League of Nations, 1933–1940*. New Haven, CT: Yale University Press.

Bartley, Tim. 2007. "Institutional Emergence in an Era of Globalization: The Rise of Transnational Private Regulation of Labor and Environmental Conditions." *American Journal of Sociology*, 113(2): 297–351.

Bauer, Stephan. 1905. *The Working of the International Office of Labor in Basel, 1901–1905*. Basel: International Office of Labor.

Bawn, Kathleen. 1999. "Constructing 'Us': Ideology, Coalition Politics, and False Consciousness." *American Journal of Political Science*, 43(2): 303–334.

Behrstock, Julian. 1987. *The Eighth Case: Troubled Times at the United Nations*. Lanham, MD: University Press of America.

Beigbeder, Yves. 1979. "The United States' Withdrawal from the International Labor Organization." *Relations Industrielles/Industrial Relations*, 34(2): 223–240.

Bellush, Bernard. 1968. *He Walked Alone: A Biography of John Gilbert Winant*. The Hague: Mouton.

Bennett, A. LeRoy, and James K. Oliver. 2002. *International Organizations: Principles and Issues*. Upper Saddle River, NJ: Prentice Hall.

Bercovitch, Jacob, and Richard Jackson. 2009. *Conflict Resolution in the Twenty-First Century: Principles, Methods, and Approaches*. Ann Arbor: University of Michigan Press.

Berthelot, Yves, and Paul Rayment. 2007. *Looking Back and Peering Forward: A Short History of the United Nations Economic Commission for Europe*. Geneva: UNECE Information Service.

Biermann, Rafael, and Joachim Koops, eds. 2017. *Palgrave Handbook on Inter-organizational Relations*. Houndmills: Palgrave.

Birn, Anne-Emanuelle. 2014a. "Philanthrocapitalism, Past and Present: The Rockefeller Foundation, the Gates Foundation, and the Setting(s) of the International/Global Health Agenda." *Hypothesis*, 12(1): e8.

2014b. "Backstage: The Relationship between the Rockefeller Foundation and the World Health Organization, Part I. 1940s–1960s." *Public Health*, 128(2): 129–140.

Blagescu, Monica, and Robert Lloyd. 2006. *Global Accountability Report: Holding Power to Account*. London: One World Trust.

Blanqui, Adolphe. 1880. *History of Political Economy in Europe, by Jérôme-Adolphe Blanqui*. Translated from the 4th French edition. London: G. Bell and Sons.

Boli, John, and George M. Thomas. 1997. "World Culture in the World Polity: A Century of International Non-Governmental Organization." *American Sociological Review*, 62(2): 171–190.

1999. *Constructing World Culture: International Nongovernmental Organizations since 1875*. Stanford, CA: Stanford University Press.

Borgwardt, Elizabeth. 2005. *A New Deal for the World: America's Vision for Human Rights*. Cambridge, MA: Belknap Press of Harvard University Press.

Borowy, Iris. 2009. *Coming to Terms with World Health: The League of Nations Health Organisation, 1921–1946*. Frankfurt am Main: Peter Lang.

Botz, Abe. n.d. Special Study #1: Social Security: A Brief History of Social Insurance. Available at www.socialwelfarehistory.com/social-security/social-security-a-brief-history-of-social-insurance, accessed February 22, 2018.

Bousquet, Françoise, Christian Casper, Tineke M. Egyedi, Bernard Gauvin, Birger Hansen, Michel Jeanson, Marine Moguen-Toursel, and Emmanuel Coblence. 2008. "L'évolution à long terme des standards vue d'Europe [The Long-Term Evolution of Standards, as Seen from Europe]." *Entreprises et histoire*, 51(2): 117–134.

Bozeman, Barry. 1987. *All Organizations Are Public: Bridging Public and Private Organizational Theories*. San Francisco, CA: Jossey-Bass.

Brinkley, Joel S. T. 1987. Reagan Appoints Privatization Unit. Retrieved from www.nytimes.com/1987/09/04/us/reagan-appoints-privatization-unit.html, accessed February 18, 2018.

British Delegation to 1919 International Labor Conference. 1934. "Memorandum on the Machinery and Procedure Required for the International Regulation of Industrial Conditions." Prepared by the British Delegation, January 15–20, 1919. In *The Origins of the International Labor Organization Vol. II*, edited by James T. Shotwell. New York: Columbia University Press, 117–125.

Brooks, Stephen G., and William Curti Wohlforth. 2008. *World Out of Balance: International Relations and the Challenge of American Primacy*. Princeton, NJ: Princeton University Press.

Brown, E. Richard. 1979. *Rockefeller Medicine Men: Medicine and Capitalism in America*. Berkeley: University of California Press.

Burley, Anne-Marie. 1993. "Regulating the World: Multilateralism, International Law, and the Protection of the New Deal Regulatory State." In *Multilateralism Matters: The Theory and Praxis of an Institutional Form*, edited by John Gerard Ruggie. New York: Columbia University Press.

Büthe, Tim. 2010. "The Power of Norms; the Norms of Power: Who Governs International Electrical and Electronic Technology?" In *Who Governs the Globe?*, edited by Deborah D. Avant, Martha Finnemore, and Susan K. Sell. Cambridge, UK: Cambridge University Press, 292–332.

Cabanes, Bruno. 2014. *The Great War and the Origins of Humanitarianism, 1918–1924.* Cambridge, UK: Cambridge University Press.

Cannon, John Ashton. 2015. *The Oxford Companion to British History.* Oxford, UK: Oxford University Press.

Carpenter, Charli. 2010. "Governing the Global Agenda: 'Gatekeepers' and 'Issue Adoption' in Transnational Advocacy Networks." In *Who Governs the Globe?*, edited by Deborah Avant, Martha Finnemore, and Susan Sell. New York: Cambridge University Press, 202–237.

Cavanagh, John. 1997. "The Global Resistance to Sweatshops." In *No Sweat: Fashion, Free Trade and the Rights of Garment Workers*, edited by Andrew Ross. New York: Verso, 39–50.

Chaplowe, Scott G., and Ruth Bamela Engo-Tjega. 2007. "Civil Society Organizations and Evaluation: Lessons from Africa." *Evaluation*, 13(2): 257–274.

Charnovitz, Steve. 1997. "Two Centuries of Participation: NGOs and International Governance." *Michigan Journal of International Law*, 18(2): 183–286.

Chave, Sidney P. W. 1984. "The Origins and Development of Public Health." In *Oxford Textbook of Public Health, Vol. 1: History, Determinants, Scope, and Strategies*, edited by Walter W. Holland, Roger Detels, and George Knox. New York: Oxford University Press, 1–20.

Checkel, Jeffrey, T. 1997. "International Norms and Domestic Politics: Bridging the Rationalist-Constructivist Divide." *European Journal of International Relations*, 3(4): 473–495.

Chiang, Pei-heng. 1981. *Non-Governmental Organizations at the United Nations.* New York: Praeger.

Chow, Jack C. 2010. "Is the WHO Becoming Irrelevant? Why the World's Premier Public Health Organization Must Change or Die." Foreign Policy, December 9, 2010. Available at http://foreignpolicy.com/2010/12/09/is-the-who-becoming-irrelevant, accessed February 18, 2018.

Churchill, Winston. 1910. *Speeches by the Rt. Hon. Winston Churchill, the Earl of Lytton, Mr. Arthur Henderson.* London, UK: Garden City Press.

Clements, Richard Barrett. 1996. *Complete Guide to ISO 14000.* Englewood Cliffs, NJ: Prentice Hall.

Cochrane, Rexmond Canning. 1966. *Measures for Progress: A History of the National Bureau of Standards.* Washington, DC: National Bureau of Standards, United States Department of Commerce.

Codex Alimentarius. 1986. "Report on Duty Travel to Brussels 12–13 November 1985." WHO Archives, C14/372/2. Rome: Codex Alimentarius.

Collier, David, and James E. Mahon. 1993. "Conceptual 'Stretching' Revisited: Adapting Categories in Comparative Analysis." *The American Political Science Review*, 87(4): 845–855.

Collingsworth, Terry, J. William Goold, and Pharis Harvey. 1994. "Time for a Global New Deal." *Foreign Affairs*, 48: 8–13.

Commission for International Labor Legislation (Commission). 1919a. "3eme séance, 5 fevrier 1919. Proces Verbal." International Labor Organization Archives, Geneva, Switzerland. P3.

1919b. "4eme séance, 6 fevrier 1919. Proces Verbal." International Labor Organization Archives, Geneva, Switzerland. P4.

1919c. "5eme séance, 7 fevrier 1919. Proces Verbal." International Labor Organization Archives, Geneva, Switzerland. P5.

1919d. "9eme séance, Lundi, 17 fevrier 1919. Proces Verbal." International Labor Organization Archives, Geneva, Switzerland. P9.

Commission of the European Communities. 1985. "Completing the Internal Market: White Paper from the Commission to the European Council." Brussels: Commission of the European Communities.

Conference du Metre. 1875. "Documents Diplomatiques de la Conference du Metre." Paris, France: Imprimerie Nationale. Available at www.bipm.org/utils/common/documents/official/Diplomatic-Conference-Metre.pdf, accessed February 21, 2019.

Conference of Allied Ministers of Education. 1945. "Minutes of the 7th Meeting of the Drafting Committee Held on 18th of April 1945." London: Conference of Allied Ministers of Education.

Conference of NGOs in Consultative Relationship with the United Nations (CONGO). 2006. "NGO Participation Arrangements at the UN and Other Agencies of the UN System." Geneva, Switzerland: CONGO.

Cooley, Alexander. 2010. "Outsourcing Authority: How Project Contracts Transform Global Governance Networks." In *Who Governs the Globe?*, edited by Deborah Avant, Martha Finnemore, and Susan Sell. New York: Cambridge University Press, 238–265.

Coonley, Howard. 1954. "The International Standards Movement." In *National Standards in a Modern Economy*, edited by Dickson Reck. New York: Harper & Brothers, 37–45.

Cronin, Bruce. 2002. "The Two Faces of the United Nations: The Tension between Intergovernmentalism and Transnationalism." *Global Governance*, 8(1): 53–71.

Cumming, Hugh S. 1946. *International Health Conference*. Archive document from Hugh S. Cumming papers at the U.S. National Library of Medicine. 325MS C.

Dahl, Robert Alan. 1961. *Who Governs?: Democracy and Power in an American City*. New Haven, CT: Yale University.

Davies, Thomas Richard. 2014. *NGOs: A New History of Transnational Civil Society*. Oxford, UK: Oxford University Press.

Davison, Henry Pomeroy. 1920. *The American Red Cross in the Great War*. New York: Macmillan.

Delevingne, Malcolm. 1934. "The Pre-War History of International Labor Legislation." In *The Origins of the International Labor Organization Vol. I*, edited by James T. Shotwell. New York: Columbia University Press, 19–54.

Dingwerth, Klaus, and Philipp Pattberg. 2006. "Global Governance as a Perspective on World Politics." *Global Governance*, 12(2): 185–203.

Dodgson, Richard, Kelley Lee, and Nick Drager. 2002. *Global Health Governance: A Conceptual Review*. London, UK: Centre on Global Change & Health, London School of Hygiene & Tropical Medicine.

Dove, Jonathan. 2016. "The AIIB and the NDB: The End of Multilateralism or a New Beginning?" *The Diplomat*, April 26, 2016. Available at https://thediplomat.com/2016/04/the-aiib-and-the-ndb-the-end-of-multilateralism-or-a-new-beginning/

Downs, Anthony. 1966. *Inside Bureaucracy*. Boston, MA: Little, Brown.

Dreher, Axel. 2006. "Does Globalization Affect Growth? Evidence from a New Index of Globalization." *Applied Economics*, 38(10): 1091–1110.

Dubin, Martin David. 1995. "The League of Nations Health Organization." In *International Health Organisations and Movements: 1918–1939*, edited by Paul Weindling. Cambridge, UK: Cambridge University Press, 56–80.

The Economist. 1945. "UNSCC," *The Economist*. Vol. 148, March 3, 1945, 286–287.

ECOSOC. 1946. "Meeting of the Preparatory Technical Commission for the International Health Conference, 24 April 1946." E/H/1. New York: ECOSOC.

Egger, Clara. 2017. "From Non-governmental to Neo-Governmental Organizations: Exploring the Impact of Donors' Strategies on Humanitarian NGOs Communication." Paper presented at the General Conference of the European Consortium for Political Research, September 6, 2017.

European Committee for Standardization (CEN). 2000, December. "New Areas of Standardization." *Newsletter 9*.

European Telecommunications Standards Institute (ETSI). 2018, February 8. "ETSI Directives, Version 38." Available at https://portal.etsi.org/directives/38_directives_feb_2018.pdf

European Union (EU). 2000, May 19. "Council Resolution of 28 October 1999 on the Role of Standardization in Europe." OJC 141.

Farley, John. 2008. *Brock Chisholm the World Health Organization and the Cold War*. Vancouver, Canada: UBC Press.

Finnemore, Martha. 1996. *National Interests in International Society*. Ithaca, NY: Cornell University Press.

Finnemore, Martha, and Kathryn Sikkink. 1998. "International Norm Dynamics and Political Change." *International Organization*, 52(4): 887–917.

Fioretos, Orfeo. 2011. "Historical Institutionalism in International Relations." *International Organization*, 65(2): 367–399.

Florini, Ann. 2003. *The Coming Democracy: New Rules for Running a New World*. Washington, DC: Island Press.

Follows, John William. 1951. *Antecedents of the International Labour Organization*. Oxford, UK: Clarendon Press.

Food and Agriculture Organization (FAO). 1962. "Joint FAO/WHO Conference on Food Standards." Geneva, Switzerland, October 1–2, 1962. Extract from Report of 11th Session of FAO Conference.

1963. "Conference of Food and Agriculture Organization of the United Nations." Twelfth Session, November 12, 1963. Report of Commission II to Plenary. C63/REP/17.

1985. Letter of R. K. Mallik, Chief of Joint FAO/WHO Food Standards Programme to Felleke Sawdu, Secretary-General of African Regional Organization for Standardization, May 31, 1985.

Forsythe, David P. 2005. *The Humanitarians: The International Committee of the Red Cross*. Cambridge, UK: Cambridge University Press.

Friedman, Elisabeth J., Kathryn Hochstetler, and Ann Marie Clark. 2005. *Sovereignty, Democracy, and Global Civil Society State-Society Relations at UN World Conferences*. Albany, NY: State University of New York Press.

Fukuyama, Francis. 1992. *The End of History and the Last Man*. London, UK: Hamilton.

Galenson, Walter. 1981. *The International Labor Organization: An American View*. Madison: University of Wisconsin Press.

George, Alexander L., and Andrew Bennett. 2005. *Case Studies and Theory Development in the Social Sciences.* Cambridge, MA: MIT Press.

Gerring, John. 1997. "Ideology: A Definitional Analysis." *Political Research Quarterly,* 50(4): 957–994.

Gest, Nathaniel, and Alexandru Grigorescu. 2010. "Interactions among Intergovernmental Organizations in the Anti-Corruption Realm." *Review of International Organizations,* 5(1): 53–72.

Glenn, John. 2009. "Welfare Spending in an Era of Globalization: The North–South Divide." *International Relations,* 23(1): 27–50.

Global Policy Forum. 1996. "ECOSOC Concludes NGO Review." Available at www.globalpolicy.org/social-and-economic-policy/social-and-economic-policy-at-the-un/ngos-and-ecosoc/31786.html, accessed March 3, 2018.

2011. "NGOs in Consultative Status with ECOSOC by Category." Available at www.globalpolicy.org/component/content/article/176-general/32119-ngos-in-consultative-status-with-ecosoc-by-category.html, accessed March 10, 2018.

Goldstein, Judith, and Robert O. Keohane. 1993. *Ideas and Foreign Policy: Beliefs, Institutions, and Political Change.* Ithaca, NY: Cornell University Press.

Goodman, Neville M. 1952. *International Health Organizations and Their Work: With a Foreword by Sir W. Wilson Jameson.* London, UK: J. & A. Churchill.

Graham, Erin R. 2015. "Money and Multilateralism: How Funding Rules Constitute IO Governance." *International Theory,* 7(1): 162–194.

Green, Jessica F. 2014. *Rethinking Private Authority: Agents and Entrepreneurs in Global Environmental Governance.* Princeton, NJ: Princeton University Press.

Greenstein, Shane M. 1992. "Invisible Hands and Visible Advisors: An Economic Interpretation of Standardization." *Journal of the American Society of Information Science,* 43(8): 538–549.

Grieco, Joseph. 1988. "Anarchy and the Limits of Cooperation: A Realist Critique of the Newest Liberal Institutionalism." *International Organization,* 42(3): 485–507.

Grigorescu, Alexandru. 2007. "Transparency of Intergovernmental Organizations: The Roles of Member-States, International Bureaucracies and Non-Governmental Organizations." *International Studies Quarterly,* 51(3): 625–648.

2015. *Democratic Intergovernmental Organizations? Normative Pressures and Decision-Making Rules.* Cambridge, UK: Cambridge University Press.

2017. "IGO Relations in the Anti-corruption Realm and in Promoting Integrity in Public Procurement." In *Palgrave Handbook on Inter-Organizational Relations,* edited by Rafael Biermann and Joachim Koops. Houndmills, UK: Palgrave, 627–647.

Grigorescu, Alexandru, and Caglayan Baser. 2019. "The Choice between Intergovernmentalism and Nongovernmentalism: Projecting Domestic Preferences to Global Governance." *World Politics,* 71(1): 88–125.

Haas, Ernst B. 1962. "System and Process in the International Labor Organization: A Statistical Afterthought." *World Politics,* 14(2): 322–352.

Haas, Mark L. 2007. *The Ideological Origins of Great Power Politics, 1789–1989.* Ithaca, NY: Cornell University Press.

Haas, Peter M. 1989. "Do Regimes Matter? Epistemic Communities and Mediterranean Pollution Control." *International Organization,* 43(3): 377–403.

Haass, Richard N. 2018. "Liberal World Order, R.I.P." Council on Foreign Relations, March 21, 2018. Available at www.cfr.org/article/liberal-world-order-rip, accessed March 5, 2019.

Hale, Thomas Nathan. 2015. *Between Interests and Law: The Politics of Transnational Commercial Disputes*. Cambridge, UK: Cambridge University Press.

Hale, Thomas N., and Charles B. Roger. 2014. "Orchestration and Transnational Climate Governance." *The Review of International Organizations*, 9(1): 59–82.

Harman, Sophie. 2009. *The World Bank, Civil Society and HIV/AIDS: Setting a Global Agenda*. London, UK: Routledge.

2012. *Global Health Governance*. London, UK: Routledge.

Harmer, Andrew. 2012. "Who's Funding WHO?" Available at http://andrewharmer.org/wp-content/uploads/2017/06/Who%E2%80%99s-funding-WHO-%E2%80%93-globalhealthpolicy.net_.pdf, accessed March 23, 2011.

Haug, Hans, Hans-Peter Gasser, Françoise Perret, and Jean-Pierre Robert-Tissot. 1993. *Humanity for All: The International Red Cross and Red Crescent Movement*. Bern, Switzerland: P. Haupt.

Hawkins, Richard. 1999. "The Rise of Consortia in the Information and Communication Technology Industries." *Telecommunications Policy*, 23: 159–173.

Hills, Jill. 2002. *The Struggle for Control of Global Communication: The Formative Century*. Urbana: University of Illinois Press.

Howard-Jones, Norman. 1978. *International Public Health between the Two World Wars: The Organizational Problems*. Geneva, Switzerland: World Health Organization.

Huntington, Samuel Phillips. 1991. *The Third Wave: Democratization in the Late Twentieth Century*. Norman: University of Oklahoma Press.

Hutchinson, John F. 1997. *Champions of Charity: War and the Rise of the Red Cross*. Boulder, CO, and Oxford, UK: Westview.

2001. *The International Relief Union*. Emmitsburg, MD: National Emergency Training Center.

Ikenberry, G. John, David A. Lake, and Michael Mastanduno. 1988. *The State and American Foreign Economic Policy*. Ithaca, NY: Cornell University Press.

Independent Commission of Experts. 2002. "Switzerland - Second World War." Available at www.uek.ch/en/schlussbericht/synthesis/ueke.pdf, accessed March 4, 2018.

Institute of Medicine. 1988. "Committee for the Study of the Future of Public Health." *Future of Public Health*. Washington, DC: National Academies Press.

International Association for Labor Legislation (ILL). 1901. Assemblee constitutive tenue a Bale les 27–28 Septembre 1901. Rapports et compte-rendu des séances. Basel, Switzerland: Association internationale pour la protection légale des travailleurs.

1906a. Compte rendu de la premiere séance de la Commission de l'Association Internationale pour la Protection Légale des Travailleurs de 17 septembre 1906. Paris, France. Nancy: Berger-Levrault & Cie, Editeurs.

1906b. Compte rendu de la troisieme séance de la Commission de l'Association Internationale pour la Protection Légale des Travailleurs de 18 septembre 1906. Paris, France. Nancy: Berger-Levrault & Cie, Editeurs.

1910. Compte rendu de la seance sixieme assemblee generale du Comite de l'Association Internationale pour la Protection Légale des Travailleurs suivi de rapports annuels de de l'Association Internationale pour la Protection Légale des Travailleurs. Paris, France. Nancy: Berger-Levrault & Cie, Editeurs.

1921. Compte rendu de la séance du lundi 17 octobre 1921. Basel, Switzerland: Association internationale pour la protection légale des travailleurs.

International Bureau of Education (IBE). 1929. Minutes of second General Assembly of Bureau of International Education, July 25, 1929.

International Committee of the Red Cross (ICRC). Various years. Annual Report. Geneva, Switzerland: International Committee of the Red Cross.

1863a. Compte rendu de la Conference Internationale reunie a Geneve les 26, 27, 28 et 29 Octobre 1863 pour etudier les moyens de pouvoir a l'insuffance du services sanitaire dans les armees en campagne. Geneva, Switzerland: Fick.

1863b. Resolutions of the Geneva International Conference. Geneva, Switzerland, October 26–29, 1863. Available at https://ihl-databases.icrc.org/applic/ihl/ihl.nsf/52d68d14de6160e0c12563da005fdb1b/1548c3c0c113ffdfc12564 1a00059c537, accessed February 21, 2018.

1948. *Report of the International Committee of the Red Cross on Its Activities during the Second World War (September 1, 1939–June 30, 1947).* Geneva, Switzerland: International Committee of the Red Cross.

1977. *The ICRC, the League and the Tansley Report: Considerations of the International Committee of the Red Cross and of the League of Red Cross Societies on the Final Report on the Reappraisal of the Role of the Red Cross.* Geneva, Switzerland: International Committee of the Red Cross.

International Electrical Congress. 1904. *Proceedings of the Chamber of Delegates Appointed by Various Governments to the International Electrical Congress.* St Louis, MO: Chamber of Delegates.

International Electrotechnical Commission (IEC). 1906. Report of Preliminary Meeting Held at the Hotel Cecil, London on Tuesday and Wednesday, June 26th and 27th, 1906. London, UK: International Electrotechnical Commission.

1909. Transactions of the Council Held in October 1908. London, UK: Phipps and Connor.

1914. *Report of Berlin Meeting Held September 1913.* London, UK: Hudson and Kearns Ltd.

1919. *Report of Fourth Plenary Meeting Held in London in October 1919.* London, UK: Gaylard and Son.

1927. Unconfirmed Minutes of the Plenary Meeting Held in Rome at the Royal Accademia Dei Lincei on Thursday, September 22, 1927.

1934. Unconfirmed Minutes of the Twelfth Meeting Held in Prague on Saturday, October 13, 1934.

1946. Unconfirmed Minutes of the Meeting held at the Maison de la Chimie, 28 bis rue St. Dominique, Paris, France, on 8th and 9th July, 1946.

1947. Unconfirmed Minutes of the Meeting Held at the Kongressshaus, Zurich, on June 16, 1947.

International Labor Organization (ILO). 1956. International Labour Conference. Thirty-ninth Session. Record of Proceedings. Geneva, Switzerland: International Labor Office.

1959. Governing Body. 143rd Session. Minutes. Geneva, Switzerland: International Labor Office.

1975. International Labour Conference. Sixtieth Session. Record of Proceedings. Geneva, Switzerland: International Labor Office.

1978. International Labour Conference. Sixty-fourth Session. Record of Proceedings. Report II. Geneva, Switzerland: International Labor Office.

1997. International Labour Conference. Eighty-fifth Session. Record of Proceedings. Geneva, Switzerland: International Labor Office.

2002a. International Labour Conference. Ninetieth Session. Record of Proceedings. Geneva, Switzerland: International Labor Office.

2002b. Governing Body Minutes of the 285th Session. Geneva, Switzerland: International Labor Office.

2009. Director General's Announcement, IGDS No. 81, Version July 14, 2009. Geneva, Switzerland: International Labor Office.

International Labour Office (ILO). 1920. *First Special International Trade Union Congress.* Geneva, Switzerland: International Labour Office.

International Labour Office (ILO). 1923. International Labour Conference. Fifth Session. October 22–29, 1923. Geneva, Switzerland: International Labor Office.

1934. "Reports of Credential of Members of the Washington Conference, November 1919." In *The Origins of the International Labor Organization Vol. II,* edited by James T. Shotwell. New York: Columbia University Press, 480–485.

1941. *Conference of the International Labour Organization: 1941, New York and Washington, DC, Record of Proceedings.* Montreal, Canada: International Labour Office.

1943. Minutes of the Ninety-First Session of the Governing Body London 16–20 September 1943. Montreal, Canada: International Labour Office.

1946. "Instrument of Amendment Adopted by the International Labour Conference at Its 29th Session." *International Labour Office Official Bulletin.* November 15, 1946, XXIX(4): 215–225.

International Office of Public Health (OIHP). 1907. *Statutes of the International Office of Public Health.* Paris, France: International Office of Public Health.

1909. Letter from French Foreign Ministry to International Office of Public Health June 29, 1909. OIHP archives, Document OIHP_A62.

1918. Letter from International Office of Public Health to all Delegates June 15, 1918. OIHP Archives, Document OIHP_A47.

1920. Annexe a la letter de l'Office International d'Hygiene Publique du 15 decembre 1920. Reglement sue le Personnel. Paris, France: International Office of Public Health.

International Organization for Standardization (ISO). 1952. Unconfirmed Minutes of the 2nd ISO General Assembly Held at New York (USA), June 20–21, 1952.

1955. Unconfirmed Minutes of the General Assembly Held at Stockholm (Sweden), June 17 and 18, 1955.

1958. Unconfirmed Minutes of the 4th ISO General Assembly Held at Harrogate (United Kingdom), June 19 and 20, 1958.

1967. Unconfirmed Minutes of the General Assembly Held at Moscow, June 26 and 27, 1967.

1970. Minutes of the 8th ISO General Assembly, Ankara 21, 22, 23, 24, and 25 September 1970.

1973. Minutes of the 9th ISO General Assembly, Washington, September 10–14, 1973.

1979. 11th ISO General Assembly, Geneva, September 17–21, 1979, Minutes.

1985. 13th ISO General Assembly, Tokyo, September 9–13, 1985, Minutes and Statements Made, Annex 22.

1988. 14th ISO General Assembly, Prague, September 19–22, 1988, Minutes, Annex 23.

1997a. Minutes of the 20th ISO General Assembly Geneva (Switzerland), September 23–24, 1997.

1997b. *Friendship among Equals: Recollections from the ISO's First Fifty Years.* Geneva, Switzerland: ISO Central Secretariat.

International Radio Consultative Committee (CCIR). 1929. First Meeting, The Hague, September/October 1929.

International Telecommunication Union (ITU). 1964. List of Recognized Private Operating Agencies, Scientific or Industrial Organizations and International Organizations Taking Part in the Work of the C.C.I.s, as of 16 February 1964. Annex No. 2 to Notification No. 933.

"Overview of the ITU's History." Available at www.itu.int/en/history/Pages/ ITUsHistory.aspx, retrieved May 30, 2018.

International Telephone Consultative Committee (CCIF). 1938. XIIth Plenary Assembly. Cairo, February 4–5, 1938. Paris, France: International Telephone Consultative Committee.

1945. XIIIth Plenary Assembly. London, October 29–30, 1945. Modifications of the Green Book of the CCIF (Cairo 1938). Paris, France: International Telephone Consultative Committee.

International Union for Conservation of Nature (IUCN). 2017. "Statutes, including Rules of Procedure of the World Conservation Congress, and Regulations." Available at www.iucn.org/sites/dev/files/iucn_statutes_and_regulations_january_2018_final-master_file.pdf, accessed March 8, 2018.

International Union of League of Nations Associations. 1921. *Report for Year 1921.* Geneva, Switzerland: International Union of League of Nations Associations.

International Union of Official Travel Organizations (IUOTO). 1969. Record of Proceedings of Intergovernmental Conference on Tourism, Sofia, Bulgaria, May 15–28, 1969. Geneva, Switzerland: IUOTO.

Inter-Parliamentary Union. 1921. Letter from Christian Lange, Secretary General of Inter-Parliamentary Union to Eric Drummond, Secretary General of the League of Nations. February 18. League of Nations Archive. Document no 11009. File no 299.

Jackson, J. 1997. Regime Theory, Epistemic Communities, and International Health Decision-Making, PhD Dissertation. University of Wales, Aberystwyth, Wales.

Jenkins, Roy. 2001. *Churchill: A Biography.* London, UK: Macmillan.

Jervis, Robert. 1976. *Perception and Misperception in International Politics.* Princeton, NJ: Princeton University Press.

Jervis, Robert, Henry R. Nau, and Randall L. Schweller. 2002. "Correspondence: Institutionalized Disagreement." *International Security*, 27(1): 174–185.

Johnson, Tana. 2016. "Cooperation, Co-Optation, Competition, Conflict: International Bureaucracies and Non-Governmental Organizations in an Interdependent World." *Review of International Political Economy*, 23(5): 737–767.

Joll, James. 1955. *The Second International, 1889–1914.* London, UK: Weidenfeld and Nicolson.

Jupille, Joseph, Walter Mattli, and Duncan Snidal. 2013. *Institutional Choice and Global Commerce*. Cambridge, UK: Cambridge University Press.

Katzenstein, Peter J., ed. 1996. *The Culture of National Security: Norms and Identity in World Politics*. New York: Columbia University Press.

Keohane, Robert O. 1984. *After Hegemony: Cooperation and Discord in the World Political Economy*. Princeton, NJ: Princeton University Press.

Keohane, Robert O., and Joseph S. Nye. 1977. *Power and Interdependence: World Politics in Transition*. Boston, MA: Little, Brown.

Keohane, Robert O., and David G. Victor. 2011. "The Regime Complex for Climate Change." *Perspectives on Politics*, 9(1): 7–23.

Kloppenberg, James T. 1988. *Uncertain Victory: Social Democracy and Progressivism in European and American Thought, 1870–1920*. New York: Oxford University Press.

Koremenos, Barbara, Charles Lipson, and Duncan Snidal. 2004. *The Rational Design of International Institutions*. Cambridge, UK: Cambridge University Press.

Kosar, Kevin R. 2008. *The Quasi Government: Hybrid Organizations with Both Government and Private Sector Legal Characteristics*. Washington, DC: Congressional Research Service, Library of Congress.

Krasner, Stephen D. 1978. *Defending the National Interest: Raw Materials Investments and U.S. Foreign Policy*. Princeton, NJ: Princeton University Press.

  1983. *International Regimes*. Ithaca, NY: Cornell University Press.

  1991. "Global Communications and National Power: Life on the Pareto Frontier." *World Politics*, 43(3): 336–366.

Kuert, Willy. 1997. "The Founding of the ISO: Things Are Going the Right Way!" In *Friendship Among Equals: Recollections from the ISO's First Fifty Years*, edited by International Organization for Standardization. Geneva, Switzerland: ISO Central Secretariat, 13–22.

Lane, Robert E. 1969. "The Meanings of Ideology." In *Power, Participation and Ideology: Readings in the Sociology of American Political Life*, edited by Calvin J. Larson. New York: McKay, 321–323.

Lavelle, Kathryn C. 2005. "Exit, Voice, and Loyalty in International Organizations: US Involvement in the League of Nations." *The Review of International Organizations*, 2(4): 371–393.

Laves, Walter H. C., and Thomson, C. A. 1957. *UNESCO: Purpose, Progress, Prospects*. Bloomington: Indiana University Press.

League of Nations. 1919. Statement of Result of Discussion with Col. Cumming, July 18, 1919. Geneva, Switzerland: League of Nations and International Health Organization.

  1920a. "Covenant of the League of Nations." Available at http://avalon.law.yale.edu/20th_century/leagcov.asp, accessed February 21, 2018.

  1920b. Draft Proposals of the Argentine Delegation for the Establishment of an International Organizations for Health and Demography with the Council of League of Nations. Geneva, Switzerland: League of Nations.

  1920c. Minutes of the Third Session of the Council of the League of Nations, April 13, 1920. Geneva, Switzerland: League of Nations.

  1922. *Bulletin of Information on the Work of International Organisations*. Geneva, Switzerland: League of Nations.

  1925a. Minutes of Fourth Health Committee Meeting, May 15, 1925. Geneva, Switzerland: League of Nations.

1925b. Proces-verbaux des travaux de la commission d'etude du projet Ciraolo, 2nd Session, Paris, France, June 27, 1925.

1926a. Minutes of the 32nd Session of the League Council of 11 December 1925. Geneva, Switzerland: League of Nations.

1926b. International Relief Union. *Official Journal*, 7(6): 845–848.

League of Nations Council. 1921. Draft Report for the Establishment of an International Office of Education, 12th session, March 1, 1921.

League of Red Cross Societies (LRCS). 1919a. Proceedings of the Medical Conference held at the invitation of the Committee of Red Cross Societies, Cannes, France, April 1–11, 1919.

1919b. Minutes of the Board of Governors of the League of Red Cross Societies. *Bulletin of League of Red Cross Societies*, 1(3).

1920. Meeting of the Board of Governors of the League of Red Cross Societies, Paris, France, March 25, 1920.

Lebow, Richard Ned, and Thomas Risse-Kappen. 1997. *International Relations Theory and the End of the Cold War*. New York: Columbia University Press.

Lee, Kelley. 2010. "Civil Society Organizations and the Functions of Global Health Governance: What Role within Intergovernmental Organizations?" *Global Health Governance: The Scholarly Journal for the New Health Security Paradigm*, 3(2). Available at http://blogs.shu.edu/ghg/files/2011/11/Lee_Civil-Society-Organizations-and-the-Functions-of-Global-Health-Governance_Spring-2010.pdf, accessed February 18, 2018.

Legge, David. 2015. WHO Shackled: Donor Control of the World Health Organization. *Third World Resurgence*, 298/299: 15–19.

Lenin, Vladimir I. 1975. "A 'Scientific' System of Sweating." In *Lenin Collected Works*, 18. Moscow: Progress Publishers, 594–595.

Ley, Anthony J. 2000. *A History of Building Control in England and Wales 1840–1990*. Coventry, UK: RICS Books.

Locke, Richard, and Kathleen Thelen. 1998. "Problems of Equivalence in Comparative Politics: Apples and Oranges, Again." *Newsletter of the APSA Organized Section in Comparative Politics*, 8(1): 1–9.

Loya, Thomas A., and John Boli. 1999. "Standardization in the World Polity: Technical Rationality over Power." In *Constructing World Culture: International Nongovernmental Organizations since 1875*, edited by John Boli and George M. Thomas. Stanford, CA: Stanford University Press, 169–197.

Lyall, Francis. 2016. *International Communications: The International Telecommunication Union and the Universal Postal Union*. London, UK: Taylor & Francis.

Lynch, Colum, and Elias Groll. 2017. "As U.S. Retreats from World Organizations, China Steps in to Fill the Void." October 6, 2017, *Foreign Policy*. Available at https://foreignpolicy.com/2017/10/06/as-u-s-retreats-from-world-organizations-china-steps-in-the-fill-the-void/

MacDonald, Nina. 1934. "Letter to Adrian Pelt, Director of Information Section. League of Nations." February 19. League of Nations Archives, 10943. File 299.

Maday, André de. 1935. *Necker, précurseur du pacifisme et de la protection ouvrière*. Brussels, Belgium: Imprimerie des travaux publics.

Mahaim, Ernest. 1904. *Association internationale pour la protection légale des travailleurs – Son histoire – son but – son oeuvre*. Basel, Switzerland: Association internationale pour la protection légale des travailleurs.

1913. *Le Droit International Ouvrier*. Paris, France: Recueil Sirey.

1934. "The Historical and Social Importance of International Labor Legislation." In *The Origins of the International Labor Organization. Volume I*, edited by James T. Shotwell. New York: Columbia University Press, 3–18.

Mahoney, James. 2000. "Path Dependence in Historical Sociology." *Theory and Society*, 29: 507–548.

Marshall, Monty G., Keith Jaggers, and Ted Robert Gurr. 2010. "Polity IV Project, Political Regime Characteristics and Transitions, 1800–2010, Dataset Users' Manual." Center for Systemic Peace.

Martens, Kerstin. 2011. "Civil Society and Accountability in the United Nations." In *Building Global Democracy?: Civil Society and Accountable Global Governance*, edited by Jan Aart Scholte. Cambridge, MA: Cambridge University Press.

Martin, Lisa L. 1992. "Interests, Power, and Multilateralism." *International Organization*, 46(4): 765–792.

Mason, Edward S., and Robert A. Asher. 1973. *The World Bank since Bretton Woods: The origins, policies, operations, and impact of the International Bank for Reconstruction and Development and the other members of the World Bank group: The International Finance Corporation, the International Development Association [and] the International Centre for Settlement of Investment Disputes.* Washington, DC: Brookings Institution.

Matthews, Jessica. 1997. "Power Shift." *Foreign Affairs*, 76(1): 50–66.

Mattli, Walter. 2003. "Public and Private Governance in Setting International Standards." In *Governance in a Global Economy: Political Authority in Transition*, edited by Miles Kahler and David A. Lake. Princeton, NJ: Princeton University Press, 199–225.

Mattli, Walter, and Tim Büthe. 2003. "Setting International Standards: Technological Rationality or Primacy of Power?" *World Politics*, 56(1): 1–42.

Maxwell, William Quentin. 1956. *Lincoln's Fifth Wheel: The Political History of the U.S. Sanitary Commission*. New York, London, UK and Toronto, Canada: Longmans, Green and Co.

Mazower, M. 2009. *No Enchanted Palace: The End of Empire and the Ideological Origins of the United Nations*. Princeton, NJ and Oxford, UK: Princeton University Press.

McCarthy, Kathleen D. 1987. "From Cold War to Cultural Development: The International Cultural Activities of the Ford Foundation, 1950–1980." *Daedalus*, 116(1): 93–117.

McCoy, David, Gayatri Kembhavi, Jinesh Patel, and Akish Luintel. 2009. "The Bill & Melinda Gates Foundation's Grant-Making Programme for Global Health." *Lancet*, 373(9675): 1645–1653.

McCoy, Jennifer L. 2001. "The Emergence of a Global Anti-corruption Norm." *International Politics*, 38: 65–90.

McCune, Lindsay. 1934. "The Problem of American Cooperation." In *The Origins of the International Labor Organization*. Volume I, edited by James T. Shotwell. New York: Columbia University Press, 331–370.

McFate, Sean. 2014. *The Modern Mercenary: Private Armies and What They Mean for World Order*. Oxford, UK: Oxford University Press.

McNair, Arnold D. 1956. Report. *International Labor Organization Official Bulletin*. (9).

McWilliam, Robert Coutts. 2002. "The Evolution of British Standards," Doctoral Dissertation, University of Reading, Reading, UK, September, 2002.

Mearsheimer, John. 1994. "The False Promise of International Institutions." *International Security*, 19(3): 5–49.

Meyer, John W., John Boli, George M. Thomas, and Francisco O. Ramirez. 1997. "World Society and the Nation-State." *American Journal of Sociology*, 103(1): 144–181.

Micklitz, Hans-W. 1998. "Review of Rönck, Rüdiger, Technische Normen als Gestaltungsmittel des Europäischen Gemeinschaftsrechts: Zulässigkeit und Praktikabilität ihrer Rezeption zur Realisierung des Gemeinsamen Marktes." *European Journal of International Law*, 9: 574–576.

Middleton, Robert W. 1980. "The GATT Standards Code." *Journal of World Trade*, 14(3): 201–219.

Miller, David H. 1928. *The Drafting of the Covenant* (Volumes I and II). New York: G. P. Putnam's Sons.

Milman-Sivan, Faina. 2009. "Representativity, Civil Society, and the EU Social Dialogue: Lessons from the International Labor Organization." *Indiana Journal of Global Legal Studies*, 16(1): 311–337.

Milner, Helen V. 1992. "International Theories of Cooperation among Nations: Strengths and Weaknesses." *World Politics*, 44(3): 466–496.

Milner, Helen V., and Dustin Tingley. 2015. *Sailing the Water's Edge: The Domestic Politics of American Foreign Policy*. Princeton, NY: Princeton University Press.

Milner, Susan. 1991. *The Dilemmas of Internationalism: French Syndicalism and the International Labour Movement 1900–1914*. Oxford, UK: Berg Publishers.

Mitrany, David. 1966. *A Working Peace System*. Chicago, IL: Quadrangle Books.

Moorehead, Caroline. 1998. *Dunant's Dream: War, Switzerland and the History of the Red Cross*. London, UK: HarperCollins.

Moravcsik, Andrew. 1997. "Taking Preferences Seriously: A Liberal Theory of International Politics." *International Organization*, 51(4): 513–553.

2010. "The New Liberalism." In *The Oxford Handbook of International Relations*, edited by Christian Reus-Smit and Duncan Snidal. New York and Oxford, UK: Oxford University Press, 234–254.

Mullins, Willard. 1972. "On the Concept of Ideology in Political Science." *American Political Science Review*, 66(2): 498–510.

Mundy, Karen. 2010. "'Education for All' and the Global Governors." In *Who Governs the Globe?*, edited by Deborah D. Avant, Martha Finnemore, and Susan K. Sell. Cambridge, UK: Cambridge University Press, 333–355.

Murdie, Amanda. 2014. *Help or Harm: The Human Security Effects of International NGOs*. Stanford, CA: Stanford University Press.

Murphy, Craig N. 2014. "Global Governance over the Long Haul." *International Studies Quarterly*, 58(1): 216–218.

1994. *International Organization and Industrial Change: Global Governance since 1850*. New York: Oxford University Press.

Murphy, Craig N., and JoAnne Yates. 2010. *The International Organization for Standardization (ISO): Global Governance through Voluntary Consensus*. London, UK: Routledge.

Mylonas, Denis. 1976. *La Genèse de l'Unesco: La Conférence des Ministres Alliés de L'éducation: 1942–1945*. Bruxelles, Belgique: E. Bruylant.

Nadvi, Khalid, and Frank Waeltring. 2004. "Making Sense of Global Standards." In *Local Enterprises in the Global Economy: Issues of Governance and Upgrading*, edited by Hubert Schmitz. Cheltenham, UK: Edward Elgar, 53–94.

Naess, Arne, Jens A. Christophersen, and Kjell Kvalø. 1956. *Democracy, Ideology and Objectivity: Studies in the Semantics and Cognitive Analysis of Ideological Controversy*. Oslo, Norway: Norwegian Research Council for Science and the Humanities.

Naim, Moses. 2009. "What Is a GONGO? How Government-Sponsored Groups Masquerade as Civil Society." *Foreign Policy*, October 13. Available at http://foreignpolicy.com/2009/10/13/what-is-a-gongo, accessed March 10, 2018.

National Industrial Conference Board (NICB). 1922. *The International Labor Organization of the League of Nations*. New York: The Century Co.

NGO Monitor. 2013a. "United States," June 11. Available at www.ngo-monitor.org/article/usa_usaid, accessed March 10, 2018.

   2013b. "The Negative Impact of U.S. Government Funding for Mideast Political NGOs," May 20. Available at www.ngo-monitor.org/article/due_diligence_and_accountability_the_negative_impact_of_u_s_government_funding_for_mideast_political_ngos, accessed March 10, 2018.

Nugent, Walter T. K. 2010. *Progressivism a Very Short Introduction*. Oxford, UK: Oxford University Press.

Nye, Joseph S., and Robert O. Keohane. 1972. *Transnational Relations and World Politics*. Cambridge, MA: Harvard.

Olsen, Figueres, José María, José Manuel Salazar-Xirinachs, and Mónica Araya. 2001. "Trade and Environment at the World Trade Organization: The Need for a Constructive Dialogue." In *The Role of the World Trade Organization in Global Governance*, edited by Gary P. Sampson. Tokyo: United Nations University Press, 155–181.

Ōmae, Ken'ichi. 1995. *The End of the Nation State: The Rise of Regional Economies*. New York: Free Press.

Opoku-Mensah, Paul. 2001. "The Rise and Rise of NGOs: Implications for Research." *Tidsskrift ved Institutt for sosiologi og statsvitenskap*, 1: 1–3.

Organization for Economic Cooperation and Development (OECD). 1999. *Regulatory Reform and International Standardization*. Paris, France: OECD Working Party of the Trade Committee.

O'Siochrú, Sean. 1995. *International Telecommunication Union and Non-governmental Organisations: The Case for Mutual Cooperation*. Dublin, Ireland: Nexus Research Cooperative Unit.

Osieke, Ebere. 1985. *Constitutional Law and Practice in the International Labour Organisation*. Dordrecht, the Netherlands: Nijhoff.

Osterhammel, Jürgen, and Niels P. Petersson. 2009. *Globalization: A Short History*. Princeton, NJ: Princeton University Press.

Oye, Kenneth A. 1986. *Cooperation under Anarchy*. Princeton, NJ: Princeton University Press.

"Parliamentary Committee of the Report of the International Conference in Paris." 1883. Report of the deputation. *Journal of the House of Lords*, 124.

Pevehouse, Jon, Timothy Nordstrom, and Kevin Warnke. 2004. "The COW-2 International Organizations Dataset, Version 2.0." *Conflict Management and Peace Science*, 21(2): 101–119.

Pfeffer, Jeffrey. 1997. *New Directions for Organization Theory Problems and Prospects.* New York: Oxford University Press.

Phelan, Edward J. 1934. "The Commission on International Labor Legislation." In *The Origins of the International Labor Organization.* Volume I, edited by James T. Shotwell. New York: Columbia University Press, 127–198.

2009. *Edward Phelan and the ILO: The Life and Views of an International Social Actor.* Geneva, Switzerland: International Labour Office.

Pickard, Bertram. 1956. *The Greater United Nations; an Essay Concerning the Place and Significance of International Non-governmental Organizations.* New York: Carnegie Endowment for International Peace.

Picquenard, Charles. 1934. "The Preliminaries of the Peace Conference: French Preparations." In *The Origins of the International Labor Organization.* Volume I, edited by James T. Shotwell. New York: Columbia University Press, 83–96.

Pierson, Paul. 2000. "Increasing Returns, Path Dependence, and the Study of Politics." *The American Political Science Review,* 94(2): 251–267.

Ping, Wang. 2011. "A Brief History of Standards and Standardization Organizations: Chinese Perspective." East-West Center Working Papers, Economics Series, 11. Available at www.eastwestenter.org/system/tdf/private/econwp117.pdf?file=1&type= node&id=32840, accessed January 31, 2019.

Polaski, Sandra. 2006. "Combining Global and Local Forces: The Case of Labor Rights in Cambodia." *World Development,* 34(5): 919–932.

Posner, Eric A., and Miguesl De Figueiredo. 2005. "Is the International Court of Justice Biased?" *Journal of Legal Studies,* 34: 599–630.

Preston, William, Edward S. Herman, and Herbert I. Schiller. 1989. *Hope & Folly: The United States and UNESCO, 1945–1985.* Minneapolis: University of Minnesota Press.

Putnam, Robert. 1988. "Diplomacy and Domestic Politics: The Logic of Two-Level Games." *International Organization.* 42(3): 427–460.

Raghavan, Chakravarthi. 2001. "HAI Voices Concern over WHO's 'Partnership' with Private Sector." Third World Network, May 13, 2001. Available at www.twnside.org.sg/title/hai.htm, accessed February 18, 2018.

Rathbun, Brian C. 2012. *Trust in International Cooperation: International Security Institutions, Domestic Politics, and American Multilateralism.* Cambridge, UK: Cambridge University Press.

Rau, Bill. 2006. "The Politics of Civil Society in Confronting HIV/AIDS." *International Affairs,* 82(2): 285–295.

Raustiala, Kal, and David G. Victor. 2004. "The Regime Complex for Plant Genetic Resources." *International Organization,* 582: 277–309.

Reck, Dickson, ed. 1956. *National Standards in a Modern Economy.* New York: Harper and Brothers.

Reimann, Kim. 2006. "A View from the Top: International Politics, Norms and the Worldwide Growth of NGOs." *International Studies Quarterly,* 50(1): 45–67.

Renoliet, Jean-Jacques. 1999. *L'Unesco Oubliée: La Société des Nations Et La Coopération Intellectuelle, 1919–1946.* Paris, France: Publications de la Sorbonne.

Reuther, Walter P. 1956. "Labor Uses Standards." In *National Standards in a Modern Economy,* edited by Dickson Reck. New York: Harper and Brothers, 303–310.

Richter, Judith. 2012. "WHO Reform and Public Interest Safeguards: An Historical Perspective." *Social Medicine*, 6(3): 141–150.

Rider, Christine, ed. 2007. *Encyclopedia of the Age of the Industrial Revolution, 1700–1920*. Westport, CN: Greenwood.

Riegelman, Carol. 1934. "War-Time Trade Unions and Socialist Proposals." In *The Origins of the International Labor Organization*. Volume I, edited by James T. Shotwell. New York: Columbia University Press, 55–82.

Ripinsky, Sergey, and Peter Van den Bossche. 2007. *NGO Involvement in International Organizations: A Legal Analysis*. London, UK: British Institute of International and Comparative Law.

Risse-Kappen, Thomas. 1991. "Public Opinion, Domestic Structure, and Foreign Policy in Liberal Democracies." *World Politics*, 43(4): 479–512.

Rixen, Thomas, Lora Anne Viola, and Michael Zürn. 2016. *Historical Institutionalism and International Relations: Explaining Institutional Development in World Politics*. Oxford, UK: Oxford University Press.

Roberts, Steven. 2012. "A History of the Telegraph Companies in Britain between 1838–1868." Available at http://distantwriting.co.uk, accessed May 30, 2018.

Rodgers, Gerry, Eddy Lee, Lee Swepston, and Jasmien Van Daele. 2009. *The International Labour Organization and the Quest for Social Justice, 1919–2009*. Geneva, Switzerland: International Labour Office.

Rodgers, Stuart, and Thomas J. Volgy. 2009. "Substituting for Democratization: A Comparative Analysis of Involvement in Regional Intergovernmental Organizations." In *Mapping the New World Order*, edited by Thomas J. Volgy, Zlatko Sabic, Petra Roter, and Andrea K. Gerlak. New York: Wiley, 148–173.

Rohde, D. 1997, September 19. "Ted Turner Plans a $1 Billion Gift for UN Agencies." Retrieved from www.nytimes.com/1997/09/19/world/ted-turner-plans-a-1-billion-gift-for-un-agencies.html, accessed March 3, 2018.

Roosevelt, Franklin D. 1941. *The Four Freedoms: Message to the 77th Congress, January 6, 1941*. Washington, DC: United States Government Publishing Office.

Rosenau, James N. 1969. *Linkage Politics: Essays on the Convergence of National and International Systems*. New York: Free Press.

1992. "Governance, Order and Change in World Politics." In *Governance without Government: Order and Change in World Politics*, edited by James N. Rosenau and Ernst-Ottawa Czempiel. Cambridge, UK: Cambridge University Press, 1–29.

1997. *Along the Domestic-Foreign Frontier: Exploring Governance in a Turbulent World*. Cambridge, UK: Cambridge University Press.

Rossello, Pedro. 1943. *Les Précurseurs du Bureau International D'éducation; Un Aspect Inédit de L'histoire de L'éducation et des Institutions Internationales*. Genève, Suisse: Bureau International D'éducation.

Ruger, Jennifer Prah. 2005. "The Changing Role of the World Bank in Global Health." *American Journal of Public Health*, 95(1): 60–70.

Ruggie, John Gerard. 1982. "International Regimes, Transactions, and Change: Embedded Liberalism in the Postwar Economic Order." *International Organization*, 36(2): 379–415.

2004. "Reconstituting the Global Public Domain – Issues, Actors, and Practices." *European Journal of International Relations*, 10(4): 499–531.

Russett, Bruce. 1993. *Grasping the Democratic Peace*. Princeton, NJ: Princeton University Press.

Sagar, David. 1999. "The Privatisation of INMARSAT: Special Problems." International Organisations and Space Law, Proceedings of the Third ECSL Colloquium, Perugia, Italy, May 6–7, 1999: 127–142. Available at http://articles.adsabs.harvard.edu/cgi-bin/nph-iarticle_query?1999ESASP.442..127S&data_type=PDF_HIGH&whole_paper=YES&type=PRINTER&filetype=.pdf, accessed July 17, 2018.

Salamon, Lester M., and Helmut K. Anheier. 1999. *Defining the Nonprofit Sector: A Cross-National Analysis*. Manchester, UK: Manchester University Press.

Sandberg, Eve. 1994. *The Changing Politics of Non-Governmental Organizations and African States*. Westport, CT and London, UK: Praeger.

Sartori, Giovanni. 1969. "Politics, Ideology, and Belief Systems." *American Political Science Review* 63(2): 398–411.

1970. "Concept Misformation in Comparative Politics." *American Political Science Review*, 64(4): 1033–1053.

Schapiro, J. Salwyn. 1923. *Modern and Contemporary European History*. New York: Houghton Mifflin.

Schechter, Michael G. 2005. *United Nations Global Conferences*. London, UK: Routledge.

Schevenels, Walther. 1956. *A Historical Precis: Forty-Five Years: International Federation of Trade Unions, 1901–1945*. Brussels, Belgium: International Federation of Trade Unions.

Schneiker, Andrea. 2017. "NGO-NGO Relations." In *Palgrave Handbook on Inter-Organizational Relations*, edited by Rafael Biermann and Joachim Koops. Houndmills, UK: Palgrave, 319–336.

Seary, Bill. 1996. "The Early History: From the Congress of Vienna to the San Francisco Conference." In *The Conscience of the World: The Influence of Non-governmental Organisations in the UN System*, edited by Peter Willetts. Washington, DC: Brookings Institution, 15–30.

Seddon, John. 2000. *The Case against ISO 9000: How to Create Real Quality in Your Organisation*. Dublin, Ireland: Oak Tree.

Sewell, James Patrick. 1975. *UNESCO and World Politics: Engaging in International Relations*. Princeton, NJ: Princeton University Press.

Shanks, Cheryl, Harold K. Jacobson, and Jeffrey H. Kaplan. 1996. "Inertia and Change in the Constellation of International Governmental Organizations, 1981–1992." *International Organization*, 50(4): 593–627.

Shultz, George. 1985. "U.S. Role in the ILO – International Labor Organization." *U.S. Department of State Bulletin*, 85: 8–15.

Singer, J. David, Stuart Bremer, and John Stuckey. 1972. "Capability Distribution, Uncertainty, and Major Power War, 1820–1965." In *Peace, War, and Numbers*, edited by Bruce Russett. Beverly Hills, CA: Sage.

Singer, J. David, and Michael Wallace. 1970. "Intergovernmental Organization and the Preservation of Peace, 1816–1964: Some Bivariate Relationships." *International Organization*, 24(3): 520–547.

Singer, Peter Warren. 2008. *Corporate Warriors: The Rise of the Privatized Military Industry*. Ithaca, NY: Cornell University Press.

Skjelsbaek, Kjell. 1971. "The Growth of International Nongovernmental Organization in the Twentieth Century." In *Transnational Relations and World Politics*, edited by Robert O. Keohane and Joseph S. Nye. Cambridge, MA: Harvard University Press, 70–92.

Slaughter, Anne-Marie. 2004. *A New World Order*. Princeton, NJ: Princeton University Press.

Smith, Brian H. 1990. *More than Altruism: The Politics of Private Foreign Aid*. Princeton, NJ: Princeton University Press.

Smythe, Elizabeth. 2009. "Whose Interests? Transparency and Accountability in the Global Governance of Food: Agribusiness, the Codex Alimentarius, and the World Trade Organization." In *Corporate Power in Global Agrifood Governance*, edited by Jennifer Clapp and Doris Fuchs. Cambridge, MA: MIT Press, 93–123.

Snidal, Duncan. 1985. "Coordination versus Prisoners' Dilemma: Implications for International Cooperation and Regimes." *The American Political Science Review* 79(4): 923–942.

Spruyt, Hendrik. 2001. "The Supply and Demand of Governance in Standard-Setting: Insights from the Past." *Journal of European Public Policy*, 8(3): 371–391.

Staples, Amy L. S. 2007. *The Birth of Development: How the World Bank, Food and Agriculture Organization, and World Health Organization Changed the World, 1945–1965*. Kent, OH: Kent State University Press.

Steffek, Jens. 2014. "The IONGO Phenomenon: How International Organizations Shape Transnational Civil Society." Paper Presented at the Annual Conference of the British International Studies Association, Dublin, Ireland, June 18–20, 2014.

Steffek, Jens, and Leonie Holthaus. 2018. "The Social-Democratic Roots of Global Governance: Welfare Internationalism from the 19th Century to the United Nations." *European Journal of International Relations*, 24(1): 106–129.

Steffek, Jens, Claudia Kissling, and Patrizia Nanz, eds. 2008. *Civil Society Participation in European and Global Governance: A Cure for the Democratic Deficit?* Basingstoke: Palgrave Macmillan.

Stewart, Margaret. 1969. *Britain and the ILO: The Story of Fifty Years*. London, UK: Her Majesty's Stationery Office.

Strange, Susan. 1982. "Cave! Hic Dragones: A Critique of Regime Analysis." *International Organization*, 36(2): 479–496.

Sturen, Olle. 1980. "Responding to the Challenge of the GATT Standards Codes." Washington, DC. March, 1980.

Suchodolski, Bogdan. 1979. *"The International Bureau of Education in the Service of Educational Development."* Paris, France: UNESCO.

Sweetser, Arthur. 1920. *The League of Nations at Work*. New York: Macmillan.

Tallberg, Jonas, Thomas Sommerer, Theresa Squatrito, and Christer Jonsson. 2013. *The Opening Up of International Organizations: Transnational Access in Global Governance*. Cambridge, UK: Cambridge University Press.

Tamm Hallström, Kristina. 2008. "ISO Expands Its Business into Social Responsibility (SR)." In *Organizing Transnational Accountability: Mobilization, Tools, Challenges*, edited by Magnus Boström and Christina Garsten. Cheltenham, UK: Edward Elgar, 46–60.

Tate, Jay. 2001. "National Varieties of Standardization." In *Varieties of Capitalism: The Institutional Foundations of Competitive Advantage*, edited by Peter A. Hall and David Soskice. New York: Oxford University Press, 442–473.

Thelen, Kathleen Ann. 1999. "Historical Institutionalism in Comparative Politics." *Annual Review of Political Science*, 2: 369–404.

Thomann, Lars. 2008. "The ILO, Tripartism, and NGOs: Do Too Many Cooks Really Spoil the Broth." In *Civil Society Participation in European and Global Governance: A Cure for the Democratic Deficit?*, edited by Jens Steffek, Claudia Kissling, and Patrizia Nanz. Basingstoke, UK: Palgrave Macmillan, 71–94.

Timmins, Nicholas. 2001. *The Five Giants: A Biography of the Welfare State*. New York: HarperCollins.

Tipton, John Bruce. 1959. *Participation of the United States in the International Labor Organization*. Champaign: University of Illinois, Institute of Labor and Industrial Relations.

Towers, Bridget A. 1987. *The Politics of Tuberculosis in Western Europe 1914–40: A Study in the Sociology of Policymaking*. London, UK: University of London.

Towers, Bridget. 1995. "Red Cross Organisational Politics, 1918–1922: Relations of Dominance and the Influence of the United States." In *International Health Organisations and Movements: 1918–1939*, edited by Paul Weindling. Cambridge, UK: Cambridge University Press, 36–55.

Tsebelis, George. 1995. "Decision Making in Political Systems: Veto Players in Presidentialism, Parliamentarism, Multicameralism and Multipartyism." *British Journal of Political Science*, 25(3): 289–325.

UNAIDS. 2009. The Governance Handbook. UNAIDS/09.15E/JC1682E. Available at www.unaids.org/sites/default/files/media_asset/JC1682_GovernanceHandbook_March2011_en.pdf, accessed March 3, 2018.

UNESCO. 1946. "Preparatory Commission, Letter from Joseph Needham, Head of Division of Natural Sciences, to Charles Le Maistre, 17th June 1946."

1951. Record of General Conference, Sixth Session, Proceedings, 1951. Paris, France: UNESCO.

2009. "Executive Board." Available at http://atom.archives.unesco.org/unesco-executive-board, accessed March 10, 2018.

2016. "Voluntary Contributions Received for Special Accounts & Other for the Period 1 January to 31 December 2015." BFM/2016/PI/H/1 at http://unesdoc.unesco.org/images/0024/002444/244459e.pdf, accessed March 3, 2018.

UNICEF. 1999. *Annual Report*. New York: UNICEF.

2009. *Annual Report*. New York: UNICEF.

Union of International Associations. 1912. *L'Union des associations internationales*. Brussels, Belgium: O. Lamberty.

2015. *Yearbook of International Organizations. 2014–2015*. 6 vols. Leiden, the Netherlands: Koninklijke Brill NV.

United Nations. 1975. United States Letter Containing Notice of Withdrawal from the International Labour Organization, U.N. Doc. A/C.5/1704, Annex.

United Nations Conference on International Organization (UNCIO). 1945. *Record of Proceedings*. Volume V. San Francisco, CA: United Nations Conference on International Organization.

United Nations General Assembly (UNGA). 1946. First Committee. Official Records. Year I. Session I. New York: United Nations.

United Nations Standards Coordinating Committee (UNSCC). 1945. UNSCC Proceedings of New York Meeting, October 8–11, 1945.

1946a. Report of the Unofficial Meeting of the UNSCC Executive Committee and ISA Council held at the Quai D'Orsay, Paris, France, on Friday, July 12, 1946.

1946b. Project Unifié de Constitution, Pour L'Organisation Internationale des Norms, July 2, 1946.

1946c. Draft Constitution Prepared in Paris by Representatives of Denmark, France, Holland, U.S.A., U.S.S.R., July 1946, Statutes.

1946d. *Report of Conference of the United Nations Standards Co-ordinating Committee Together with Delegates from Certain Other Standards Bodies Held in London at the Institution of Civil Engineers 14th–26th October, 1946.* London, UK: Central Office of the UNSCC.

United States Department of Commerce. 1929. *Standards Yearbook 1929.* Washington, DC: United States Government Printing Office.

1980. *Standardization in France.* Washington, DC: United States Department of Commerce.

United States Department of State. 1946. Verbal Note from U.S. Secretary of State to French Ambassador in Washington, DC. January 29, 1946.

UN-NGO. 1998. "IRENE UPDATE." New York. Available at http://unpan1.un.org/intradoc/groups/public/documents/un/unpan011533.pdf, accessed March 10, 2018.

Valleix, Claude. 1998. "Interpol." *International Criminal Police Review*, 4: 177–194.

Vernon, Raymond. 1971. *Sovereignty at Bay: The Multinational Spread of U.S. Enterprises.* New York: Basic Books.

Wallace, Michael, and David J. Singer. 1970. "Intergovernmental Organization in the Global System, 1815–1964: A Quantitative Description." *International Organization*, 24(2): 239–287.

Walther, Henri. 1965. "Révision de la Convention de Mannheim Pour la Navigation du Rhin." *Annuaire Français de Droit International*, 11: 810–822.

Waltz, Kenneth N. 1979. *Theory of International Politics.* Reading, MA: Addison-Wesley.

Weart, Spencer R. 1998. *Never at War.* New Haven, CT: Yale University Press.

Weidlein, Edward R., and Vera Reck. 1956. "A Million Years of Standards." In *National Standards in a Modern Economy*, edited by Dickson Reck. New York: Harper and Brothers, 5–20.

Weindling, Paul. 1995. *International Health Organisations and Movements: 1918–1939.* Cambridge, MA: Cambridge University Press.

Weiss, Thomas G., and Rorden Wilkinson. 2014. "Rethinking Global Governance? Complexity, Authority, Power, Change." *International Studies Quarterly*, 58(1): 207–215.

Wendt, Alexander. 1992. "Anarchy Is What States Make of It: The Social Construction of Power Politics." *International Organization*, 46(2): 391–425.

1995. "Constructing International Politics." *International Security*, 20(1): 71–81.

White, Lyman Cromwell. 1951. *International Non-Governmental Organisations.* New Brunswick, Canada: Rutgers University Press.

Willemin, Georges, Roger Heacock, and Jacques Freymond. 1984. *The International Committee of the Red Cross.* Boston, MA: Martinus Nijhoff.

Willetts, Peter. 1996. *The Conscience of the World: The Influence of Non-governmental Organisations in the UN System.* Washington, DC: Brookings Institution for the David Davies Memorial Institute of International Studies.

2000. "From 'Consultative Arrangements' to 'Partnership': The Changing Status of NGOs in Diplomacy at the UN." *Global Governance*, 6(2): 191–212.

2011. *Non-governmental Organizations in World Politics: The Construction of Global Governance.* Milton Park, UK, Abingdon, UK and Oxon, UK: Routledge.

Winslow, Charles Edward Amory. 1923. *The Evolution and Significance of the Modern Public Health Campaign. (An address.).* New Haven, CT: Yale University Press.

World Health Organization (WHO). 1946. "Constitution of the World Health Organization." Available at www.who.int/governance/eb/who_constitution_en.pdf.

1947a. Minutes of Meeting of World Health Organization Interim Committee, Fourth Session of the Committee on Relations, Sub-committee on Negotiations with UNESCO Subcommittee, September 5, 1947. World Health Organization Archives. 954_1_4.

1947b. Letter of United States Representative Interim Commission, World Health Organization to Mr. Brock Chisholm, Executive Secretary, Interim Commission, World Health Organization, May 12, 1947. World Health Organization Archives. Registry 1-1-2.

1948a. *Guide Book for Delegates.* Geneva, Switzerland: First World Health Assembly.

1948b. Proposals for the Formation of an Appeals Service of the WHO Secretariat. December 1948. World Health Organization Archives. 208_1_1.

1949a. Memorandum from G. E. Hill to M. Hafezi Regarding a Proposed Inter-agency Fundamental Program, August 9, 1949. World Health Organization Archives. 1-1-2, 4–8.

1949b. Memorandum from B. Howell to G. E. Hill Regarding a Proposed Inter-agency Fundamental Program, August 24, 1949. World Health Organization Archives. 1-1-2, 18.

1950a. Memo for Director General's Office, March 30, 1950.

1950b. Memorandum from Milton Siegel to Brock Chisholm, May 2, 1950. 4_4_66.

1956. Memorandum: Renewal of Panel Members/Experts Advisory Panel on the International Pharmacopoeia, October 18, 1956. WHO Archives: P5/136/1.

1957. Note of meeting between WHO Director-General and Mr. Gowen, United States Representative to International Organizations, Geneva on February 19, 1957. N-51/180/2-USA.

1963. Report on the Ninth General Conference of Consultative Non-governmental Organizations, Geneva, Switzerland, 28 June–1 July 1963. World Health Organization Archives N61/86/6.

Joint FAO-WHO Food Standards Program, Eighth Meeting of the Executive Committee of the Codex Alimentarius Commission, June 14–16, 1966, Agenda Item 11 – Trust Fund 40: Revenue 1965. ALINORM/EXEC/66/5, May 1966.

1971. Executive Board, Triennial Report of Non-Governmental Organizations in Special Relations with WHO 1969–1971, November 26, 1971, EB49/17.

1975a. Note for the Record: Meeting with Nongovernmental Organizations, June 24, 1975. World Health Organization Archives. N61/348/3(1).

1975b. Inter-office Memorandum: Strengthening of Collaboration between NGOs and WHO, November 7, 1975. World Health Organization Archive N61/348/1 (1).

1975c. USAID/WHO Coordination Meeting, Geneva, July 9–10, 1975, Summary Report. World Health Organization Archive B12/372/2AID.

1976. Memorandum of Dr. E. Helander, Medical Officer SHS to Director SHS and Chief CWO on Strengthening of Collaboration between Non-Governmental Organizations and WHO, April 9, 1976. World Health Organization Archive N61/348/1.

1988. Letter Addressed to David Magrath, Chief, Biologicals Section, World Health Organization by Charles Guthrie, Operations Director, Commonwealth Laboratories. WHO Archives B3/449/1.

1994. Review of Draft on Codex Alimentarius. WHO Archives: C14/372/2.

2013. "Top 20 Voluntary Contributors 2012–2013." Geneva, Switzerland: World Health Organization. Available at www.who.int/about/funding/top20.pdf, accessed March 10, 2018.

2016. "Framework of engagement with non-State actors, 69th World Health Assembly. WHA69.10. Agenda item 11.3, 28 May 2016." Available at www.who.int/about/collaborations/non-state-actors/A69_R10-FENSA-en.pdf?ua=1, accessed February 18, 2018.

Yates, JoAnne, and Craig N. Murphy. 2007. "Coordinating International Standards: The Formation of the ISO. Massachusetts Institute of Technology (MIT)." Sloan School of Management, Working papers. 10.2139/ssrn.962455.

2008. "Charles Le Maistre: Entrepreneur in international standardization." *Entreprises Et Histoire / Publ. Avec Le Soutien De L'Institut D'Histoire De L'Industrie*, 51: 10–27.

Youde, Jeremy. 2012. *Global Health Governance*. Malden, MA: Polity Press.

Zakaria, Fareed. 1997. "The Rise of Illiberal Democracy." *Foreign Affairs*, 76(6): 22–43.

Zaracostas, John. 1997. "White House Insists on Efforts for Global Standards of Labor." *Women's Wear Daily*, June 13, 1997, 18.

Zürn, Michael. 2018. *A Theory of Global Governance: Authority, Legitimacy, and Contestation*. Oxford, UK: Oxford University Press.

Index

Note: Page numbers in italic and bold refer to figures and tables, respectively.

Lightning Source UK Ltd.
Milton Keynes UK
UKHW010043260920
370559UK00004B/13